THE

CLINTON

Foreign Policy
Reader

THE

CLINTON
Foreign Policy Reader

Presidential Speeches with Commentary

Edited by
Alvin Z. Rubinstein
Albina Shayevich and
Boris Zlotnikov

M.E. Sharpe
Armonk, New York
London, England

Library of Congress Cataloging-in-Publication Data

Clinton, Bill, 1946–
    The Clinton foreign policy reader : presidential speeches with commentary / edited by
Alvin Z. Rubinstein, Albina Shayevich, Boris Zlotnikov.
        p. cm.
        Includes bibliographical references and index.
        ISBN 0-7656-0583-X (c : alk. paper)
        1. United States—Foreign relations—1993– 2. Clinton, Bill, 1946– —Views on
    foreign relations. I. Rubinstein, Alvin Z. II. Shayevich, Albina, 1979– III.
    Zlotnikov, Boris, 1979– IV. Title.

E885.C545 2000   99-059587
327.73—dc21   CIP

Printed in the United States of America

The paper used in this publication meets the minimum requirements of
American National Standard for Information Sciences
Permanence of Paper for Printed Library Materials,
ANSI Z 39.48-1984.

∞

BM (c)   10   9   8   7   6   5   4   3   2   1

Contents

Preface

William Jefferson Clinton is the first American president of the post-Cold War era. With the end of the systemic rivalry between the United States and the Soviet Union, which lasted from 1945 to 1991, we entered a period of US global hegemony. According to Secretary of State Madeleine Albright, the United States is now "the indispensable nation," the one whose "work is never done." Even less triumphalist officials and observers maintain that the world needs US leadership without which nothing major can be achieved.

Over the course of his terms in office, President Clinton has set in motion a pattern of US policy initiatives and responses that will affect US foreign policy for years to come—and perhaps not always with the consequences that were intended. Most of the issues with which he has contended, though seemingly carry-overs from the Cold War era, are in fact substantively very different. Whether they involve Russia or China, the Middle East or the United Nations, ethnic conflicts or weapons of mass destruction, the issues are new, unresolved, troublesome, far-reaching, and present challenging moral and political dilemmas.

As we complete this work, America is enjoying unparalleled prosperity, sustained by the longest and largest economic expansion in the twentieth century. Americans have a general feeling that there are no serious threats for the United Sates to worry about, that globalization heralds a century of American preeminence, and that economics reign, perhaps.

Our aim in assembling this collection of President Clinton's foreign policy speeches is to introduce students and other readers to the principal, evolving foreign policy choices that are likely to dominate the agenda of American policymakers for the next decade or more. In order to understand the problems confronting future administrations, it will be essential to know their background in the first post-Cold War years. The speeches have been edited to exclude extraneous remarks, such as salutations expressions of friendship, and reiterations of general principles about democracy, free markets, and support for human rights. They have been organized thematically to provide intellectual focus and facilitate analytical assessment. Each chapter begins with an original essay presenting essential information about the international and domestic context within which the President's speech was delivered and tentatively examining its inherent policy implications. We have sought to make as self-contained, integrated, and coherent an assessment of Clinton's foreign policy as is feasible within the book's structure; and by offering selections from presidential statements, we seek to encourage the reader to reach an independent judgment about the President's expressed aims, the means used, and the attendant consequences.

The international system is undergoing a series of revolutionary transformations, and so, too, are the policies of its most prominent and powerful actor. It is time to reassess familiar themes in light of the new ways in which they have been and are constantly changing.

The authors are deeply appreciative of the interest and assistance of Patricia Kolb. From the beginning of this enterprise, her many thoughtful suggestions and editorial expertise were invaluable. Working with her, and her colleagues at M.E. Sharpe, has been a professional pleasure.

Alvin Z. Rubinstein
Albina Shayevich
Boris Zlotnikov

THE

CLINTON

Foreign Policy
Reader

1. Strategic Outlook for a New World Order

When William Jefferson Clinton took office in January 1993, the international environment was different from any that Americans had known since the 1920s: there were no serious military threats and there was an opportunity to look inward and attend to pressing domestic problems. Elected at a time of transition from a bipolar era to an era of unchallenged US military supremacy and global influence, Clinton was determined to tackle long-standing internal challenges—getting control of burgeoning budget deficits, righting imbalances in trade relationships, downsizing defense expenditures, enhancing industrial competitiveness, and establishing preeminence in the field of information technology. He faced an extensive array of domestic difficulties, as Franklin D. Roosevelt had sixty years earlier when he took office during the world wide depression of the 1930s. The centerpiece of Clinton's domestic agenda was to be a comprehensive and all-encompassing reform of the existing patchwork system of health care.

Clinton's stewardship began at a time of unprecedented international change. The former Soviet Union, a dangerous adversary for decades, had imploded in December 1991, a victim of self-destruction by its own ruling elite, and was no longer a threat. Japan had emerged as a formidable economic-industrial-financial superpower, but was nevertheless an ally dependent on America's nuclear protection. China was intent on a sweeping program of modernization and gave mixed signals as to its long-term aims, but clearly wanted trade, not tensions. There were unresolved regional conflicts around the world, but none seemed likely to trigger a wider war. The proliferation of weapons of mass destruction remained a source of concern and frustration, and there was the knotty question of what to do about Saddam Hussein's Iraq. But as far as one could see, there were few threatening clouds on the foreign policy horizon.

Clinton brought to his new office a keen appreciation of the twin challenges of globalization and the revolution in cyberspace. Both were rapidly changing the way economic wealth was produced, accumulated, and distributed, with, as yet, only hints of their long-term economic, social, cultural, and political consequences. The first US president born after World War II was to lead the country into a new age of constant techno-. logical innovation. It was fitting, therefore, that his first major foreign policy statement be devoted to the demanding competitive challenges that faced America in the global economic arena (Speech 1-1).

Distinguished by its clarity, scope, and command of detail, Clinton's speech analyzed the problems that had to be overcome and laid out a series of steps designed to deal with them. It established the administration's international economic agenda and basic approach for the next few years; and by the end of the decade, the President would be able to claim that he had brought an end to deficit spending, ushered in a period of budgetary surpluses, reduced unemployment, and curbed inflation, as his administration led the way to the greatest sustained period of economic growth and prosperity in modern American history.

In 1993, although the economy was slowly improving, Clinton failed to obtain congressional approval for his national health insurance plan, and international political mini-crises increasingly intruded on his domestic agenda. Troubles in Russia, Somalia, Haiti, and Bosnia demanded presidential attention. Smart, articulate, impressively informed, and energetically involved as Clinton could be in domestic matters, he seemed unfocused, almost unengaged, and ad hoc in his response to foreign policy issues. Critics lamented the absence of a coherent vision or strategic outlook. The prospering international economy was proving no cure-all for the world's security concerns, ethnic conflicts, and brushfire outbreaks of hostilities.

In September 1993 the essentials of a strategic vision were laid out by the key figures in the Clinton administration: the President, National Security Adviser Anthony Lake, Secretary of State Warren Christopher, and UN ambassador Madeleine Albright. The President and his National Security Council (NSC) adviser spoke a few days apart, but their combined presentations constituted a package that contained many of the essentials of Clinton's foreign policy (Speeches 1-2 and 1-3). Warren Christopher and Madeleine Albright also made policy statements during this period, but their speeches contained nothing that was not in those of the President and Mr. Lake, and so are not included here.

The President talked about democracy, free markets, "reducing suffering, fostering sustainable development, and improving health and living conditions, particularly for our world's children." This was liberalism, globalized. He lauded the United Nations for its peacekeeping activities and hailed it as the instrument that "holds the promise to resolve many of this era's conflicts." Urging the United Nations to undertake much-needed fiscal and organizational reforms, he promised to press Congress for increased funding. Running through his speech was an emphasis on the importance of multilateralism as epitomized by an active and engaged United Nations.

Anthony Lake also spoke of the central roles of democratization and market economics in efforts to promote peace, stability, and prosperity; but he gave a decidedly American spin to his pitch. Calling American values universal, he spoke of the need to adopt a strategy of enlargement of the world's democracies, as a replacement for the Cold War strategy of containment of Soviet imperial expansion. He cited the lowering of barriers to humanitarian interventions since the end of the Cold War and argued that "we should not oppose using our military forces for humanitarian purposes simply because these missions do not resemble major wars for control of territory."

Despite this statement by his national security adviser, less than a month later President Clinton pulled US troops out of Somalia after eighteen Rangers were killed in a gun fight against a local warlord in Mogadishu.

Close observers of the Washington scene reported a struggle between Lake and Christopher to define the President's approach to foreign policy. Whereas Lake pushed a "strategy of enlargement" with a globalist, moralist, and interventionist thrust, Christopher espoused a "strategy of active engagement" with an emphasis on certain key geographic regions, notably, Russia, Western Europe, East Asia, and the Middle East. Both of these officials subscribed to the tenets of economic liberalism, and a strong strain of Wilsonian idealism permeated their outlooks, but there were differences between them.

Throughout the spring of 1994 the White House considered a number of draft proposals for a national security strategy, as it tried to reconcile the different perspectives of the State Department, the Pentagon, and other departments of government. After repeated delays and revisions, in July 1994 the administration issued President Clinton's first comprehensive strategy document, *A National Security Strategy of Engagement and Enlargement* (Speech 1-4). As the title suggests, and as was often to be the case, the President, unable to reach a decision, chose to straddle the issue in the hope that over time essentially opposing points of view could be reconciled. Since then, the formulations and general objectives outlined in the strategy document, which is sent to Congress annually (usually in February), have changed little and may be assumed to reflect the President's continuing basic outlook on foreign policy.

Since the prefaces to these documents are issued with the President's signature, they are especially significant. Two points merit mention, by way of shedding light on how the President's thinking evolved. First, in contrast to the preface to the initial report of July 1994, all subsequent prefaces to the annual reports made mention, early on, of the role of the use of force. This material has a strong unilateralist bent that is at variance with the multilateralist approach cultivated in many of the administration's other statements. Thus, from 1995 on, the President stated that military force was integral to the conduct of US foreign policy. For example, in the report that year he said:

> The United States recognizes that we have a special responsibility that goes along with being a great power. Our global interests and our historic ideals impel us to oppose those who would endanger the survival or well-being of their peaceful neighbors. Nations should be able to expect that their borders and their sovereignty will always be secure. At the same time, this does not mean we or the international community must tolerate gross violations of human rights within those borders.
>
> When our national security interests are threatened, we will, as America always has, use diplomacy when we can, but force if we must. We will act with others when we can, but alone when we must. We recognize, however, that while force can defeat an aggressor, it cannot solve underlying problems. Democracy and economic prosperity can take root in a struggling society only through local solutions carried out by the society itself. We must use military force selectively, recognizing that its use may do no more than provide a window of opportunity for a society—and diplomacy—to work.
>
> We therefore will send American troops abroad only when our interests and our values are sufficiently at stake. When we do so, it will be with clear objectives to which we are firmly committed and which—when combat is likely—we have the means to achieve decisively. To do otherwise, risks those objectives and endangers our troops. These requirements are as pertinent for humanitarian and other non-traditional interventions today as they were for previous generations during prolonged world wars....

The President added that, while the costs and benefits of any operation must be continually reassessed as it unfolds, "reflexive calls for withdrawal of our forces when casualties are incurred would simply encourage rogue" regimes.

Second, dependence on these annual reports for an assessment of the Clinton administration's approach to international problems could well lead to the conclusion that for the White House multilateralism had little to do with the United Nations, but was primarily a matter of economic policy, to be pursued partially through global organizations such as the International Monetary Fund (IMF), World Bank, and World Trade Organization (WTO), and partially on a bilateral basis with key trading partners such as Canada, Japan, Mexico, and China. To the extent that multilateralism also involved military-political cooperation, it was linked to our allies in NATO and in the Far East, Japan, and South Korea. In practice, however, the matter was more complicated because internal documents in the Clinton White House dealing with peacekeeping operations showed an inclination toward substantial (but not exclusive) reliance on the United Nations. The inherent contradictions between the annual National Strategy reports and in-house, ad hoc, case-by-case presidential directives complicate attempts to interpret the course of US foreign policy; they also give insight into the continuing internal "debate" in the White House over what constitutes the "national interest."

Each president redefines the national interest in light of the new threats, challenges, and opportunities that he sees facing the nation. In the absence of a formidable military adversary, the term becomes more difficult to elucidate, for example, under what circumstances should the United States use force to promote human rights or intervene on behalf of beleaguered ethnic minorities. After the 1994 strategy report, President Clinton offered no new broad overview of strategic security policy.

After the 1994 statement, whenever a difficult problem was perceived to challenge what the President considered to be a "vital interest," he delivered a speech in which he responded to the specific issue. Such was the case in February 1999: after one year of avoiding press conferences or venues in which he might be subjected to questions about his personal relationship with a former White House intern, and one month after the impeachment charges brought by the House of Representatives failed to obtain a two-thirds vote for conviction in the Senate, President Clinton, speaking in San Francisco about foreign policy, used the occasion to draw attention to the rising tensions with Yugoslavia over its treatment of the Muslim Albanians living in the province of Kosovo (Speech 1-5). Few paid heed. The economy was booming; no Americans were dying in combat. Yet Clinton's assessment of the major problems facing the United States in 1999 was far more sober than the speeches that had ushered in his Presidency.

1-1 Liberal Internationalism: America and the Global Economy

Speech at American University
Washington DC
February 26, 1993

... Thirty years ago in the last year of his short but brilliant life, John Kennedy came to this university to address the paramount challenge of that time: the imperative of pursuing peace in the face of nuclear confrontation. Many Americans still believe it was the finest speech he ever delivered. Today I come to this same place to deliver an address about what I consider to be the great challenge of this day: the imperative of American leadership in the face of global change.

Over the past year I have tried to speak at some length about what we must do to update our definition of national security and to promote it and to protect it and to foster democracy and human rights around the world. Today, I want to allude to those matters, but to focus on the economic leadership we must exert at home and abroad as a new global economy unfolds before our eyes.

Twice before in this century, history has asked the United States and other great powers to provide leadership for a world ravaged by war. After World War I, that call went unheeded. Britain was too weakened to lead the world to reconstruction. The United States was too unwilling. The great powers together turned inward as violent, totalitarian power emerged. We raised trade barriers. We sought to humiliate rather than rehabilitate the vanquished. And the result was instability, inflation, then depression and ultimately a second World War.

After the second War, we refused to let history repeat itself. Led by a great American President, Harry Truman, a man of very common roots but uncommon vision, we drew together with other Western powers to reshape a new era. We established NATO to oppose the aggression of communism. We rebuilt the American economy with investments like the GI Bill and a national highway system. We carried out the Marshall Plan to rebuild war-ravaged nations abroad. General MacArthur's vision prevailed in Japan, which built a massive economy and a remarkable democracy. We built new institutions to foster peace and prosperity: the United Nations, the International Monetary Fund, the World Bank, the General Agreement on Tariffs and Trade, and more.

These actions helped to usher in four decades of robust economic growth and collective security. Yet the Cold War was a draining time. We devoted trillions of dollars to it, much more than many of our more visionary leaders thought we should have. We posted our sons and daughters around the world. We lost tens of thousands of them in the defense of freedom and in the pursuit of a containment of communism....

The change confronting us in the 1990s is in some ways more difficult than previous times because it is less distinct. It is more complex and in some ways the path is less clear to most of our people still today, even after twenty years of declining relative productivity and a decade or more of stagnant wages and greater effort.

The world clearly remains a dangerous place. Ethnic hatreds, religious strife, the proliferation of weapons of mass destruction, the violation of human rights flagrantly in altogether too many places around the world still call on us to have a sense of national security in which our national defense is an integral part. And the world still calls on us to promote democracy, for even though democracy is on the march in many places in the world, you and I know that it has been thwarted in many places, too. And yet we still face, overarching everything else, this amorphous but profound challenge in the way humankind conducts its commerce.

We cannot let these changes in the global economy carry us passively toward a future of insecurity and instability. For change is the law of life. Whether you like it or not, the world will change much more rapidly in your lifetime than it has in mine. It is absolutely astonishing the speed with which the sheer volume of knowledge in the world is doubling every few years. And a critical issue before us and especially before the young people here in this audience is whether you will grow up in a world where change is your friend or your enemy.

We must challenge the changes now engulfing our world toward America's enduring objectives of peace and prosperity, of democracy and human dignity. And we must work to do it at home and abroad.

It is important to understand the monumental scope of these changes. When I was growing up, business was mostly a local affair. Most farms and firms were owned locally; they borrowed locally; they hired locally; they shipped most of their products to neighboring communities or states within the United States. It was the same for the country as a whole. By and large, we had a domestic economy.

But now we are woven inextricably into the fabric of a global economy. Imports and exports, which accounted for about $1 in $10 when I was growing up, now represent $1 in every $5. Nearly three-quarters of the things that we make in America are subject to competition at home or abroad from foreign producers and foreign providers of services. Whether we see it or not, our daily lives are touched everywhere by the flows of commerce that cross national borders as inexorably as the weather.

Capital clearly has become global. Some $3 trillion of capital race around the world every day. And when a firm wants to build a new factory, it can turn to financial markets now open twenty-four hours a day, from London to Tokyo, from New York to Singapore. Products have clearly become more global. Now if you buy an American car, it may be an American car built with some parts from Taiwan, designed by Germans, sold with British-made advertisements, or a combination of others in a different mix.

Services have become global. The accounting firm that keeps the books for a small business in Wichita may also be helping new entrepreneurs in Warsaw. And the same fast food restaurant that your family goes to or at least that I go to also may well be serving families from Manila to Moscow and managing its business globally with information technologies, and satellites.

Most important of all, information has become global and has become king of the global economy. In earlier history, wealth was measured in land, in gold, in oil, in machines. Today, the principal measure of our wealth is information: its quality, its quantity, and the speed with which we acquire it and adapt to it. We need more than anything else to measure our wealth and our potential by what we know and by what we can learn and what we can do with it. The value and volume of information has soared; the half-life of new ideas has trumped....

We are in a constant race toward innovation that will not end in the lifetime of anyone in this room. What all this means is that the best investment we can make today is in the one resource firmly rooted in our own borders. That is, in the education, the skills, the reasoning capacity, and the creativity of our own people....

The truth of our age is this and must be this: Open and competitive commerce will enrich us as a nation. It spurs us to innovate. It forces us to compete. It connects us with new customers. It promotes global growth without which no rich country can hope to grow wealthier. It enables our producers who are themselves consumers of services and raw materials to prosper. And so I say to you in the face of all the pressures to do the reverse, we must compete, not retreat.

Our exports are especially important to us. As bad as the recent recession was, it would have gone on for twice as long had it not been for what we were able to sell to other nations. Every $1 billion of our exports creates nearly 20,000 jobs here, and we now have over 7 million export-related jobs in America. They tend to involve better work and better pay. Most are in manufacturing, and on average, they pay almost $3,500 more per year than the average American job. They are exactly the kind of jobs we need for a new generation of Americans.

American jobs and prosperity are reason enough for us to be working at mastering the essentials of the global economy. But far more is at stake, for this new fabric of commerce will also shape global prosperity or the lack of it, and with it, the prospects of people around the world for democracy, freedom, and peace.

We must remember that even with all our problems today, the United States is still the world's strongest engine of growth and progress. We remain the world's largest producer and its largest and most open market. Other nations, such as Germany and Japan, are moving rapidly. They have done better than we have in certain areas. We should respect them for it, and where appropriate, we should learn from that. But we must also say to them, "You, too, must act as engines of global prosperity." Nonetheless, the fact is that for now and for the foreseeable future, the world looks to us to be the engine of global growth and to be the leaders.

Our leadership is especially important for the world's new and emerging democracies. To grow and deepen their legitimacy, to foster a middle class and a civic culture, they need the ability to tap into a growing global economy. And our security and our prosperity will be greatly affected in the years ahead by how many of these nations can become and stay democracies.

All you have to do to know that is to look at the problems in Somalia, to look at Bosnia, to look at the other trouble spots in the world. If we could make a garden of democracy and prosperity and free enterprise in every part of this globe, the world would be a safer and a better and a more prosperous place for the United States and for all of you to raise your children in....

Cooperation among the major powers toward world growth is not working well at all today. And most of all, we simply haven't done enough to prepare our own people and to produce our own resources so that we can face with success the rigors of the new world. We can change all that if we have the will to do it. Leonardo da Vinci said that God sells all things at the price of labor. Our labor must be to make this change.

I believe there are five steps we can and must take to set a new direction at home and to help create a new direction for the world.

First, we simply have to get our own economic house in order. I have outlined a new national economic strategy that will give America the new direction we require to meet our challenges. It seeks to do what no generation of Americans has ever been called upon to do before: to increase investment in our productive future and to reduce our deficit at the same time....

Second, it is time for us to make trade a priority element of American security. For too long, debates over trade have been dominated by voices from the extremes. One says governments should build walls to protect firms from competition. Another says government should do nothing in the face of foreign competition, no matter what the dimension and shape of that competition is, no matter what the consequences are in terms of job losses, trade dislocations, or crushed incomes. Neither view takes on the hard work of creating a more open trading system that enables us and our trading partners to prosper. Neither steps up to the task of empowering our workers to compete or of ensuring that there is some compact of shared responsibility regarding trade's impact on our people or of guaranteeing a continuous flow of investment into emerging areas of new technology which will create the high-wage jobs of the twenty-first century....

Our trade policy will be part of an integrated economic program, not just something we use to compensate for the lack of a domestic agenda. We must enforce our trade laws and our agreements with all the tools and energy at our disposal. But there is much about our competitive posture that simply cannot be straightened out by trade retaliation. Better educated and trained workers, a lower deficit, stable, low interest rates, a reformed health care system, world-class technologies, revived cities: These must be the steel of our competitive edge. And there must be a continuing quest by business and labor and, yes, by Government for higher and higher and higher levels of productivity....

We also know that regional and bilateral agreements provide opportunities to explore new kinds of trade concerns, such as how trade relates to policies affecting the environment and labor standards and the antitrust laws. And these agreements, once concluded, can act as a magnet including other countries to drop barriers and to open their trading systems.

The North American Free Trade Agreement is a good example. It began as an agreement with Canada, which I strongly supported, which has now led to a pact with Mexico as well. That agreement holds the potential to create many, many jobs in America over the next decade if it is joined with others to ensure that the environment, that living standards, that working conditions, are honored, that we can literally know that we are going to raise the condition of people in America and in Mexico. We have a vested interest in a wealthier, stronger Mexico, but we need to do it on terms that are good for our people.

We should work with organizations, such as the Asian-Pacific Economic Cooperation Forum, to liberalize our trade across the Pacific as well....

Third, it is time for us to do our best to exercise leadership among the major financial powers to improve our coordination on behalf of global economic growth. At a time when capital is mobile and highly fungible, we simply cannot afford to work at cross-purposes with the other major industrial democracies. Our major partners must work harder and more closely with us to reduce interest rates, stimulate investment, reduce structural barriers to trade, and to restore robust global growth. And we must look anew at institutions we use to chart our way in the global economy and ask whether they are serving our interest in this new world or whether we need to modify them or create others....

Fourth, we need to promote the steady expansion of growth in the developing world, not only because it's in our interest but because it will help them as well. These nations are a rapidly expanding market for our products. Some 3 million American jobs flow from exports to the developing world. Indeed, because of unilateral actions taken by Mexico over the last few years, the volume of our trade has increased dramatically, and our trade deficit has disappeared.

Our ability to protect the global environment and our ability to combat the flow of illegal narcotics also rests in large measure on the relationships we develop commercially with the developing world....

The final step we must take, my fellow Americans, is toward the success of democracy in Russia and in the world's other new democracies. The perils facing Russia and other former Soviet republics are especially acute and especially important to our future. For the reductions in our defense spending that are an important part of our economic program over the long run here at home are only tenable as long as Russia and the other nuclear republics pose a diminishing threat to our security and to the security of our allies and the democracies throughout the world. Most worrisome is Russia's precarious economic condition. If the economic reforms begun by President Yeltsin are abandoned, if hyperinflation cannot be stemmed, the world will suffer.

Consider the implications for Europe if millions of Russian citizens decide they have no alternative but to flee to the West where wages are fifty times higher. Consider the implication for the global environment if all the Chernobyl-style nuclear plants are forced to start operating there without spare parts, when we should be in a phased stage of building them down, closing them up, cleaning them up. If we are willing to spend trillions of dollars to ensure communism's defeat in the Cold War, surely we should be willing to invest a tiny fraction of that to support democracy's success where communism failed....

1-2 Globalism and Interdependence

Address to the Forty-eighth Session of
the United Nations General Assembly
New York, New York
September 27, 1993

... I come before you as the first American President born after the founding of the United Nations. Like most of the people in the world today, I was not even alive during the convulsive World War that convinced humankind of the need for this organization, nor during the San Francisco Conference that led to its birth. Yet I have followed the work of the United Nations throughout my life, with admiration for its accomplishments, with sadness for its failures, and conviction that through common effort our generation can take the bold steps needed to redeem the mission entrusted to the UN forty-eight years ago.

I pledge to you that my Nation remains committed to helping make the UN's vision a reality. The start of this General Assembly offers us an opportunity to take stock of where we are, as common shareholders in the progress of humankind and in the preservation of our planet.

It is clear that we live at a turning point in human history. Immense and promising changes seem to wash over us every day. The Cold War is over. The world is no longer divided into two armed and angry camps. Dozens of new democracies have been born.

It is a moment of miracles. We see Nelson Mandela stand side by side with President de Klerk, proclaiming a date for South Africa's first nonracial election. We see Russia's first popularly elected President, Boris Yeltsin, leading his nation on its bold democratic journey. We have seen decades of deadlock shattered in the Middle East, as the Prime Minister of Israel and the Chairman of the Palestine Liberation Organization reached past enmity and suspicion to shake each other's hands and exhilarate the entire world with the hope of peace.

We have begun to see the doomsday welcome of nuclear annihilation dismantled and destroyed. Thirty-two years ago, President Kennedy warned this chamber that humanity lived under a nuclear sword of Damocles that hung by the slenderest of threads. Now the United States is working with Russia, Ukraine, Belarus, and others to take that sword down, to lock it away in a secure vault where we hope and pray it will remain forever.

It is a new era in this hall as well. The superpower standoff that for so long stymied the United Nations work almost from its first day has now yielded to a new promise of practical cooperation. Yet today we must all admit that there are two powerful tendencies working from opposite directions to challenge the authority of nation states everywhere and to undermine the authority of nation states to work together.

From beyond nations, economic and technological forces all over the globe are compelling the world towards integration. These forces are fueling a welcome explosion of entrepreneurship and political liberalization. But they also threaten to destroy the insularity and independence of national economies, quickening the pace of change and making many of our people feel more insecure. At the same time, from within nations, the resurgent aspirations of ethnic and religious groups challenge governments on terms that traditional nation states cannot easily accommodate.

These twin forces lie at the heart of the challenges not only to our National Government but also to all our international institutions. They require all of us in this room to find new ways to work together more effectively in pursuit of our national interests and to think anew about whether our institutions of international cooperation are adequate to this moment....

When this organization was founded forty-eight years ago, the world's nations stood devastated by war or exhausted by its expense. There was little appetite for cooperative efforts among nations. Most people simply wanted to get on with their lives. But a farsighted generation of leaders from the United States and elsewhere rallied the world. Their efforts built the institutions of postwar security and prosperity.

We are at a similar moment today. The momentum of the Cold War no longer propels us in our daily actions. And with daunting economic and political pressures upon almost every nation represented in this room, many of us are turning to focus greater attention and energy on our domestic needs and problems, and we must. But putting each of our economic houses in order cannot mean that we shut our windows to the world. The pursuit of self-renewal, in many of the world's largest and most powerful economies, in Europe, in Japan, in North America, is absolutely crucial because unless the great industrial nations can recapture their robust economic growth, the global economy will languish....

Let me start by being clear about where the United States stands. The United States occupies a unique position in world affairs today. We recognize that, and we welcome it. Yet, with the Cold War over, I know many people ask whether the United States plans to retreat or remain active in the world and, if active, to what end. Many people are asking that in our own country as well. Let me answer that question as clearly and plainly as I can. The United States intends to remain engaged and to lead. We cannot solve every problem, but we must and will serve as a fulcrum for change and a pivot point for peace.

In a new era of peril and opportunity, our overriding purpose must be to expand and strengthen the world's community of market-based democracies. During the Cold War we sought to contain a threat to the survival of free institutions. Now we seek to enlarge the circle of nations that live under those free institutions. For our dream is of a day when the opinions and energies of every person in the world will be given full expression, in a world of thriving democracies that cooperate with each other and live in peace.

With this statement, I do not mean to announce some crusade to force our way of life and doing things on others or to replicate our institutions, but we now know clearly that throughout the world, from Poland to Eritrea, from Guatemala to South Korea, there is an enormous yearning among people who wish to be the masters of their own economic and political lives. Where it matters most and where we can make the greatest difference, we will, therefore, patiently and firmly align ourselves with that yearning....

We will support the consolidation of market democracy where it is taking new root, as in the states of the former Soviet Union and all over Latin America. And we seek to foster the practices of good government that distribute the benefits of democracy and economic growth fairly to all people.

We will work to reduce the threat from regimes that are hostile to democracies and to support liberalization of nondemocratic states when they are willing to live in peace with the rest of us.

As a country that has over 150 different racial, ethnic and religious groups within our borders, our policy is and must be rooted in a profound respect for all the world's religions and cultures. But we must oppose everywhere extremism that produces terrorism and hate. And we must pursue our humanitarian goal of reducing suffering, fostering sustainable development, and improving the health and living conditions, particularly for our world's children.

On efforts from export control to trade agreements to peacekeeping, we will often work in partnership with others and through multilateral institutions such as the United Nations. It is in our national interest to do so. But we must not hesitate to act unilaterally when there is a threat to our core interests or to those of our allies....

Let me talk more about what I believe we must do in each of these three categories: nonproliferation, conflict resolution, and sustainable development.

One of our most urgent priorities must be attacking the proliferation of weapons of mass destruction, whether they are nuclear, chemical, or biological, and the ballistic missiles that can rain them down on populations hundreds of miles away. We know this is not an idle problem. All of us are still haunted by the pictures of Kurdish women and children cut down by poison gas. We saw SCUD missiles dropped during the Gulf War that would have been far graver in their consequence if they had carried nuclear weapons. And we know that many nations still believe it is in their interest to develop weapons of mass destruction or to sell them or the necessary technologies to others for financial gain.

More than a score of nations likely possess such weapons, and their number threatens to grow. These weapons destabilize entire regions. They could turn a local conflict into a global human and environmental catastrophe. We simply have got to find ways to control these weapons and to reduce the number of states that possess them by supporting and strengthening the IAEA and by taking other necessary measures.

I have made nonproliferation one of our Nation's highest priorities. We intend to weave it more deeply into the fabric of all of our relationships with the world's nations and institutions. We seek to build a world of increasing pressures for nonproliferation but increasingly open trade and technology for those states that live by accepted international rules....

As we reduce our nuclear stockpiles, the United States has also begun negotiations toward a comprehensive ban on nuclear testing. This summer I declared that to facilitate these negotiations, our Nation would suspend our testing if all other nuclear states would do the same. Today, in the face of disturbing signs, I renew my call on the nuclear states to abide by that moratorium as we negotiate to stop nuclear testing for all time.

I am also proposing new efforts to fight the proliferation of biological and chemical weapons. Today, only a handful of nations has ratified the Chemical Weapons Convention. I call on all nations, including my own, to ratify this accord quickly so that it may enter into force by January 13th, 1995. We will also seek to strengthen the biological weapons convention by making every nation's biological activities and facilities open to more international students.

I am proposing as well new steps to thwart the proliferation of ballistic missiles. Recently, working with Russia, Argentina, Hungary, and South Africa, we have made significant progress toward that goal. Now, we will seek to strengthen the principles of the missile technology control regime by transforming it from an agreement on technology transfer among just twenty-three nations to a set of rules that can command universal adherence.

We will also reform our own system of export controls in the United States to reflect the realities of the post-Cold War world, where we seek to enlist the support of our former adversaries in the battle against proliferation.

At the same time that we stop deadly technologies from falling into the wrong hands, we will work with our partners to remove outdated controls that unfairly burden legitimate commerce and unduly restrain growth and opportunity all over the world.

As we work to keep the world's most destructive weapons out of conflict, we must also strengthen the international community's ability to address those conflicts themselves. For as we all now know so painfully, the end of the Cold War did not bring us to the millennium of peace. And indeed, it simply removed the lid from many cauldrons of ethnic, religious, and territorial animosity.

The philosopher, Isaiah Berlin, has said that a wounded nationalism is like a bent twig forced down so severely that when released, it lashes back with fury. The world today is thick with both bent and recoiling twigs of wounded communal identities.

This scourge of bitter conflict has placed high demands on United Nations peacekeeping forces. Frequently the blue helmets have worked wonders. In Namibia, El Salvador, the Golan Heights, and elsewhere, UN peacekeepers have helped to stop the fighting, restore civil authority, and enable free elections....

Many still criticize UN peacekeeping, but those who do should talk to the people of Cambodia, where the UN's operations have helped to turn the killing fields into fertile soil through reconciliation. Last May's elections in Cambodia marked a proud accomplishment for that war-weary nation and for the United Nations. And I am pleased to announce that the United States has recognized Cambodia's new government.

UN peacekeeping holds the promise to resolve many of this era's conflicts. The reason we have supported such missions is not, as some critics in the United States have charged, to subcontract American foreign policy but to strengthen our security, protect our interests, and to share among nations the costs and effort of pursuing peace. Peacekeeping cannot be a substitute for our own national defense efforts, but it can strongly supplement them....

In recent weeks in the Security Council, our Nation has begun asking harder questions about proposals for new peacekeeping missions: Is there a real threat to international peace? Does the proposed mission have clear objectives? Can an end point be identified for those who will be asked to participate? How much will the mission cost? From now on, the United Nations should address these and other hard questions for every proposed mission before we vote and before the mission begins.

The United Nations simply cannot become engaged in every one of the world's conflicts. If the American people are to say yes to UN peacekeeping, the United Nations must know when to say no. The United Nations must also have the technical means to run a modern world-class peacekeeping operation. We support the creation of a genuine UN peacekeeping headquarters with a planning staff, with access to timely intelligence, with a logistics unit that can be deployed on a moment's notice, and a modern operations center with global communications.

And the UN's operations must not only be adequately funded but also fairly funded. Within the next few weeks, the United States will be current in our peacekeeping bills. I have worked hard with the Congress to get this done. I believe the United States should lead the way in being timely in its payments, and I will work to continue to see that we pay our bills in full. But I am also committed to work with the United Nations to reduce our Nation's assessment for these missions.

The assessment system has not been changed since 1973. And everyone in our country knows that our percentage of the world's economic pie is not as great as it was then. Therefore, I believe our rates should be reduced to reflect the rise of other nations that can now bear more of the financial burden. That will make it easier for me as President to make sure we pay in a timely and full fashion.

Changes in the UN's peacekeeping operations must be part of an even broader program of United Nations reform....

I applaud the initial steps the Secretary General has taken to reduce and to reform the United Nations bureaucracy. Now, we must all do even more to root out waste. Before this General Assembly is over, let us establish a strong mandate for an Office of Inspector General so that it can attain a reputation for toughness, for integrity, for effectiveness. Let us build new confidence among our people that the United Nations is changing with the needs of our times.

Ultimately, the key for reforming the United Nations, as in reforming our own Government, is to remember why we are here and whom we serve. It is wise to recall that the first words of the UN Charter are not "We, the government," but, "We, the people of the United Nations." That means in every country the teachers, the workers, the farmers, the professionals, the fathers, the mothers, the children, from the most remote village in the world to the largest metropolis, they are why we gather in this great hall. It is their futures that are at risk when we act or fail to act, and it is they who ultimately pay our bills....

1-3 From Containment to Enlargement

Speech of Assistant to the President for National Security
Affairs Anthony Lake at Johns Hopkins University
Washington DC
September 21, 1993

Let us begin by taking stock of our new era. Four facts are salient. First, America's core concepts—democracy and market economics—are more broadly accepted than ever. Over the past ten years the number of democracies has nearly doubled. Since 1970, the number of significant command economies dropped from ten to three.

This victory of freedom is practical, not ideological: billions of people on every continent are simply concluding, based on decades of their own hard experience, that democracy and markets are the most productive and liberating ways to organize their lives....

Both processes strengthen each other: democracy alone can produce justice, but not the material goods necessary for individuals to thrive; markets alone can expand wealth, but not that sense of justice without which civilized societies perish....

The second feature of this era is that we are its dominant power. Those who say otherwise sell America short. The fact is, we have the world's strongest military, its largest economy and its most dynamic, multiethnic society. We are setting a global example in our efforts to reinvent our democratic and market institutions. Our leadership is sought and respected in every corner of the world. As Secretary Christopher noted yesterday, that is why the parties to last week's dramatic events chose to shake hands in Washington. Around the world, America's power, authority and example provide unparalleled opportunities to lead.

Moreover, absent a reversal in Russia, there is now no credible near-term threat to America's existence. Serious threats remain: terrorism, proliferating weapons of mass destruction, ethnic conflicts and the degradation of our global environments....

America's challenge today is to lead on the basis of opportunity rather than fear. The third notable aspect of this era is an explosion of ethnic conflicts. As Senator Moynihan and others have noted, the end of the World War and the collapse of various repressive regimes has removed the lid from numerous caldrons of ethnic, religious or factional hatreds. In many states of the former Soviet Union and elsewhere, there is a tension between the desire for ethnic separatism and the creation of liberal democracy, which alone can safely accommodate and even celebrate differences among citizens. A major challenge to our linking, our policies and our international institutions in this era; the fact that most conflicts are taking place within rather than among nations.

These conflicts are typically highly complex; at the same time, their brutality will tug at our consciences. We need a healthy wariness about our ability to shape solutions for such disputes, yet at times our interests or humanitarian concerns will impel our unilateral or multilateral engagement.

The fourth feature of this new era is that the pulse of the planet has accelerated dramatically and with it the pace of change in human events. Computers, faxes, fiber optic cables and satellites all speed the flow of information. The measurement of wealth, and increasingly wealth itself, consists in bytes of data that move at the speed of light.

The accelerated pace of events is neither bad nor good. Its sharp consequences can cut either way. It means both doctors and terrorists can more quickly share their technical secrets. Both pro-democracy activists and skinhead anarchists can more broadly spread their views. Ultimately, the world's acceleration creates new and diverse ways for us to exert our influence, if we choose to do so—but increases the likelihood that, if we do not, rapid events, instantly reported, may overwhelm us....

From Containment to Enlargement

In such a world, our interests and ideals compel us not only to be engaged, but to lead. And in a real-time world of change and information, it is all the more important that our leadership be steadied around our central purpose.

That purpose can be found in the underlying rationale for our engagement throughout this century. As we fought aggressors and contained communism, our engagement abroad was animated both by calculations of power and by this belief: to the extent democracy and market economics hold sway in other nations, our own nation will be more secure, prosperous and influential, while the broader world will be more humane and peaceful.

The expansion of market-based economics abroad helps expand our exports and create American jobs, while it also improves living conditions and fuels demands for political liberalization abroad. The addition of new democracies makes us more secure because democracies tend not to wage war on each other or sponsor terrorism. They are more trustworthy in diplomacy and do a better job of respecting the human rights of their people.

These dynamics lay at the heart of Woodrow Wilson's most profound insights; although his moralism sometimes weakened his argument, he understood that our own security is shaped by the character of foreign regimes. Indeed, most Presidents who followed Republicans and Democrats alike, understood we must promote democracy and market economics in the world—because it protects our interests and security and because it reflects values that are both American and universal.

Throughout the Cold War, we contained a global threat to market democracies; now we should seek to enlarge their reach, particularly in places of special significance to us.

The successor to a doctrine of containment must be a strategy of enlargement—enlargement of the world's free community of market democracies.

We must not allow this overarching goal to drive us into overreaching actions. To be successful, a strategy of enlargement must provide distinctions and set priorities. It must combine our broad goals of fostering democracy and markets with our more traditional geostrategic interests. And it must suggest how best to expend our large but nonetheless limited national security resources: financial, diplomatic and military.

In recent years, discussions about when to use force have turned on a set of vital questions, such as whether our forces match our objectives; whether we can fight and win in a time that is acceptable; whether we have a reasonable exit if we do not; whether there is public and congressional support. But we have overlooked a prior, strategic question—the question of "where"—which sets the context for such military judgments.

I see four components to a strategy of enlargement.

- First, we should strengthen the community of major market democracies—including our own—which constitutes the core from which enlargement is proceeding.
- Second, we should help foster and consolidate new democracies and market economies, where possible, especially in states of special significance and opportunity.
- Third, we must counter the aggression—and support the liberalization—of states hostile to democracy and markets.
- Fourth, we need to pursue our humanitarian agenda not only by providing aid, but also by working to help democracy and market economics take root in regions of greatest humanitarian concern....

Strengthening the Community of Major Market Democracies

Let me review each of the four components of this strategy in greater detail....

That renewal starts at home. Our efforts to empower our people, revive our economy, reduce our deficit and re-invent our government have profound implications for our global strength and the attractiveness of democracy and markets around the world. Our domestic revival will also influence how much of their hard-earned money Americans will commit to our engagement abroad....

... We are in the early stages of as great a change in the global economy as we faced at the end of World War II. And with hard times in all our nations, we face the possibility of creating vicious rather than virtuous circles of international economic action. Unless the major market democracies act together updating international economic institutions, coordinating macroeconomic policies and striking hard but fair bargains on the ground rules of open trade—the fierce competition of the new global economy, coupled with the end of our common purpose from the Cold War, could drive us into prolonged stagnation or even economic disaster.

The military problem involves NATO. For half a century, NATO has proved itself the most effective military alliance in human history. If NATO is to remain an anchor for European and Atlantic stability, as the President believes it must, its members must commit themselves to updating NATO's role in this new era. Unless NATO is willing over time to assume a broader role, then it will lose public support, and all our nations will lose a vital bond of transatlantic and European security. That is why, at the NATO summit that the president has called for this January, we will seek to update NATO, so that there continues behind the enlargement of market democracies an essential collective security.

Fostering New Democracies and Market Economies

Beyond seeing to our base, the second imperative for our strategy must be to help democracy and markets expand and survive in other places where we have the strongest security concerns and where we can make the greatest difference. This is not a democratic crusade; it is a pragmatic commitment to see freedom take hold where that will help us most. Thus, we must target our effort to assist states that affect our strategic interests, such as those with large economies, critical locations, nuclear weapons or the potential to generate refugee flows into our own nation or into key friends and allies. We must focus our efforts where we have the most leverage. And our efforts must be demand-driven—they must focus on nations whose people are pushing for reform or have already secured it.

The most important example is the former Soviet Union—and it fits the criteria I just noted. If we can support and help consolidate democratic and market reforms in Russia and the other newly independent states, we can help turn a former threat into a region of valued diplomatic and economic partners. In addition, our efforts in Russia, Ukraine and the other states raise the likelihood of continued reductions in nuclear arms and compliance with international non-proliferation accords....

The "Backlash" States

The third element of our strategy of enlargement should be to minimize the ability of states outside the circle of democracy and markets to threaten it.

Democracy and market economics have always been subversive ideas to those who rule without consent. These ideas remain subversive today. Every dictator, theocrat, kleptocrat or central planner in an unelected regime has reason to fear their subjects will suddenly demand the freedom to make their own decisions.

We should expect the advance of democracy and markets to trigger forceful reactions from those whose power is not popularly derived. The rise of Burma's democracy movement led to the jailing of its most vocal proponent, Aung San Suu Kyi. Russia's reforms have aroused the resistance of the nomenklatura.

Centralized power defends itself. It not only wields tools of state power such as military force, political imprisonment and torture, but also exploits the intolerant energies of racism, ethnic prejudice, religious persecution, xenophobia, and irredentism. Those whose power is threatened by the spread of democracy and markets will always have a personal stake in resisting those practices with passionate intensity.

When such leaders sit atop regional powers, such as Iran and Iraq, they may engage in violence and lawlessness that threatens the United States and other democracies. Such reactionary, "backlash" states are more likely to sponsor terrorism and traffic in weapons of mass destruction and ballistic missile technologies. They are more likely to suppress their own people, foment ethnic rivalries and threaten their neighbors....

Our policy toward such states, so long as they act as they do, must seek to isolate them diplomatically, militarily, economically and technologically. It must stress intelligence, counterterrorism, and multilateral export controls. It also must apply global norms regarding weapons of mass destruction and ensure their enforcement. While some of these efforts will be unilateral, international rules are necessary and may be particularly effective in enforcing sanctions, transparency and export controls, as the work of the IAEA in Iraq demonstrates....

The Humanitarian Agenda

The fourth part of a strategy of enlargement involves our humanitarian goals, which play an important supporting role in our efforts to expand democracy and markets. Our humanitarian actions nurture the American public's support for our engagement abroad. Our humanitarian efforts also can stimulate democratic and market development in many areas of the world. Ultimately, the world trusts our leadership in that broader effort in part because it witnesses our humanitarian deeds: it knows that our responses to hunger and suffering, from Bangladesh to Somalia to Chernobyl, are an expression of who we are as a nation. Our humanitarian efforts must continue to include a broad array of programs—economic and military assistance, disaster relief, and projects to assist education, nutrition and health....

While there will be increasing calls on us to help stem bloodshed and suffering in ethnic conflicts, and while we will always bring our diplomacy to bear, these criteria suggest there will be relatively few intranational ethnic conflicts that justify our military intervention. Ultimately, on these and other humanitarian needs, we will have to pick and choose.

Where we can make a difference, as in Somalia and Northern Iraq, we should not oppose using our military forces for humanitarian purposes simply because these missions do not resemble major wars for control of territory. Such missions will never be without risk, but as in all other aspects of our security policy, our military leadership is willing to accept reasonable risks in the service of our national objectives....

Current Foreign Policy Debates in Perspective

What does a strategy of enlargement tell us about the major foreign policy debates we hear today? Above all, it suggests many of those debates are overdrawn. The headlines are dominated by Bosnia, Somalia, and "multilateralism." A strategy of enlargement suggests our principal concerns should be strengthening our democratic core in North America, Europe and Japan; consolidating and enlarging democracy and markets in key places; and addressing backlash states such as Iran and Iraq. Our efforts in Somalia and Bosnia are important expressions of our overall engagement; but they do not by themselves define our broader strategy in the world.

The conflict in Bosnia deserves American engagement: it is a vast humanitarian tragedy; it is driven by ethnic barbarism; it stemmed from aggression against an independent state; it lies alongside the established and emerging market democracies of Europe and can all too easily explode into a wider Balkan conflict....

It is why we remain committed to helping implement an acceptable and enforceable peace accord, and through that commitment, encourage its achievement. But while we have clear reasons to engage and persist, they do not obliterate other American interests involving Europe and Russia, and they do not justify the extreme costs of taking unilateral responsibility for imposing a solution....

I believe strongly that our foreign policies must marry principle and pragmatism. We should be principled about our purposes but pragmatic about our means.

Today some suggest that multilateralism should be our presumptive mode of engagement. Others suggest that it is inherently flawed—dragging us into minor conflicts where we have no interest and blocking us from acting decisively where we do have an interest.

This debate is important but dangerous in the rigidity of the doctrines that are asserted. Few who bemoan multilateralism today object to NATO, the IMF, or the GATT. And it is beyond debate that multilateral action has certain advantages: it can spread the costs of action, as in our efforts to support Russian reform; it can foster global support, as with our coalition in the Gulf War; it can ensure comprehensiveness as in our export control regimes; and it can succeed where no nation, acting alone, could have done so, as in Cambodia. I would go further and state my personal hope that the habits of multilateralism may one day enable the rule of law to play a far more civilizing role in the conduct of nations, as envisioned by the founders of the United Nations.

But for any official with responsibilities for our security policies, only one overriding factor can determine whether the US should act multilaterally or unilaterally, and that is America's interests. We should act multilaterally where doing so advances our interests—and we should act unilaterally when that will serve our purpose. The simple question in each instance is this: what works best?

The Case for Engagement

I believe there is a more fundamental foreign policy challenge brewing for the United States. It is a challenge over whether we will be significantly engaged abroad at all. As I suggested at the outset, in many ways, we are returning to the divisions and debates about our role in the world that are as old as our Republic. On one side is protectionism and limited foreign engagement; on the other is active American engagement abroad on behalf of democracy and expanded trade.

The last time our nation saw that classic division was just after World War II. It pitted those Democrats and Republicans whose creativity produced the architectures of post-war prosperity and security against those in both parties who would have had us retreat within the isolated shell we occupied in the 1920s and 1930s. The internationalists won those debates, in part because they could point to a unitary threat to America's interests and because the nation was entering a period of economic security.

Today's supporters of engagement abroad have neither of those advantages. The threats and opportunities are diffuse, and our people are deeply anxious about their economic fate. Rallying Americans to bear the costs and burdens of international engagement is no less important. But it is much more difficult....

1-4 Advancing Our Interests Through Engagement and Enlargement

A National Security Strategy of
Engagement and Enlargement
The White House
July 1994

... Enhancing our Security

The US government is responsible for protecting the lives and personal safety of Americans, maintaining our political freedom and independence as a nation and providing for the well-being and prosperity of our nation. No matter how powerful we are as a nation, we cannot secure these basic goals unilaterally. Whether the problem is nuclear proliferation, regional instability, the reversal of reform in the former Soviet empire, or unfair trade practices, the threats and challenges we face demand cooperative, multinational solutions. Therefore, the only responsible US strategy is one that seeks to ensure US influence over and participation in collective decisionmaking in a wide and growing range of circumstances.

An important element of our security preparedness depends on durable relationships with allies and other friendly nations. Accordingly, a central thrust of our strategy of engagement is to sustain and adapt the security relationships we have with key nations around the world. These ties constitute an important part of an international framework that will be essential to ensuring cooperation across a broad range of issues. Within the realm of security issues, our cooperation with allies includes such activities as: conducting combined training and exercises, coordinating military plans and preparations, sharing intelligence, jointly developing new systems, and controlling exports of sensitive technologies according to common standards....

Deciding When and How to Employ US Forces

Our strategy calls for the development and deployment of American military forces in the United States and abroad to respond to key dangers

—those posed by weapons of mass destruction, regional aggression and threats to the stability of states.

Although there may be many demands for US involvement, the need to husband scarce resources suggests that we must carefully select the means and level of our participation in particular military operations. It is unwise to specify in advance all the limitations we will place on our use of force, but it is appropriate to identify several basic principles that will guide our decisions on when to use force.

First, and foremost, our national interests will dictate the pace and extent of our engagement. In all cases, the costs and risks of US military involvement must be judged to be commensurate with the stakes involved. In those specific areas where our vital or survival interests—those of broad, overriding importance to the survival, security and vitality of our national entity—are at stake, our use of force will be decisive and, if necessary, unilateral. In other situations posing a less immediate threat, our military engagement must be targeted selectively on those areas that most affect our national interests—for instance, areas where we have a sizable economic stake or commitments to allies, and areas where there is a potential to generate substantial refugee flows into our nation or our allies.

Second, as much as possible, we will seek the help of our allies or of relevant multilateral institutions. If our most important national interests are at stake, we are prepared to act alone. But especially on those matters touching directly the interests of our allies, there should be a proportional commitment from them.

Third, in every case, we will consider several critical questions before committing military force. Have we considered nonmilitary means that offer a reasonable chance of success? What types of US military capabilities should he brought to bear, and is the use of military force carefully matched to our political objectives? Do we have reasonable assurance of support from the American people and their elected representatives? Do we have timelines and milestones that will reveal the extent of success or failure, and, in either case, do we have an exit strategy?

Fourth, our engagement must meet reasonable cost and feasibility thresholds. We will be more inclined to act where there is reason to believe that our action will bring lasting improvement. On the other hand, our involvement will he more circumscribed when other regional or multilateral actors are better positioned to act than we are. Even in these cases, however, the United States will be actively engaged at the diplomatic level....

Combatting the Spread and Use of Weapons of Mass Destruction and Missiles

Weapons of mass destruction—nuclear, biological, and chemical—along with the missiles that deliver them, pose a major threat to our security and that of our allies and other friendly nations. Thus, a key part of our strategy is to seek to stem the proliferation of such weapons and to develop an effective capability to deal with these threats. We also need to maintain robust strategic nuclear forces while seeking to implement existing strategic arms agreements.

Nonproliferation and Counterproliferation

A critical priority for the United States is to stem the proliferation of nuclear weapons and other weapons of mass destruction and their missile delivery systems. Countries' weapons programs, and their levels of cooperation with our nonproliferation efforts, will be among our most important criteria in judging the nature of our bilateral relations.

As a key part of our effort to control nuclear proliferation, we seek the indefinite extension of the Nonproliferation Treaty (NPT) beyond 1995 and its universal application. Achieving a Comprehensive Test Ban Treaty as soon as possible, ending the unsafeguarded production of fissile materials for nuclear weapons purposes and strengthening the Nuclear Suppliers Group and the International Atomic Energy Agency (IAEA) are important goals. They complement our comprehensive efforts to discourage the accumulation of fissile materials, to seek to strengthen controls and constraints on those materials, and over time, to reduce world-wide stocks.

To combat missile proliferation, the United States seeks prudently to broaden membership of the Missile Technology Control Regime (MTCR). The Administration supports the prompt ratification and earliest possible entry in force of the Chemical Weapons Convention (CWC) as well as new measures to deter violations of and enhance compliance with the Biological Weapons Convention (BWC). We also support improved export controls for nonproliferation purposes both domestically and multilaterally.

The proliferation problem is global, but we must tailor our approaches to specific regional contexts. We are leading international efforts to bring North Korea into compliance with its nonproliferation obligations, including the NPT, IAEA safeguards, and the North-South denuclearization accord. We will continue efforts to prevent Iran from advancing its weapons of mass destruction objectives and to thwart Iraq from reconstituting its previous programs. The United States seeks to cap, reduce and, ultimately, eliminate the nuclear and missile capabilities of India and Pakistan. In the Middle East and elsewhere, we encourage regional arms control agreements that address the legitimate security concerns of all parties. These tasks are being pursued with other states that share our concern for the enormous challenge of stemming the proliferation of such weapons....

Peace Operations

In addition to preparing for major regional contingencies, we must prepare our forces for peace operations to support democracy or conflict resolution. The United States, along with others in the international community, will seek to prevent and contain localized conflicts before they require a military response. US support capabilities such as airlift, intelligence, and global communications, have often contributed to the success of multilateral peace operations, and they will continue to do so. US combat units are less likely to be used for most peace operations, but in some cases their use will be necessary or desirable and justified by US national interests as guided by the Presidential Decision Directive, "US Policy on Reforming Multilateral Peace Operations," and outlined below.

Multilateral peace operations are an important component of our strategy. From traditional peacekeeping to peace enforcement, multilateral peace operations are sometimes the best way to prevent, contain, or resolve conflicts that could otherwise be far more costly and deadly....

At the same time, however, we must recognize that peace operations make demands on the UN that exceed the organization's current capabilities. The United States is working with the UN headquarters and other member states to ensure that the UN embarks only on peace operations that make political and military sense and that the UN is able to manage effectively those peace operations it does undertake. We support the creation of a professional UN peace operations headquarters with a planning staff, access to timely intelligence, a logistics unit that can be rapidly deployed and a modern operations center with global communications. The United States is committed to working with the United Nations to see that we pay our bills in full, while reducing our nation's proportional assessment for these missions.

When deciding whether to support a particular UN peace operation, the United States will insist that fundamental questions be asked before new obligations are undertaken. These include an assessment of the threat to international peace and security, a determination that the peace operation serves US interests as well as assurance of an international community of interests for dealing with that threat on a multilateral basis, identification of clear objectives, availability of the necessary resources, and identification of an operation's endpoint or criteria for completion.

Most UN peacekeeping operations do not involve US forces. On those occasions when we consider contributing US forces to a UN peace operation, we will employ rigorous criteria, including the same principles that would guide any decision to employ US forces. In addition, we will ensure that the risks to US personnel and the command and control arrangements governing the participation of American and foreign forces are acceptable to the United States.

The question of command and control is particularly critical. There may be times when it is in our interest to place US troops under the temporary operational control of a competent UN or allied commander. The United States has done so many times in the past—from the siege of Yorktown in the Revolutionary War to the battles of Desert Storm. However, under no circumstances will the President ever relinquish his command authority over US forces....

Integrated Regional Approaches

The United States is a genuinely global power. Our policy toward each of the world's regions reflects our overall strategy tailored to their unique challenges and opportunities. This section highlights the application of our strategy to each of the world's regions; our broad objectives and thrust, rather than an exhaustive list of all our policies and interests. It illustrates how we integrate our commitment to the promotion of democracy and the enhancement of American prosperity with our security requirements to produce a mutually reinforcing policy.

Europe and Eurasia

... The first and most important element of our strategy in Europe must be security through military strength and cooperation. The Cold War is over, but war itself is not over.

As we know, it rages in the former Yugoslavia. While that war does not pose an immediate threat to our security or warrant unilateral US involvement, US policy is focussed on four goals: preventing the spread of the fighting into a broader European war that could threaten both allies and the stability of new democratic states in Central and Eastern Europe; stemming the destabilizing flow of refugees from the conflict; halting the slaughter of innocents; and helping to confirm NATO's central role in post-Cold War Europe....

With the adoption of the US initiative, partnership for Peace, at the January 1994 summit, NATO is playing an increasingly important role in our strategy of European integration, extending the scope of our security cooperation to the new democracies of Europe. Twenty-one nations, including Russia, have already joined the partnership, which will pave the way for a growing program of military cooperation and political consultation. Partner countries are sending representatives to NATO headquarters near Brussels and to a military coordination cell at Mons—the site of SHAPE. Joint exercises will take place later this year in Poland and the Netherlands.

In keeping with our strategy of enlargement, PFP is open to all former members of the Warsaw Pact as well as other European states. Each partner will set the scope and pace of its cooperation with NATO. During his trip to Europe in July, the President reaffirmed his commitment to NATO's future expansion, with PFP the best path toward NATO membership. The aim of NATO's future expansion, however, will not be to draw a new line in Europe further east, but to expand stability, democracy, prosperity and security cooperation to an ever-broader Europe.

The second element of the new strategy for Europe is economic. The United States seeks to build on vibrant and open market economies, the engines that have given us the greatest prosperity in human history over the last several decades in Europe and in the United States. To this end, we strongly support the process of European integration embodied in the European Union, seek to deepen our partnership with the EU in support of our economic goals but also commit ourselves to the encouragement of bilateral trade and investment in countries not part of the EU....

The third and final imperative of this new strategy is to support the growth of democracy and individual freedoms that has begun in Russia, the nations of the former Soviet Union and Europe's former communist states. The success of these democratic reforms makes us all more secure; they are the best answers to the aggressive nationalism and ethnic hatreds unleashed by the end of the Cold War. Nowhere is democracy's success more important to us all than in these countries.

East Asia and the Pacific

East Asia is a region of growing importance for US security and prosperity; nowhere are the strands of our three-pronged strategy more intertwined, nor is the need for continued US engagement more evident. Now more than ever, security, open markets and democracy go hand in hand in our approach to this dynamic region. President Clinton envisions an integrated strategy—a New Pacific Community—which links security requirements with economic realities and our concern for democracy and human rights....

As the first pillar of our New Pacific Community, we are pursuing stronger efforts to combat the proliferation of weapons of mass destruction on the Korean peninsula and in South Asia. We have instituted new regional dialogues on the full range of common security challenges. Our goal is to integrate, not isolate the region's powers and to find solutions, short of conflict, to the area's continuing security challenges....

We are working with Japan to bring about the implementation of the 1993 Framework Agreement to ensure that the economic leg of that relationship is as healthy and vibrant as our political and security links. We are developing a broader engagement with the People's Republic of China that will encompass both our economic and strategic interests. That policy is best reflected in our decision to delink China's Most Favored Nation status from its record on human rights. We are also working to facilitate China's development of a more open market economy that accepts international trade practices. Given its growing economic potential and already sizable military force, it is essential that China not become a security threat to the region. To that end, we are strongly promoting China's participation in regional security mechanisms to reassure its neighbors and assuage its own security concerns. And we are seeking to gain further cooperation from China in controlling the proliferation of weapons of mass destruction.

We are also moving to take advantage of evolving multilateral mechanisms. The APEC summit, hosted by President Clinton last year, is vivid testimony to the possibilities of stimulating regional economic cooperation.

The third pillar of our policy in building a new Pacific community is to support the wave of democratic reform sweeping the region. The new democratic states of Asia will have our strong support as they move forward to consolidate and expand democratic reforms. Some have argued that democracy is somehow unsuited for Asia or at least for some Asian nations—that human rights are relative and that they simply mask Western culturalism and imperialism. These voices are wrong. It is not Western imperialism, but the aspirations of Asian peoples themselves that explain the growing number of democracies and the growing strength of democracy movements everywhere in Asia. It is an insult to the spirit, the hopes, and the dreams of the people who live and struggle in those countries to assert otherwise....

The Middle East, Southwest and South Asia

The United States has enduring interests in the Middle East, especially pursuing a comprehensive breakthrough to Middle East peace, assuring the security of Israel and our Arab friends, and maintaining the free flow of oil at reasonable prices. Our strategy is harnessed to the unique characteristics of the region and our vital interests there, as we work to extend the range of peace and stability, while implementing a strategy of dual containment of Iraq and Iran as long as those states pose a threat to US interests, to other states in the region, and to their own citizens....

We have made solid progress in the past year. The President's effort helped bring about an historic first—the handshake of peace between Prime Minister Rabin and Chairman Arafat on the White House lawn. The President will bring Prime Minister Rabin and King Hussein to Washington for an historic meeting to advance the peace process further. But our efforts have not stopped there; on other bilateral tracks and through regional dialogue we are working to foster a durable peace and a comprehensive settlement, while our support for economic development can bring hope to all the peoples of the region.

In Southwest Asia, the United States will maintain its longstanding presence, which has been centered on naval vessels in and near the Persian Gulf and prepositioned combat equipment. Since Operation Desert Storm, temporary deployments of land-based aviation forces, ground forces and amphibious units have supplemented our posture in the Gulf region.

While we hold out the hand of cooperation and assistance to the nations of the region that choose peace, we are firm in our determination to contain and resist those who foster conflict. We have instituted a new dual containment strategy aimed at both Iraq and Iran....

Africa

Africa is one of our greatest challenges for a strategy of engagement and enlargement. Throughout Africa, the US policy seeks to help support democracy, sustainable economic development and resolution of conflicts through negotiation, diplomacy and peacekeeping. New policies will focus on efforts to strengthen civil societies and mechanisms for conflict resolution, particularly where ethnic, religious, arid political tensions are acute. In particular, we intend to focus on identifying and addressing the root causes of conflicts and disasters before they erupt.

The nexus of economic, political, social, ethnic and environmental challenges lacing Africa can lead to a sense of "Afro-pessimism." We will instead seek to simultaneously address these challenges and create a synergy that can stimulate development, resurrect societies and build hope. Throughout the continent—in Rwanda, Burundi, Mozambique, Angola, Liberia, Sudan and elsewhere—we encourage peaceful resolution of internal disputes to promote long-term stability and development of the region. We also encourage democratic reform in nations like Nigeria and Zaire to allow the people of these countries to enjoy responsive government....

1-5 On the Eve of the Millennium

Speech on Foreign Policy
San Francisco, California
February 26, 1999

... There is still the potential for major regional wars that would threaten our security. The arms race between India and Pakistan reminds us that the next big war could still be nuclear. There is a risk that our former adversaries will not succeed in their transitions to freedom and free markets. There is a danger that deadly weapons will fall into the hands of a terrorist group or an outlaw nation and that those weapons could be chemical or biological. There is a danger of deadly alliances among terrorists, narco-traffickers, and organized criminal groups. There is a danger of global environmental crises and the spread of deadly diseases. There is a danger that global financial turmoil will undermine open markets, overwhelm open societies, and undercut our own prosperity.

We must avoid both the temptation to minimize these dangers and the illusion that the proper response to them is to batten down the hatches and protect America against the world. The promise of our future lies in the world. Therefore, we must work hard with the world to defeat the dangers we face together and to build this hopeful moment together, into a generation of peace, prosperity, and freedom. Because of our unique position, America must lead with confidence in our strengths and with a clear vision of what we seek to avoid and what we seek to advance.

Our first challenge is to build a more peaceful twenty-first century world. To that end, we're renewing alliances that extend the area where wars do not happen and working to stop the conflicts that are claiming lives and threatening our interests right now.

The century's bloodiest wars began in Europe. That's why I've worked hard to build a Europe that finally is undivided, democratic, and at peace. We want all of Europe to have what America helped build in Western Europe, a community that upholds common standards of human rights, where people have the confidence and security to invest in the future, where nations cooperate to make war unthinkable.

That is why I have pushed hard for NATO's enlargement and why we must keep NATO's doors open to new democratic members, so that other nations will have an incentive to deepen their democracies. That is why we must forge a partnership between NATO and Russia, between NATO and Ukraine; why we are building a NATO capable not only of deterring aggression against its own territory but of meeting challenges to our security beyond its territory, the kind of NATO we must advance at the fiftieth anniversary summit in Washington this April.

We are building a stronger alliance with Japan, and renewing our commitment to deter aggression in Korea and intensifying our efforts for a genuine peace there....

It's easy, for example, to say that we really have no interests in who lives in this or that valley in Bosnia or who owns a strip of brushland in the Horn of Africa or some piece of parched earth by the Jordan River. But the true measure of our interests lies not in how small or distant these places are or in whether we have trouble pronouncing their names. The question we must ask is, what are the consequences to our security of letting conflicts fester and spread? We cannot, indeed, we should not, do everything or be everywhere. But where our values and our interests are at stake and where we can make a difference, we must be prepared to do so. And we must remember that the real challenge of foreign policy is to deal with problems before they harm our national interests....

It is in our interest to be a peacemaker, not because we think we can make all these differences go away, but because in over 200 years of hard effort here at home and with bitter and good experiences around the world, we have learned that the world works better when differences are resolved by the force of argument rather than the force of arms.

That is why I am proud of the work we have done to support peace in Northern Ireland and why we will keep pressing the leaders there to observe not just the letter but the spirit of the Good Friday accords.

It is also why I intend to use the time I have remaining in this office to push for a comprehensive peace in the Middle East, to encourage Israelis and Palestinians to reach a just and final settlement, and to stand by our friends for peace, such as Jordan. The people of the Middle East can do it, but time is precious, and they can't afford to waste any more of it. In their hearts, they know there can be no security or justice for any who live in that small and sacred land until there is security and justice for all who live there. If they do their part, we must do ours.

We will also keep working with our allies to build peace in the Balkans. Three years ago, we helped to end the war in Bosnia. A lot of doubters then thought it would soon start again. But Bosnia is on a steady path toward renewal and democracy. We've been able to reduce our troops there by 75 percent as peace has taken hold, and we will continue to bring them home.

The biggest remaining danger to this progress has been the fighting and the repression in Kosovo. Kosovo is, after all, where the violence in the former Yugoslavia began, over a decade ago, when they lost the autonomy guaranteed under Yugoslav law. We have a clear national interest in ensuring that Kosovo is where this trouble ends. If it continues, it almost certainly will draw in Albania and Macedonia, which share borders with Kosovo, and on which clashes have already occurred....

Here's where we are. The Kosovar Albanian leaders have agreed in principle to a plan that would protect the rights of their people and give them substantial self-government. Serbia has agreed to much, but not all, of the conditions of autonomy and has so far not agreed to the necessity of a NATO-led international force to maintain the peace there.

Serbia's leaders must now accept that only by allowing people in Kosovo control over their day-to-day lives—as, after all, they had been promised under Yugoslav law—it is only by doing that can they keep their country intact. Both sides must return to the negotiations on March 15, with clear mandate for peace. In the meantime, President Milosevic should understand that this is a time for restraint, not repression, and if he does not, NATO is prepared to act.

Now, if there is a peace agreement that is effective, NATO must also be ready to deploy to Kosovo to give both sides the confidence to lay down their arms. Europeans would provide the great bulk of such a force, roughly 85 percent, but if there is a real peace, America must do its part as well.

Kosovo is not an easy problem. But if we don't stop the conflict now, it clearly will spread. And then we will not be able to stop it, except at far greater cost and risk.

A second challenge we face is to bring our former adversaries, Russia and China, into the international system as open, prosperous, stable nations. The way both countries develop in the coming century will have a lot to do with the future of our planet.

For fifty years, we confronted the challenge of Russia's strength. Today, we must confront the risk of a Russia weakened by the legacy of communism and also by its inability at the moment to maintain prosperity at home or control the flow of its money, weapons, and technology across its borders....

The Russian people will decide their own future. But we must work with them for the best possible outcome with realism and with patience. If Russia does what it must to make its economy work, I am ready to do everything I can to mobilize adequate international support for them. With the right framework, we will also encourage foreign investment in its factories, its energy fields, its people. We will increase our support for small business and for the independent media. We will work to continue cutting our two nations' nuclear arsenals and help Russia prevent both its weapons and its expertise from falling into the wrong hands. The budget I have presented to Congress will increase funding for this critical threat reduction by 70 percent over the next five years.

The question China faces is how best to assure its stability and progress. Will it choose openness and engagement? Or will it choose to limit the aspirations of its people without fully embracing the global rules of the road? In my judgment, only the first path can really answer the challenges China faces....

China's leaders know more economic reform is needed, and they know reform will cause more unemployment, and they know that can cause unrest. At the same time, and perhaps for those reasons, they remain unwilling to open up their political system, to give people a peaceful outlet for dissent.

Now, we Americans know that dissent is not always comfortable, not always easy, and often raucous. But I believe that the fact that we have peaceful, orderly outlets for dissent is one of the principal reasons we're still around here as the longest lasting freely elected Government in the world. And I believe, sooner or later, China will have to come to understand that a society, in the world we're living in, particularly a country as great and old and rich and full of potential as China, simply cannot purchase stability at the expense of freedom.

On the other hand, we have to ask ourselves, what is the best thing to do to try to maximize the chance that China will take the right course, and that, because of that, the world will be freer, more peaceful, more prosperous in the twenty-first century? I do not believe we can hope to bring change to China if we isolate China from the forces of change. Of course, we have our differences, and we must press them. But we can do that and expand our cooperation through principled and purposeful engagement with China, its government, and its people.

Our third great challenge is to build a future in which our people are safe from the dangers that arise, perhaps halfway around the world, dangers from proliferation, from terrorism, from drugs, from the multiple catastrophes that could arise from climate change.

Each generation faces the challenges of not trying to fight the last war. In our case, that means recognizing that the more likely future threat to our existence is not a strategic nuclear strike from Russia or China but the use of weapons of mass destruction by an outlaw nation or a terrorist group.

In the last six years, fighting that threat has become a central priority of American foreign policy. Here, too, there is much more to be done. We are working to stop weapons from spreading at the source, as with Russia. We are working to keep Iraq in check so that it does not threaten the rest of the world or its region with weapons of mass destruction. We are using all the means at our disposal to deny terrorists safe havens, weapons, and funds. Even if it takes years, terrorists must know there is no place to hide....

Many of these subjects are new and unfamiliar and may be frightening. As I said when I gave an address in Washington not very long ago about what we were doing on biological and computer security and criminal threats, it is important that we have the right attitude about this. It is important that we understand that the risks are real, and they require, therefore, neither denial nor panic. As long as people organize themselves in human societies, there will be organized forces of destruction who seek to take advantage of new means of destroying other people....

We are working to develop a national missile defense system which could, if we decide to deploy it, be deployed against emerging ballistic missile threats from rogue nations. We are bolstering the global agreements that curb proliferation. That's the most important thing we can be doing right now. This year, we hope to achieve an accord to strengthen compliance with the convention against biological weapons.

It's a perfectly good convention, but frankly, it has no teeth. We have to give it some. And we will ask our Senate to ratify the Comprehensive Test Ban Treaty to stop nations from testing nuclear weapons so they're constrained from developing new ones. Again, I say: I implore the United States Senate to ratify the Comprehensive Test Ban Treaty this year. It is very important for the United States and the world.

Our security and our safety also depends upon doing more to protect our people from the scourge of drugs. To win this fight, we must work with others, including and especially Mexico. Mexico has a serious drug problem, increasingly affecting more of its own young people. No one understands this better than President Zedillo. He described it as the number one threat to his country's security, its people, its democracy. He is working hard to establish clean government, true democracy, and the rule of law. He is working hard to tackle the corruption traffickers have wrought....

As I certified to Congress today, Mexico is cooperating with us in the battle for our lives. And I believe the American people will be safer in this, as in so many other ways, if we fight drugs with Mexico, rather than walk away.

Another global danger we face is climate change. As far as we can tell, with all the scientific evidence available, the hottest years our planet has ever experienced were 1997 and 1998. The two hottest years recorded in the last several—excuse me—nine of the ten hottest years recorded in the last several centuries occurred in the last decade.

Now, we can wait and hope and do nothing and try to ignore what the vast majority of scientists tell us is a pattern that is fixed and continuing. We could ignore the record-breaking temperatures, the floods, the storms, the droughts that have caused such misery. Or we can accept that preventing the disease and destruction climate change can bring will be infinitely cheaper than letting future generations try to clean up the mess, especially when you consider that greenhouse gases, once emitted into the atmosphere, last and have a destructive environmental effect for at least a hundred years.

We took a giant step forward in 1997, when we helped to forge the Kyoto agreement. Now we're working to persuade developing countries that they, too, can and must participate meaningfully in this effort without forgoing growth. We are also trying to persuade a majority in the United States Congress that we can do the same thing....

Our fourth challenge is to create a world trading and financial system that will lift the lives of ordinary people on every continent around the world or, as it has been stated in other places, to put a human face on the global economy. Over the last six years, we've taken giant steps in opening the global trading system. The United States alone has concluded over 270 different trade agreements. Once again, we are the world's largest exporting nation. There is a lot more to be done....

The question is what to do about it. Some of the folks outside who were protesting when I drove up were saying by their signs that they believe globalization is inherently bad, and there's no way in the wide world to put a human face on the global economy. But if you look at the facts of the last thirty years, hundreds of millions of people have had their economic prospects advanced on every continent because they have finally been able to find a way to express their creativity in positive terms and produce goods and services that could be purchased beyond the borders of their nation....

I don't want to minimize the complexity of this challenge. As nations began to trade more and as investment rules began to permit people to invest in countries other than their own more, it became more and more necessary to facilitate the conversion of currencies. Whenever you do that, you will create a market against risk, just in the transfer of currencies. Whenever you do that, you will have people that are moving money around because they think the value of the money itself will change and profit might be gained in an independent market of currency exchange.

It is now true that on any given day, there is $1 and 1/2 trillion of currency exchange in the world. Many, many, many times more than the actual value of the exchange of goods and services. And we have got to find a way to facilitate the movement of money, without which trade and investment cannot occur, in a way that avoids these dramatic cycles of boom and then bust, which have led to the collapse of economic activity in so many countries around the world.

We found a way to do it in the United States after the Great Depression. And thank goodness we have never again had a Great Depression, even though we've had good times and bad times. That is the challenge facing the world financial system today.

The leading economies have got a lot of work to do. We have to do everything we can, not just the United States, but Europe and Japan, to spur economic growth. Unless there is a restoration of growth, all the changes in the financial rules we make will not get Asia, Latin America, countries—Russia—out of their difficulties.

We have to be ready to provide quick and decisive help to nations committed to sound policies. We have to help nations build social safety nets so that, when they have inevitable changes in their economic conditions, people at least have the basic security they need to continue to embrace change and advance the overall welfare of society.

We have to encourage nations to maintain open, properly financed— excuse me—properly regulated financial systems so that decisions are shaped by informed market decisions and not distorted by corruption. We also have to take responsible steps to reform the global financial architecture for the twenty-first century....

Our fifth challenge has to keep freedom as a top goal for the world of the twenty-first century....

Therefore, beyond economics, beyond the transformation of the great countries to economic security—Russia and China—beyond even many of our security concerns, we also have to recognize that we can have no greater purpose than to support the right of other people to live in freedom and shape their own destiny. If that right could be universally exercised, virtually every goal I have outlined today would be advanced....

2. Dealing with Russia

When Mikhail Gorbachev resigned as Soviet President on Christmas Day, 1991, the Union of Soviet Socialist Republics (USSR) collapsed. Its core republic, Russia, led by Boris Yeltsin, emerged as a nation-state, ending 450 years of imperial expansion. The sudden end of the bipolar international system, which had structured world politics since 1945, introduced a critical change into the strategic environment and called for a rethinking of the US national security policy. A new era in US-Russian relations was beginning.

In his memoirs, Secretary of State James A. Baker III describes Soviet President Gorbachev's uncomprehending despair at the state of affairs ten days before he resigned and Yeltsin's firm sense of growing power. In his discussion with Yeltsin, Baker mapped out a course that augured well for the future. Yeltsin, he wrote, agreed to work with the other former Soviet republics to control nuclear weapons, to curb nuclear proliferation, and to push quickly for ratification of the Strategic Arms Reduction Treaty (START) and the Conventional Forces in Europe Treaty (CFE). Baker found Yeltsin reassuring, forthcoming, informed.

However, although Washington was dealing with a politically congenial ruler in post-communist Russia, it was virtually indifferent to the strategic opportunity at hand. Now that the Cold War was over, it seemed as if Washington had lost interest in Russia. For ambiguous reasons, President George Bush was slow to mobilize the resources of the West and Japan to help Yeltsin embark on his professed project of transforming and democratizing Russia.

Ironically, it took former President Richard Nixon to focus public attention on the challenge that Russia posed for the United States. In a speech on March 11, 1992, Nixon stressed the importance of helping Russia move toward a "free-market economy" and making the most of Yeltsin's leadership. In retrospect, his words seem almost prophetic:

> Yeltsin is the most pro-Western leader in Russian history. Under those circumstances, then, he deserves our help. Charity, it is said, begins at home, and I agree. But aid to Russia, just speaking of Russia specifically, is not charity. We have to realize that if Yeltsin fails, the alternative is not going to be somebody better—it's going to be somebody infinitely worse. We have to realize that if Yeltsin fails, the new despotism, which will take its place, will mean that the peace dividend is finished, we will have to rearm, and that's going to cost infinitely more than would the aid that we provide at the present time.

A month later, goaded to action, President Bush pressed the major industrial nations (known as the Group of Seven or G-7), the International Monetary Fund (IMF), and the World Bank to put together a financial package of $24 billion to help Russia in 1992. The money was not wisely spent: most of it went for commodity credits, to forestall food shortages, rather than debt repayment, currency stabilization, and major economic reforms. By the end of that first year, Russia's reformers had already been discredited, and Yeltsin's opponents in the Russian parliament were gaining influence.

In the United States, 1992 was an election year. Both President Bush and candidate Clinton recognized the saliency of domestic concerns and shared a desire to downplay foreign affairs. Clinton advocated aid for Russia in a few of his speeches, but his focus remained the domestic economy. The net effect was that Russia was relegated to the sidelines for most of the presidential campaign, and Washington paid little attention to the promised financial package for Russia or the efforts of the beleaguered Russian reformers to introduce a market-oriented economy.

Once in office, President Clinton did somewhat better by Russia than his predecessor had. He defended Yeltsin against his opponents in the parliament when they threatened him with impeachment in March 1993: "I want to reiterate that the United States supports the historic movement toward democratic political reform in Russia. President Yeltsin is the leader of that process," Clinton stated during a news conference on March 23, 1993. One week later, in remarks to the American Society of Newspaper Editors, he spoke at length about Russia, situating its anticipated transformation in the general context of the global economy (Speech 2-1). In several places, the President linked economic reform with enhanced security, and showed how both were intrinsic to what the United States sought to promote in relations with Russia.

During their first summit meeting, held in early April 1993 in Vancouver, Canada, Clinton and Yeltsin discussed arms control issues and economic assistance. Clinton offered financial aid as a demonstration of confidence (Speech 2-2), but the package that he put together sounded more impressive that it was in reality. By the end of the year, only a small fraction of the announced aid had arrived, and once again the utilization of the financial assistance did not produce the desired results.

In the summer and early fall of 1993, President Yeltsin faced a new challenge from the parliament, where opponents again called for his ouster. On September 21, an irate and frustrated Yeltsin dissolved the parliament. In response, the parliament impeached Yeltsin. The Russian military took the side of the President and on his orders besieged the parliament building on October 3 – 4. The military's support proved decisive. On December 12, 1993, elections were held to ratify a new constitution and elect a new parliament, called the Duma. To Yeltsin's disappointment, however, two contentious opposition groups, the ultra-nationalist Liberal Democratic Party and the Communist Party, came to dominate the new Duma. Although the new constitution, approved on the same day, significantly expanded the President's powers at the Duma's expense, the low voter turnout of about 55 percent, and the fact that only 58.4 percent of the voters favored ratification, clearly indicated Yeltsin's diminished popularity with the electorate.

Throughout the constitutional crisis in Russia, Clinton tried to demonstrate his support for, and confidence in, the Russian President (Speech 2-3). He provided a psychological boost intended to affirm the importance attributed by Washington to Yeltsin's survival, but the actual impact may have been minor, considering the subsequent success of Yeltsin's opponents in the elections for the new Duma. Simultaneously, Clinton did little to expand or accelerate the flow of promised aid to Yeltsin when the latter most needed it. There is every reason to believe that Yeltsin looked to Washington for the wherewithal to finance Russia's economic transformation and provide the population with a safety net against any further drastic decline in living standards or increase in unemployment. However, Clinton remained focused on domestic issues. In foreign policy an array of issues—the UN peacekeeping operations in Somalia and Haiti, Israeli-Palestinian developments, and outreach to China—all acted to limit his attention to what Yeltsin desperately needed from the United States during that critical period.

A number of other developments, both American and Russian, that were later to have profound implications for US policy toward Russia and US-Russian relations started to unfold in late 1993 and early 1994. On the American side, two may be noted. First, Clinton selected a political approach to Russia that did not anticipate the difficulties that country would experience in its attempted democratization and economic transformation.

Clinton seemed to underestimate the challenge of trying to forge a "special relationship" with Yeltsin and failed to appreciate the obstacles that had to be surmounted before Russia could turn around its troubled economy.

Second, Clinton adopted a pyramid of positions that eventually led to NATO's expansion in 1999. In response to pressure from allies in Western Europe and friendly governments in the Czech Republic and Poland, in particular, Clinton—paying little heed to the triumph of nationalist and anti-Western forces in the December 1993 Duma elections—signaled his commitment to enlarging NATO in the years ahead. The first step in this direction was taken at a NATO summit meeting in Brussels on January 10 – 11, 1994, where Clinton announced the Partnership for Peace (PFP) proposal, holding out the prospect of eventual NATO membership for the countries of Central and Eastern Europe and the republics of the former Soviet Union, including Russia. For the moment, the timing and criteria were left open. Meanwhile, under pressure from his opponents, Yeltsin became a critic of NATO's PFP program. In December 1994, at the Budapest meeting of the Organization of Security and Cooperation in Europe (OSCE), an all-European venue for discussing European security issues, Yeltsin lashed out at NATO for taking Russia too lightly and warned of a "Cold Peace."

On the Russian side, the reformers had lost control. By 1994, Yeltsin's policies were more accurately characterized as holding the line—and the reins of power—than pushing basic reforms. Loans received from the International Monetary Fund as a result of US support went to paying off existing debts and to rewarding Kremlin favorites: corruption and cronyism were endemic. The economy continued to show negative growth: indeed, from 1992 to 1999 there was not a single year in which the Gross National Product of Russia increased. A Duma hostile to Yeltsin and to major reforms crippled efforts to develop a coherent national policy. All of this made the task of coordinating assistance to Russia more difficult.

Yeltsin's prestige at home and with the United States was also tarnished by his flawed policy toward Chechnya and the failure of the Russian military to suppress the attempted secession of that autonomous Muslim region of southern Russia. Chechnya had been troublesome ever since the 1830s, when it was absorbed into the Tsarist Empire. In the waning months of Soviet rule, a Chechen nationalist leadership headed by Djokhar Dudaev, a former General in the Soviet Air Force, proclaimed Chechnya's independence. Emboldened by Moscow's initial permissiveness in 1992 and 1993, the Chechens stopped paying taxes to the federal central government, siphoned off oil that was transiting the region and used the proceeds to purchase weapons, and became heavily involved in drug trafficking and other criminal activity.

In December 1994, assured by his military advisers that the Russian Army would quickly rout the Chechens, Yeltsin moved to end the separatist challenge. But instead of a fast campaign, Moscow found itself in a costly war, which raged on until the summer of 1996 when Yeltsin, newly reelected, agreed to an uneasy peace, and the final status of Chechnya was deferred until the year 2001. Throughout the war, Russian troops were consistently outfought and outmaneuvered by the Chechens, Russia's domestic situation worsened, and Yeltsin's prestige plummeted.

On several occasions, President Clinton deplored the developments in Chechnya, but simultaneously reaffirmed faith in Yeltsin's leadership. For example, during a news conference on March 3, 1995, President Clinton was asked to provide a measure of his confidence in Yeltsin in light of the latter's failure to end the fighting in Chechnya. Clinton responded by stating, "I have dealt directly with him in urging a change and a moderation of policy there, and I will continue to do that. My confidence level in him is strong," thereby avoiding any criticism that could be used to weaken the Russian President.

Meanwhile, US-Russian relations were in a holding pattern. An opportunity for some initiative presented itself during Clinton's state visit to Russia in May 1995, on the occasion of the fiftieth anniversary of the Allied victory over Nazi Germany. In a major speech to the students of Moscow State University, President Clinton reaffirmed his commitment to a partnership between the United States and Russia (Speech 2-4). He acknowledged the difficulties that Russia was experiencing in shifting to a market-oriented economy and carrying out painful reforms, but urged it to persist, noting that much progress had already been made. To the students the President made the case for a continuing commitment to the political process, strengthening and safeguarding a democratic system. He praised Yeltsin, doubtless seeking to enhance his prospects in the Russian Presidential elections scheduled for mid-1996. As so often in the previous two years, Clinton equated Russian democracy with President Yeltsin, thus personalizing US-Russian relations, perhaps inordinately.

The May 1995 summit, however, marked only a temporary repair of the deteriorating relationship between Moscow and Washington. In late August 1995, US-led NATO air strikes against the Bosnian Serbs, which helped end the bitter fighting in Bosnia's civil war, infuriated the Duma, which was pro-Serb and highly suspicious of US policy aims. The strikes also nudged Yeltsin, for electoral reasons, to adopt a harder line against NATO's unilateralist use of force and its disregard of Moscow's insistence that only the UN Security Council could approve military measures against a member state.

Yeltsin was reelected in June 1996, but his second term in office witnessed a further decline in US-Russian relations. Beset by serious health problems, Russia's ailing economy, and Kremlin in-fighting that often assumed scandalous proportions, Yeltsin also had little to show for his foreign policy. In important measure, his growing coolness toward Washington paralleled Clinton's acceleration of the timetable for NATO's enlargement, announced in late October 1996, on the eve of the US Presidential election.

Aware of Moscow's growing estrangement over this issue, Clinton sought to allay Yeltsin's concerns. In December 1996, the North Atlantic Council, NATO's authoritative political body, stated that the alliance did not intend to deploy nuclear weapons on the territory of the new members. A month later, in a further effort to reassure Russia, consultations began between NATO and Russian officials to draft a document that would signify a budding partnership. To settle the final points in dispute, Clinton and Yeltsin met in Helsinki, Finland, on March 20 – 21, 1997.

The resulting NATO-Russia Founding Act, signed in Paris on May 27, 1997, gave Russia "a voice but not a veto" in NATO affairs. It held the two parties to be equal partners, but said little about implications for the nuclear and conventional arms control talks then underway. President Clinton again emphasized that NATO was not a threat to Russia, that a "historic change in relationship between Russia and NATO" was taking place, and that NATO was rebuilding itself and "will be an alliance directed no longer against a hostile bloc of nations but instead designed to advance the security of every democracy in Europe, NATO's old members, new members, and nonmembers alike" (Speech 2-5). However, notwithstanding this statement, and like-minded ones from other NATO leaders, Russian politicians and analysts voiced bitter criticisms after the NATO Summit Meeting in Madrid in July 1997 voted to extend membership to Poland, Hungary, and the Czech Republic. They questioned the need for NATO's continued existence, much less its enlargement, in light of the end of the Cold War and any threat to Europe; deplored the repolarization of Europe that they saw implicit in NATO's expansion; and called on the Russian government to look to Russia's security needs. Simultaneously, the Duma deferred consideration of the ratification of START II—a crucial step in nuclear arsenal reductions—which had already been ratified by the US Senate.

In spite of the growing split between the two nations, Clinton continued to support aid for Russia, noting its persistent efforts to develop democratic and market-oriented institutions and processes. On May 29, 1998, for example, in a statement on Russia's economic situation, Clinton maintained that "Russia's new economic plan puts in place a solid strategy for fiscal reform. It gives Russian officials the authority they need to collect taxes, crack down on companies that ignore their obligations to the

Government, and control spending in line with revenues. The United States will continue to encourage strong IMF and World Bank engagement in support of reform." In another statement two days later, he endorsed additional conditional financial support for Russia from international financial institutions, "as necessary, to promote stability, structural reforms, and growth in Russia." Clinton's comments were intended to help Yeltsin at a time when Russia's economic condition and policies were occasioning widespread concern abroad about the direction of Russia's economy.

Clinton's upbeat comments, however, could not change Russia's economic reality. The Russian government managed to prop up the ruble throughout 1997, but Yeltsin's policies, or lack thereof, could juggle just so much for just so long. On August 17, 1998, the ruble was devalued by a staggering 80 percent following the government's decision to discontinue purchasing rubles on currency exchanges. The meltdown precipitated a free-fall in Russia's financial markets and a run on the banks, and jeopardized the very future of these fledgling institutions. The general public's increasing mistrust in Yeltsin's government, lack of unanimity among the leading politicians about how to proceed, and intensifying calls for a rethinking of economic policy created formidable obstacles on Russia's path toward a free-market democracy.

The economic crisis also triggered a political challenge to Yeltsin in the Duma. Though Yeltsin surmounted the immediate problem, which centered on his nominee for the position of prime minister, the ongoing hostility between the executive and legislative branches of government promised ongoing political paralysis as well as economic disinvestment by foreigners.

In the midst of this crisis, President Clinton visited Moscow in fulfillment of an earlier commitment and offered not only a strong endorsement of Yeltsin, who was facing another impeachment effort, but also a far-ranging, straightforward exposition on the difficulties of and necessity for patience, perseverance, and honestly facing the difficult choices required if Russia's economy was to recover (Speech 2-6). The speech was as much sermon as substance. Clinton said that Russia's troubles were temporary and amounted to nothing that the great Russian nation could not overcome. He also asserted that the whole world was interested in Russia's success and that turning against democracy would be a grave mistake.

On the following day, September 2, 1998, Presidents Clinton and Yeltsin issued the Joint Statement on Common Security Challenges (Speech 2-7), in which they summed up their achievements and outlined plans for future cooperation in the field of security. Though the statement promised extensive cooperation on numerous issues, it was a futile attempt to build a bridge across the widening gulf of interests, to demonstrate to the general public that the "strategic partnership"—a term coined by George Bush in 1992—was still in effect. In truth, however, most aspects of the relationship between the two countries were put on hold.

New tensions were not long in surfacing, this time over the US air attacks against Iraq on December 17, 1998, triggered by Saddam Hussein's defiance of the UN inspectors assigned to uncover Iraq's hidden caches of nuclear, chemical, and biological agents and equipment, capable of being turned into weapons. Russia's prime minister objected to the attack on grounds that the United States had initiated its bombing of Iraq even though the UN Security Council was still discussing what to do about Saddam's violations.

The notion of a US-Russian "strategic partnership" became even more problematic when NATO undertook a bombing campaign against Yugoslavia in late March 1999 over the Milosevic regime's handling of the ethnic Albanian problem in Serbia's province of Kosovo. Relations between Washington and Moscow underwent some tense moments during NATO's ten weeks of sustained heavy bombing. Yeltsin denounced NATO's "aggression," as did Chinese leaders. The Duma shelved discussion of the START II treaty indefinitely. And soon after the attacks ceased and Yugoslavia's President, Slobodan Milosevic, accepted the slightly less punitive terms that Russia helped negotiate with NATO, the Russian military conducted its most extensive battle exercises since the collapse of the Soviet Union. Russia openly acknowledged that it was predicating future defense plans on a "first-use" policy, that is, a readiness to use tactical nuclear weapons against an invading force or a force threatening its security. Even though Russian troops joined the UN-sponsored but NATO-dominated force occupying Kosovo, pending a political settlement, in almost all other respects the US-Russia relationship had reached an impasse.

2-1 A Conspectus for Russia's Entry Into the Global Economy

Remarks to the American Society of Newspaper Editors
Annapolis, Maryland
April 1, 1993

... I want to talk to you about the events in Russia, about our policies toward the newly independent states of the former Soviet Union, and about my meetings with President Boris Yeltsin this weekend. But first, I wish to speak about America's purposes in the world....

Nowhere is ... engagement more important than in our policies toward Russia and the newly independent states of the former Soviet Union. Their struggle to build free societies is one of the great human dramas of our day. It presents the greatest security challenge for our generation and offers one of the greatest economic opportunities of our lifetime. That's why my first trip out of the country will be to Vancouver, to meet with President Yeltsin.

Over the past month, we have seen incredibly tumultuous events in Russia. They've filled our headlines and probably confused our heads. President Yeltsin has been at loggerheads with the People's Congress of Deputies. Heated political standoffs have obstructed economic change. Meanwhile, neighboring states, such as Ukraine and the Baltic nations, have watched Russia anxiously while they grapple with their own reforms and while they deal with economic problems equally severe....

Well, I know that we cannot guarantee the future of reform in Russia or any of the other newly independent states. I know and you know that ultimately, the history of Russia will be written by Russians and the future of Russia must be charted by Russians. But I would argue that we must do what we can. We must act now, not out of charity, but because it is a wise investment, a wise investment building on what has already been done and looking to our own future. While our efforts will entail new costs, we can reap even larger dividends for our safety and our prosperity if we act now.

To understand why, I think we must grasp the scope of the transformation now occurring in Russia and the other states. From Vilnius on the

Baltic to Vladivostok on the Pacific, we have witnessed a political miracle, genuinely historic and heroic deeds without precedent in all of human history. The other two world-changing events of this century, World Wars I and II, exacted a price of over 60 million lives. By contrast, look at this world-changing event. It has been remarkably bloodless, and we pray that it remains so.

Now free markets and free politics are replacing repression. Central Europe is in command of its own fate. Lithuania, Latvia, and Estonia are again independent. Ukraine, Armenia, and other proud nations are free to pursue their own destinies.

The heart of it all is Russia. Her rebirth has begun. A great nation, rich in natural and human resources and unbelievable history, has once again moved to rejoin the political and economic cultures of the West. President Yeltsin and his fellow reformers throughout Russia are courageously leading three modern Russian revolutions at once to transform their country: from a totalitarian state into a democracy; from a command economy into a market; from an empire into a modern nation-state that freely let go of countries once under their control and now freely respect their integrity.

Russia's rebirth is not only material and political; it is genuinely spiritual....

Nothing could contribute more to global freedom, to security, to prosperity than the peaceful progression of this rebirth of Russia. It could mean a modern state, at peace not only with itself but with the world. It could mean one productively and prosperously integrated into a global economy, a source of raw materials and manufactured products and a vast market for American goods and services. It could mean a populous democracy contributing to the stability of both Europe and Asia.

The success of Russia's renewal must be a first-order concern to our country because it confronts us with four distinct opportunities. First, it offers us an historic opportunity to improve our own security. The danger is clear if Russia's reforms turn sour, if it reverts to authoritarianism or disintegrates into chaos. The world cannot afford the strife of the former Yugoslavia replicated in a nation as big as Russia, spanning eleven time zones with an armed arsenal of nuclear weapons that is still very vast....

Now, we could at last face a Europe in which no great power, not one, harbors continental designs. Think of it: land wars in Europe cost hundreds of thousands of American lives in the twentieth century. The rise of a democratic Russia, satisfied within her own boundaries, bordered by other peaceful democracies, could ensure that our Nation never needs to pay that kind of price again.

We also face the opportunity to increase our own security by reducing the chances of nuclear war. Russia still holds over 20,000 strategic and tactical nuclear warheads. Ukraine, Belarus, and Kazakhstan have nuclear weapons on their own soil as well. We are implementing historic arms control agreements that for the first time will radically reduce the number of strategic nuclear weapons. Now, by supporting Russia's reforms, we can help to turn the promise of those agreements into a reality for ourselves and for our children, and for the Russians and their children, too.

Second, Russia's reforms offer us the opportunity to complete the movement from having an adversary in foreign policy to having a partner in global problem solving. Think back to the Cold War. Recall the arenas in which we played out its conflicts: Berlin, Korea, the Congo, Cuba, Vietnam, Nicaragua, Angola, Afghanistan. We competed everywhere. We battled the Soviets at the UN. We tracked each other's movements around the globe. We lost tens of thousands of our finest young people to hold freedom's line. Those efforts were worthy. But their worth was measured in prevention more than in creation, in the containment of terror and oppression rather than the advancement of human happiness and opportunity.

Now reflect on what has happened just since Russia joined us in a search for peaceful solutions. We cooperated in the United Nations to defeat Iraqi aggression in Kuwait. We cosponsored promising peace talks in the Mideast. We worked together to foster reconciliation in Cambodia and El Salvador. We joined forces to protect the global environment. Progress of this kind strengthens our security and that of other nations. If we can help Russia to remain increasingly democratic, we can leave an era of standoff behind us and explore expanding horizons of progress and peace.

Third, Russia's reforms are important to us because they hold one of the keys to investing more in our own future. America's taxpayers have literally spent trillions of dollars to prosecute the Cold War. Now we can reduce that pace of spending, and indeed, we have been able to reduce that pace of spending, not only because the arms of the former Soviet Union pose a diminishing threat to us and our allies. If Russia were to revert to imperialism or were to plunge into chaos, we would need to reassess all our plans for defense savings. We would have to restructure our defenses to meet a whole different set of threats than those we now think will occur. That means billions of dollars less for other uses: less for creating new businesses and new jobs; less for preparing our children for the future; less for the new technologies of the twenty-first century which our competitors in Germany, Japan, and elsewhere are pouring money into right now, hoping they can capture the high wage jobs of the future. Therefore, our ability to put people first at home requires that we put Russia and its neighbors first on our agenda abroad.

Fourth, Russia's reforms offer us an historic opportunity. Russia, after all, is in a profound economic crisis today. But it is still an inherently rich nation. She has a wealth of oil and gas and coal and gold and diamonds and timbers for her own people to develop. The Russian people are among the most well educated and highly skilled in the world. They are good people sitting on a rich land. They have been victimized by a system which has failed them. We must look beyond the Russia of today and see her potential for prosperity. Think of it: a nation of 150 million people able to trade with us in a way that helps both our peoples. Russia's economic recovery may be slow, but it is in the interest of all who seek more robust global growth to ensure that, aided by American business and trade, Russia rises to her great economic potential....

America's position is unequivocal. We support democracy. We support free markets. We support freedom of speech, conscience, and religion. We support respect for ethnic minorities in Russia and for Russian and other minorities throughout the region.

I believe it is essential that we act prudently but urgently to do all that we can to strike a strategic alliance with Russian reform. My goal in Vancouver will be that. And that will be my message to the man who stands as the leader of reform, Russia's democratically elected President, Boris Yeltsin. I won't describe today all the specific ideas that I plan to discuss with him. And of course, I don't know all those that he will discuss with me. But I want to tell you the principles on which our efforts to assist reform will rest.

First, our investments in Russian reform must be tangible to the Russian people. Support for reform must come from the ground up. And that will only occur if our efforts are broadly dispersed and not focused just on Moscow. I plan to talk with President Yeltsin about measures intended to help promote the broad development of small businesses, to accelerate privatization of state enterprises, to assist local food processing and distribution efforts, and to ease the transition to private markets. Our goal must be to ensure that the Russian people soon come to feel that they are the beneficiaries of reform and not its victims. We must help them to recognize that their sufferings today are not the birth pangs of democracy and capitalism but the death throes of dictatorship and communism.

Second, our investments in Russian reform must be designed to have lasting impact. Russia's economic vessel is too large and leaky for us to bail it out. That's not what's at issue here. Our challenge is to provide some tools to help the Russians do things that work for themselves. A good example is Russia's energy sector. Russia is one of the world's largest oil producers; yet millions of barrels of the oil Russia pumps each month seep out of the system before ever reaching the market. Just the leakage from Russia's natural gas pipelines could supply the entire State of Connecticut. The Russians must make many reforms to attract energy investments. And by helping to introduce modern drilling practices and to repair Russia's energy infrastructure, we can help Russia regain a large and lasting source of hard currency. Over the long run, that effort can help to protect the environment as well and to moderate world energy prices. We have a direct interest in doing that.

Third, our people must do what we can to have people-to-people initiatives, not just government-to-government ones. We have entered a new era in which the best way to achieve many of our goals abroad is not through diplomats or dollars but through private citizens who can impart the skills and habits that are the lifeblood of democracy and free markets. We intend to expand efforts for retired American business executives to work with Russian entrepreneurs to start new businesses. We intend to work so that our farmers can teach modern farming practices; so that our labor leaders can share the basics of trade unionism; so that Americans experienced in grassroots activities can impart the techniques that ensure responsive government; so that our Armed Forces can engage in more exchanges with the Russian military; and so that thousands and thousands of young Russians who are reform's primary beneficiaries and reform's primary constituency—so that they can come to our country and study our government, our economy, and our society, not because it's perfect but because it's a great example of a democracy at work.

Fourth, our investments in reform must be part of a partnership among all the newly independent states and the international community. They must be extended in concert with measures from our allies, many of whom have at least as much stake in the survival of Russian democracy as we do. Working through the international financial institutions, we can do great things together that none of us can do by ourselves.

This principle is especially important as we help Russia to stabilize its currency and its markets. Russia's central bank prints too many rubles and extends too many credits. The result is inflation that has been nearly 1 percent a day. Inflation at such levels gravely imperils Russia's emerging markets....

Fifth, we must emphasize investments in Russia that enhance our own security. I want to talk with President Yeltsin about steps we can take together to ensure that denuclearization continues in Russia and her neighboring states. We will explore new initiatives to reassure Ukraine so that it embraces the START Treaty, and to move toward the goal of the Lisbon Protocol agenda, which was intended to ensure that Russia is the only nuclear-armed successor state to the Soviet Union. Ukraine will play a special role in the realization of these objectives, and we recognize our interest in the success of reform in Ukraine and the other new states. I'll talk with President Yeltsin about new efforts to realize the two-thirds reduction in United States and Soviet strategic nuclear arsenals envisioned under

START. And I'll suggest steps both of us can take to stem the proliferation of weapons of mass destruction, something that will be a major, major cause of concern for years to come.

Sixth, we must recognize that our policies toward Russia and the other states comprise a long-term strategy. It may take years to work completely. That was the key to our success in the Cold War. We were in it for the long run, not to win every day, not to know what every development in every country would be. We had clear principles, clear interests, clear values, a clear strategy, and we were in it for the long run. As the Soviets veered from the terror of Stalin to the thaw of Khrushchev, to the gray days of Brezhnev, to the perestroika of Gorbachev, our purpose always remained constant: containment, deterrence, human freedom.

Our goals must remain equally fixed today: above all, our security and that of our allies but also democracy, market economies, human rights, and respect for international law. In this regard, I welcome President Yeltsin's assurance that civil liberties will be respected and continuity in Russia's foreign policy maintained as Russia strives to determine her own future.

The path that Russia and the other states take toward reform will have rough stretches. Their politics may seem especially tumultuous today, in part because it's so much more public than in decades past, thanks to the television and to the other mass media. Then, the ruler of the Kremlin had only subjects; now, the ruler of the Kremlin has constituents, just like me, and it's a lot more complicated. We must be concerned over every retreat from democracy but not every growing pain within democracy....

2-2 A Gesture of Confidence

News Conference With President Boris Yeltsin of Russia
Vancouver, Canada
April 4, 1993

... In our discussions, President Yeltsin and I reached several important agreements on the ways in which the United States and the other major industrialized democracies can best support Russian reforms. First are programs that can begin immediately. I discussed with President Yeltsin the initiatives totaling $1.6 billion intended to bolster political and economic reforms in Russia. These programs already are funded. They can provide immediate and tangible results for the Russian people.

We will invest in the growth of Russia's private sector through two funds to accelerate privatization and to lend to new small private businesses. We will resume grain sales to Russia and extend $700 million in loans for Russia to purchase American grain. We will launch a pilot project to help provide housing and retraining for the Russian military officers as they move into jobs in the civilian economy.

Because the momentum for reform must come upward from the Russian people, not down from their government, we will expand exchanges between American farmers, business people, students, and others with expertise working directly with the Russian people. And we agreed to make a special effort to promote American investment, particularly in Russia's oil and gas sectors. To give impetus to this effort, we will ask Vice President Gore and Russian Prime Minister Chernomyrdin to chair a new commission on energy and space.

Second, beyond these immediate programs, the President and I agreed that our partnership requires broader perspectives and broader cooperative initiatives, which I will discuss with the Congress when I return home. We expect to do more than we are announcing today in housing and technical assistance, in nuclear safety and cooperation on the environment, and in important exchanges.

Third, this challenge we face today is clearly not one for the United States and Russia alone. I have asked our allies in the G-7 to come forward with their own individual bilateral initiatives. Canada and Britain have already done so, and I expect others to follow.

President Yeltsin and I also discussed plans for the G-7 nations to act together in support of Russia's reforms....

Beyond these economic initiatives, the President and I discussed a broad agenda of cooperation in foreign affairs. We reaffirmed our commitment to safe dismantlement and disposal of nuclear weapons. We discussed the need to strengthen the Non-Proliferation Treaty and to assure that Ukraine along with Belarus and Kazakhstan ratify the START Treaty and accede to the NPT as non-nuclear-weapons states. I stress that we want to expand our relationships with all the new independent states.

We also agreed to work in concert to help resolve regional crises, to stem weapons of proliferation, to protect the global environment, and to address common challenges to international peace, such as the tragic violence in Bosnia, advancing the promising peace talks we have cosponsored in the Mideast, and continuing our cooperation to end the regional conflicts of the Cold War era....

2-3 An Affirmation of Support

Statement on the Situation in Russia
Washington DC
September 21, 1993

From the beginning of my administration, I have given my full backing to the historic process of political and economic reform now underway in Russia. I remain convinced that democratic reforms and the transition to a market economy hold the best hope for a better future for the people of Russia.

The actions announced today by President Yeltsin in his address to the Russian people underscore the complexity of the reform process that he is leading. There is no question that President Yeltsin acted in response to a constitutional crisis that had reached a critical impasse and had paralyzed the political process.

As the democratically elected leader of Russia, President Yeltsin has chosen to allow the people of Russia themselves to resolve this impasse. I believe that the path to elections for a new legislature is ultimately consistent with the democratic and reform course that he has charted.

I called President Yeltsin this afternoon to seek assurances that the difficult choices that he faces will be made in a way that ensures peace, stability, and an open political process this autumn. He told me that it is of the utmost importance that the elections he has called be organized and held on a democratic and free basis.

In a democracy, the people should finally decide the issues that are at the heart of political and social debate. President Yeltsin has made this choice, and I support him fully. I have confidence in the abiding wisdom of the Russian people to make the right decision regarding their own future.

2-4 A Message of Hope and Encouragement

Remarks to Students of Moscow State University
Moscow, Russia
May 10, 1995

... The United States supports the forces of democracy and reform here in Russia, because it is in our national interest to do so. I have worked hard to make this post-Cold War world a safer and more hopeful peace for the American people. As President, that is my job. That is every president's job. But I have had the opportunity, unlike my recent predecessors, to work with Russia instead of being in opposition to Russia. And I want to keep it that way....

Both our nations are destroying thousands of nuclear weapons at a faster rate than our treaties require. We have removed the last nuclear weapons from Kazakhstan. And Ukraine and Belarus will soon follow. We are cooperating with you to prevent nuclear weapons and bomb-making materials from falling into the hands of terrorists and smugglers. We are working together to extend indefinitely the Nuclear Nonproliferation Treaty, the cornerstone of our efforts to stop the spread of nuclear weapons.

Your progress on the economic front is also important. I have seen reports that more than 60 percent of your economy is now in private hands. Inflation is dropping, and your government is taking sensible steps to control its budget deficit. Managers work to satisfy customers and to make profits. Employees, more and more, search for the best jobs at the highest wages. And every day, despite hardship and uncertainty, more and more Russian people are able to make decisions in free markets rather than having their choices dictated to them.

We have supported these reforms. They are good for you, but they are also good for the United States and for the rest of the world, for they bring us together and move us forward.

I know there are severe problems. There are severe problems in your transition to a market economy. I know, too, that in anywhere free markets exist, they do not solve all social problems. They require policies that can ensure economic fairness and basic human decency to those who need and deserve help.

Finally, I know that all democracies, the United States included, face new challenges, from the emergence of the global economy and the information age, as well as from the threats posed by the proliferation of weapons of mass destruction, by organized crime, and by terrorism.

But the answer is not to back away from democracy or to go back to isolation. The answer is not to go back to defining your national interest in terms that make others less secure. The answer is to stay on this course, to reap the full benefits of democracy, and to work on these problems with those of us who have a stake in your success, because your success makes us safer and more prosperous as well.

That success, I believe, depends upon three things; First, continuing to strengthen your democracy; second, improving your economy and reducing social and economic problems; and third, establishing your role in the world in a way that enhances your economic and national security interest—not at the expense of your friends and neighbors, but in cooperation with them.

First, the work of building democracy never ends. The democratic system can never be perfected, because human beings are not perfect. In America today, we are engaged in a renewed debate over which decision should be made by our national government and which ones should be made locally or by private citizens on their own, unimpeded by government.

We argue today over the proper roles of the different branches of government, and we argue over how we can be strengthened, not weakened by the great diversity in our society. These are enduring challenges that all democracies face.

But no element among them is more fundamental than the holding of free elections. In our meetings today, President Yeltsin once again pledged to keep on schedule, both a new round of parliamentary elections in December and the presidential election next June. He has shown that he understands what has often been said about a new democracy; the second elections are even more important than the first, for the second elections establish a pattern of peaceful transition of power.

Therefore, I urge all Russians who have the right to vote to exercise that vote this year and next year. Many people sacrificed so that you could have this power. I address that plea especially to the young people in this room and throughout your great nation.

Your future is fully before you. And these elections will shape that future. Do not fall into the trap that I hear even in my own country of believing that your vote does not count. It does count. It will count if you cast it. And if you do not count—cast it, that will count for something, too. So I urge you to exercise the vote.

But the heart of a democracy does not lie in the ballot box alone. That is why it is also important that your generation continues to demand and support a free and independent press. Again, this can be a difficult, even dangerous process, as the people in your press know all too well...

There is another challenge, a challenge of building tolerance, for tolerance too lies at the heart of any democracy. Few nations on earth can rival Russia's vast human and natural resources, or her diversity. Within your borders live more than 100 different ethnic groups. Scores of literary, cultural and artistic traditions thrive among your people. And in the last few years, millions have returned to their faiths, seeking refuge in their stability and finding hope in their teachings. These are vital signs of democracy taking root.

Given your nation's great diversity, it would have been easy along this path to surrender to the cries of extremists, who in the name of patriotism have tried to rally support by stirring up fear among different peoples. But you have embraced, instead, the cause of tolerance. The vast majority of Russians have rejected those poisonous arguments and bolster your young, fragile democracy.

When Americans and others in the West look back on the events of the last four years, we are struck by the remarkably peaceful nature of your revolutionary transition, your accomplishment to go through a massive social and political upheaval, and the breakup of an empire with so little brutality and bloodshed has few precedents in history. Your restraint was a critical factor in paving the way for Russia to take its place in the global community, a modern state at peace with itself and its neighbors.

Now it is against this backdrop, this great achievement that we Americans have viewed the tragedy in Chechnya. As I told President Yeltsin earlier today, this terrible tragedy must be brought to a rapid and peaceful conclusion. Continued fighting in that region can only spill more blood and further erode support for Russia among her neighbors around the world.

Holding free elections, ensuring a free and independent press, promoting tolerance of diversity—these are some of the difficult tasks of building a democracy. They are all important.

But these efforts also depend upon your economic reforms. Your efforts on the political front will benefit from efforts on the economic front that generate prosperity and give people a greater stake in a democratic future.

To too many people in this country, I know that economic reform has come to mean hardship, uncertainty, crime and corruption. Profitable enterprise, once owned by the state, have been moved into private hands, sometimes under allegedly questionable circumstances. The demands of extortionists have stopped some would-be entrepreneurs from even going into business. And when the heavy hand of totalitarianism was lifted from your society, many structures necessary for a free market to take shape were not there and organized crime was able to move into the vacuum.

These are real and urgent concerns. They demand an all-out battle to create a market based on law, not lawlessness; a market that rewards merit, not malice. Economic reform must not be an excuse for the privileged and the strong to prey upon the weak.

To help your government break the power of those criminals, our Federal Bureau of Investigation has opened an office here in Moscow. And we are cooperating with your government's attempts to strengthen the integrity of your markets.

Pressures in the market economy are also leaving some people behind, people whose needs are not being met and who are not able to compete and win, while some of the richest are said to pay no taxes at all. Those Russians who lose their jobs or who live in poverty deserve an economic and social safety net that is strong enough to break their fall and keep them going until they can get back on their feet.

Finally, market economies require discipline. Cutting inflation helps families struggling to become members of the new Russian middle class so they need not fear the future. Continuing your country's recent record of more realistic budgets is vital to achieving long-term economic stability....

Finally, Russia's success at political and economic reform at home requires an approach to the world that reinforces your progress and enhances your security. Russia and the United States must work together in this regard. We must work for our common security.

More than anything else, that is what my meeting with President Yeltsin today was all about, and we made progress in many areas. I would like to report them to you. First, Russia agreed to implement its Partnership for Peace with NATO. And I agreed now to press NATO to begin talks on a special relationship with Russia.

The United States has made it clear that we favor a strong continuing NATO that any admission of new members be based on the principles we have articulated, along with our partners. It must be gradual and deliberate and open, and consistent with the security interests of all of our partners for peace, including Russia.

My goal since I became President has been to use the fact that the Cold War is over to unify Europe for the first time in its history, and that is what we must all be working for. President Yeltsin's decision to join the Partnership for Peace will support that move toward security and unity.

Second, the United States strongly believes that there should be no future nuclear cooperation with Iran. We believe that is in Russia's interest. Today, President Yeltsin said that Russia would not sell enrichment technology or training to Iran because that could clearly be used to develop a nuclear capacity. And that should be more important to you than to us because you are closer to Iran than we are....

Next, we agreed to immediately work to see if we could get our respective parliamentary bodies to ratify the START II Treaty this year so that we could continue to reduce our nuclear arsenals; and after START II is ratified, to consider further reductions in the nuclear arsenals of the United States and Russia to make your future safer. We also agreed to a statement of principles on one of the most difficult issues in our security relationship—how we define so-called theatre missile defenses in the context of our Anti-ballistic Missile Treaty designed, again, to make us both safer.

And finally ... the United States and Russia agreed that we must work much harder in sharing information, sharing technology, sharing research in the areas of combatting terrorism and organized crime....

2-5 Friends at Last?

Remarks at a Signing Ceremony
for the NATO-Russia Founding Act
Paris, France
May 27, 1997

... Ladies and gentlemen, on this beautiful spring day in Paris, in the twilight of the twentieth century, we look toward a new century with a new Russia and a new NATO, working together in a new Europe of unlimited possibility. The NATO-Russia Founding Act we have just signed joins a great nation and history's most successful alliance in common cause for a long-sought but never before realized goal: a peaceful, democratic, undivided Europe....

For all of us, this is a great day. From now on, NATO and Russia will consult and coordinate and work together. Where we all agree, we will act jointly, as we are in Bosnia where a Russian brigade serves side by side with NATO troops, giving the Bosnian people a chance to build a lasting peace. Deepening our partnership today will make all of us stronger and more secure.

The historic change in the relationship between NATO and Russia grows out of a fundamental change in how we think about each other and our future. NATO's member states recognize that the Russian people are building a new Russia, defining their greatness in terms of the future as much as the past. Russia's transition to democracy and open markets is as difficult as it is dramatic. And its steadfast commitment to freedom and reform has earned the world's admiration.

In turn, we are building a new NATO. It will remain the strongest alliance in history, with smaller, more flexible forces, prepared to provide for our defense but also trained for peacekeeping. It will work closely with other nations that share our hopes and values and interests through the Partnership For Peace. It will be an alliance directed no longer against a hostile bloc of nations but instead designed to advance the security of every democracy in Europe, NATO's old members, new members, and nonmembers alike.

I know that some still see NATO through the prism of the Cold War and that especially in NATO's decision to open its doors to Central Europe's new democracy, they see a Europe still divided, only differently divided. But I ask them to look again. For this new NATO will work with Russia, not against it. And by reducing rivalry and fear, by strengthening peace and cooperation, by facing common threats to the security of all democracies, NATO will promote greater stability in all of Europe, including Russia. And in turn, that will increase the security of Europe's North American partners, the United States and Canada as well.

We establish this partnership because we are determined to create a future in which European security is not a zero-sum game, where NATO's gain is Russia's loss and Russia's strength is our alliance's weakness. That is old thinking; these are new times. Together, we must build a new Europe in which every nation is free and every free nation joins in strengthening the peace and stability for all.

Half a century ago, on a continent darkened by the shadow of evil, brave men and women in Russia and the world's free nations fought a common enemy with uncommon valor. Their partnership forged in battle, strengthened by sacrifice, cemented by blood, gave hope to millions in the West and in Russia that the grand alliance would be extended in peace. But in victory's afterglow, the freedom the Russian people deserved was denied them. The dream of peace gave way to the hard reality of Cold War, and our predecessors lost an opportunity to shape a new Europe, whole and free.

Now we have another chance. Russia has opened itself to freedom. The veil of hostility between East and West has lifted. Together we see a future of partnership too long delayed that must no longer be denied. The founding act we signed captures the promise of this remarkable moment. Now we must implement it in good faith, so that future generations will live in a new time that escapes the twentieth century's darkest moments and fulfills its most brilliant possibilities....

2-6 Exhorting Russia— Once Again

Remarks to Students of Moscow
University of International Relations
Moscow, Russia
September 1, 1998

Russia's great ally in World War II, our President, Franklin Roosevelt, said that democracy is a never-ending seeking for better things. For Americans, that means, in good times and bad, we seek to widen the circle of opportunity, to deepen the meaning of our freedom, to build a stronger national community.

Now, what does all that got to do with Russia in 1998? Your history is much longer than ours and so rich with accomplishment, from military victories over Napoleon and Hitler to the literary achievements of Pushkin, Tolstoy, Chekhov, Pasternak, and so many others, to great achievements in art, music dance, medicine, science, space flight. Yet for all your rich, long history, it was just seven years ago that Russia embarked on its own quest for democracy, liberty, and free markets—just seven years ago—a journey that is uniquely your own and must be guided by your own vision of Russia's democratic destiny.

Now you are at a critical point on your journey. There are severe economic pressures and serious hardships which I discussed in my meetings with your leaders this morning. The stakes are enormous. Every choice Russia makes today may have consequences for years and years to come. Given the facts before you, I have to tell you that I do not believe there are any painless solutions, and indeed, an attempt to avoid difficult solutions may only prolong and worsen the present challenges.

First, let me make a couple of points. The experience of our country over the last several years, and especially in the last six years, proves that the challenges of the global economy are very great, but so are its rewards. The Russian people have met tremendous challenges in the past. You can do it here. You can build a prosperous future. You can build opportunity and jobs for all the people of this land who are willing to work for them if you stand strong and complete, not run from but complete the transformation you began seven years ago.

The second point I want to make is the rest of the world has a very large stake in your success. Today about a quarter of the world's people are struggling with economic challenges that are profound—the people of your country; the people in Japan, who have had no economic growth for five years—it's still a very wealthy country, but when they don't have any growth, it's harder for all other countries that trade with them who aren't so wealthy to grow—other countries in Asia. And now we see when there are problems in Russia or in Japan or questions about the economy of China, you see all across the world—the stock market in Latin America drops; you see the last two days we've had big drops in the American stock market.

What does that say? Well, among other things, it says, whether we like it or not, we must build the future together, because, whether we like it or not, we are going to be affected by what we do. We will be affected by what you do; you will be affected by what we do. We might as well do it together and make the most of it....

And that's what I want to talk to you about today: How can we move in the right direction? When I look at all the young people here today—and I have read about you and your background—young people from all over Russia, seizing the possibilities of freedom to chart new courses for yourselves and your nation, making a difference by building businesses from modest loans and innovative ideas, by taking technologies created for weapons and applying them to human needs, by finding creative government solutions to complex problems, by improving medical care and fighting disease, by publishing courageous journalism, exposing abuses of power, producing literature and art and scholarship, changing the way people see their own lives, organizing citizens to fight for justice and human rights and a cleaner environment, reaching out to the world. In this room today, there are young people doing all those things. That should give you great reason to hope.

You are at the forefront of building a modern Russia. You are a new generation. You do represent the future of your dreams. Your efforts today will not only ensure better lives for yourselves but for your children and generations that follow.

I think it is important to point out, too, that when Russia chose freedom, it was not supposed to benefit only the young and well educated, the rich and well connected; it was also supposed to benefit the men and women who worked in factories and farms and fought the wars of the Soviet era, those who survive today on pensions and Government assistance. It was also supposed to benefit the laborers and teachers and soldiers who work every day but wait now for a paycheck.

The challenge is to create a new Russia that benefits all responsible citizens of this country. How do you get there? I do not believe it is by reverting to the failed policies of the past. I do not believe it is by stopping the reform process in midstream, with a few Russians doing very well but far more struggling to provide for their families. I believe you will create the conditions of growth if, but only if, you continue to move decisively along the path of democratic, market-oriented, constructive revolution.

The Russian people have made extraordinary progress in the last seven years. You have gone to the polls to elect your leaders. Some 65 to 70 percent of you freely turn out in every election. People across Russia are rebuilding diverse religious traditions, launching a wide range of private organizations. Seventy percent of the economy now is in private hands. Not bureaucrats but consumers determine what goods get to stores and where people live. You have reached out to the world with trade and investment, exchanges of every kind, and leadership in meeting security challenges around the globe.

Now you face a critical moment. Today's financial crisis does not require you to abandon your march toward freedom and free markets. Russians will define Russia's future, but there are clear lessons, I would argue, from international experience. Here's what I think they are.

First, in tough times governments need stable revenues to pay their bills, support salaries, pensions, and health care. That requires decisive action to ensure that everyone pays their fair share of taxes. Otherwise, a few pay too much, many pay too little, the government is in the hole and can never get out, and you will never be able to have a stable economic policy. It is tempting for everyone to avoid wanting to pay any taxes. But if everyone will pay their fair share, the share will be modest and their incomes will be larger over the long run because of the stability and growth it will bring to this Russian economic system.

Second, printing money to pay the bills and bail out the banks does not help. It causes inflation and ultimately will make the pain worse. Third, special bailouts for a privileged few come at the expense of the whole nation.

Fourth, fair, equitable treatment of creditors today will determine their involvement in a nation tomorrow. The people who loan money into this nation must be treated fairly if you want them to be loaning money into this nation four years, five years, ten years hence.

These are not radical theories, they are simply facts proven by experience. How Russia reacts to them will fundamentally affect your future. Surviving today's crisis, however difficult that may be, is just the beginning. To create jobs, growth, and higher income, a nation must convince its own citizens and foreigners that they can safely invest. Again, experience teaches what works: fair tax laws and fair enforcement; easier transferability of land; strong intellectual property rights to encourage innovation; independent courts enforcing the law consistently and upholding contract rights; strong banks that safeguard savings; securities markets that protect investors; social spending that promotes hope and opportunity and a safety net for those who in any given time in an open market economy will be dislocated; and vigilance against hidden ties between government and business interests that are inappropriate.

Now, this is not an American agenda. I will say it again: This is not an American agenda. These are the imperatives of the global marketplace, and you can see them repeated over and over and over again. You can also see the cost of ignoring them in nation after nation after nation.

Increasingly, no nation, rich or poor, democratic or authoritarian, can escape the fundamental economic imperatives of the global market. Investors and entrepreneurs have a very wide and growing range of choices about where they put their money. They move in the direction of openness, fairness, and freedom. Here, Russia has an opportunity. At the dawn of a new century there is a remarkable convergence; increasingly, the very policies that are needed to thrive in the new economy are also those which deepen democratic liberty for individual citizens.

This is a wealthy country. It is rich in resources. It is richer still in people. It has done a remarkable job of providing quality education to large numbers of people. You have proven over and over and over again in ways large and small that the people of this country have a sense of courage and spirit, an unwillingness to be beat down and to give up. The future can be very, very bright.

But we can't ignore the rules of the game, because if there is a system of freedom, you cannot take away and no country, not even the United States with the size of our economy, no country is strong enough to control what millions and millions and millions of people decide freely to do with their money. But every country will keep a large share of its own citizens' money and get a lot of money from worldwide investors if it can put in place systems that abide by the rules of international commerce. And all Russia needs is its fair share of this investment. You have the natural wealth. You have the people power. You have the education. All you need is just to get your fair share of the investment....

... To get your fair share of investment, you have to play by the rules that everyone else has to play by. That's what this whole crisis is about. No one could ever have expected your country to be able to make this transition without pain. You've only been at this seven years.

Look at any European country that has had an open market society for decades and decades and decades. They have hundreds, indeed thousands, of little organizations, they have major national institutions that all tend to reinforce these rules that I talked about earlier. Don't be discouraged, but don't be deterred. Just keep working until you get it in place.

Once you get it in place, Russia will take off like a rocket, because you have both natural resources and people resources.

Now, I think it's important to point out, however, that economic strength—let's go back to the rules—it depends on the rule of law. If somebody from outside a country intends to put money into a foreign country, they want to know what the rules are. What are the terms on which my money is being invested? How will my investment be protected? If I lose money, I want to know it's because I made a bad decision, not because the law didn't protect my money. It is very important. Investors, therefore, seek honest government, fair systems—fair for corporations and consumers, where there are strong checks on corruption and abuse of authority and openness in what the rules are on how investment capital is handled....

You must have a state that is strong enough to control abuses: violence, theft, fraud, bribery, monopolism. But it must not be so strong that it can limit the legitimate rights and dreams and creativity of the people. That is the tension of creating the right kind of democratic market society.

The bottom line is that the American people very much want Russia to succeed. We value your friendship. We honor your struggle. We want to offer support as long as you take the steps needed for stability and progress. We will benefit greatly if you strengthen your democracy and increase your prosperity....

I was amazed there were some doubters back in America who said perhaps I shouldn't come here because these are uncertain times politically and economically. And there are questions being raised in the American press about the commitment of Russia to the course of reform and democracy. It seems to me that anybody can get on an airplane and take a trip in good times and that friends come to visit each other in challenging and difficult times.

I come here as a friend, because I believe in the future of Russia. I come here also because I believe someone has to tell the truth to the people, so that you're not skeptical when your political leaders tell you things that are hard to hear. There is no way out of playing by the rules of the international economy if you wish to be a part of it. We cannot abandon the rules of the international economy. No one can.

There is a way to preserve the social safety net and the social contract and to help the people who are too weak to succeed. There is a way to do that. And there are people who will help to do that. But it has to be done. So I come here as a friend. I come here because I know that the future of our children and the future of Russia's young people are going to be entwined, and I want it to be a good future. And I believe it can be....

2-7 A Bridge Over the Widening Gulf

Joint Statement on Common Security Challenges
Moscow, Russia
September 2, 1998

We, the Presidents of the United States of America and of the Russian Federation, declare that cooperation between the US and Russia will be of the greatest import in the twenty-first century for promoting prosperity and strengthening security throughout the world. In this connection, we reaffirm that the United States of America and the Russian Federation are natural partners in advancing international peace and stability. We have devoted particular attention to intensifying joint efforts to eliminate threats inherited from the Cold War and to meet common security challenges at the threshold of the twenty-first century.

We understand that the most serious and pressing danger is the proliferation of nuclear, biological, chemical, and other types of weapons of mass destruction, the technologies for their production, and their means of delivery. Given the increasing interdependence of the modern world, these threats are becoming transnational and global in scope; they affect not only the national security of the United States and the Russian Federation, but also international stability. We reaffirm the determination of the US and Russia to cooperate actively and closely with each other, as well as with all other interested countries, to avert and reduce this threat by taking new steps, seeking new forms of collaboration, and strengthening generally recognized international norms.

We recognize that more must be done and today we have taken a number of steps to enhance not only our security, but global security as well. We are declaring our firm commitment to intensifying negotiations toward early completion of the Biological Weapons Convention Protocol. We are embarking on new and important cooperation to further lessen the risks of false warnings of missile attacks. And, we have agreed on principles to guide our cooperation in the management and disposition of plutonium from nuclear weapons programs so that it can never again be used in a nuclear weapon.

Common commitments have made the US and Russia partners in developing the foundations of an international non-proliferation regime, including the Treaty on the Non-Proliferation of Nuclear Weapons, IAEA safeguards, the Convention on Biological and Toxin Weapons, and the Comprehensive Test Ban Treaty. Russia and the US reaffirm their commitment to the goal of having all countries accede to the Treaty on the Non-Proliferation of Nuclear Weapons in its present form, without amendments. They are also committed to the strengthened guidelines of the Nuclear Suppliers Group. As participants in the Conference on Disarmament, they jointly achieved success in the negotiations of the Chemical Weapons Convention and of the Comprehensive Test Ban Treaty, and call upon all countries to accede to these treaties. Guided by these obligations, they have taken substantial practical steps to reduce the global nuclear threat and control transfers of sensitive technology.

They remain deeply concerned about the nuclear tests in South Asia and reaffirm US and Russian commitments to coordinate closely support for all steps set forth in the Joint Communique of the "P-5", as endorsed by the G-8 and the UN Security Council.

The START Treaty and Presidents' nuclear arms reduction initiatives in 1991-92 will help to ensure the ultimate goal of nuclear disarmament and enhance international security. We have together eliminated more than 1,700 heavy bombers and missile launchers, including more than 700 launch silos, 45 submarines capable of launching nuclear missiles, and deactivated or eliminated more than 18,000 strategic and tactical nuclear warheads. Reaffirming our commitment to strict compliance with our obligations under the START I and ABM Treaties, we declare our resolve to collaborate in expediting the entry into force of the START II Treaty. Immediately after Russian ratification of START II, the US and Russia will begin negotiations regarding lower levels within the framework of a START III Treaty....

We reaffirm our commitment to further cooperation on export controls as an essential part of ensuring non-proliferation. Our governments recently created an additional mechanism for cooperation in the field of exports of sensitive technology. To this end, at our meeting today we agreed to establish expert groups on nuclear matters, missile and space technology, catch-all and internal compliance, conventional weapons transfers controls, as well as law enforcement, customs matters, and licensing in order to enhance cooperation and to implement specific bilateral assistance and cooperative projects. These groups will be formed within the next month and begin practical activities without delay. A protected communications channel between senior officials of both countries has also been established, which will ensure the rapid and confidential exchange of information on non-proliferation matters.

We reaffirmed the importance of the Conventional Armed Forces in Europe Treaty (CFE) and its fundamental contribution to stability, predictability and cooperation in Europe....

The US and Russia remain committed to jointly building an enduring peace based upon the principles of democracy and the indivisibility of security. They reaffirm the common objective of strengthening security and stability in the interest of all countries, and combating aggressive nationalism and preventing abuses of human rights. They will consult with each other and strive to cooperate in averting and settling conflicts and in crisis management. In this regard, we attach great importance to operational military cooperation, in both bilateral and multilateral settings, between the armed forces of the US and Russia. We are pleased to note that definite progress has been achieved in the area of defense cooperation, particularly in strengthening nuclear security and in implementation of the Cooperative Threat Reduction Program.

We recognize that the soundness of an increasingly interdependent world financial and economic system affects the well-being of people in all countries. We agree on the importance to the international community of the success of economic and structural reform in Russia.

Strengthening environmental protection in the twenty-first century is imperative in order to protect natural systems on which humanity depends. Russia and the US will work together to resolve the global climate problem, to preserve the ozone layer, to conserve biodiversity, and to ensure the sustainable management of forests and other natural resources. We underscored the necessity of deepening broad based international and bilateral cooperation in this area.

We declare that terrorism in all its forms and manifestations, irrespective of its motives, is utterly unacceptable....

We agreed to intensify joint efforts to counteract the transnational threats to our economies and security, including those posed by organized crime, the narcotics trade, the illegal arms trade, computer and other high-technology crime, and money laundering. We agreed to establish a bilateral law enforcement working group that will meet on a regular basis, and we agreed to step up law enforcement efforts and improve the public information system to eradicate trafficking in women and children. We agreed that the United States and Russia will take an active part in working out an effective UN convention to combat transnational organized crime. We welcome Russia's hosting of a G-8 transnational crime conference at the ministerial level in Moscow in 1999.

We recognize the importance of promoting the positive aspects and mitigating the negative aspects of the information technology revolution now taking place, which is a serious challenge to ensuring the future strategic security interests of our two countries. As part of the efforts to resolve these problems the US and Russia have already held productive discussions within the framework of the Defense Consultative Group on resolving the potential Year 2000 computer problem. The US and Russia are committed to continuing consultations and to studying the wider consequences of this computer problem in order to resolve issues of mutual interest and concern.

We declare that the common security challenges on the threshold of the twenty-first century can be met only by consistently mobilizing the efforts of the entire international community. All available resources must be utilized to do so. In the event that it is necessary, the world community must promptly take effective measures to counter such threats. The US and Russia will continue to play a leadership role bilaterally and multilaterally to advance common objectives in the area.

3. NATO Enlargement: Origins and Implications

President Clinton came to office at a time when there was a pressing need to rethink the security of Europe. Since the signing of the North Atlantic Treaty in Washington, DC on April 4, 1949, NATO had existed to deter Soviet aggression, reassure the West Europeans of America's commitment to their independence, and nurture an environment that encouraged economic recovery. NATO not only kept the Russians out, the Germans down, and the Americans in Europe, it also provided the secure setting for a grand reconciliation between France and Germany and laid the foundations for the historic integration of the West European countries in a European Union (EU). The collapse of the USSR and the end of the Cold War in December 1991 raised serious questions about the future of the alliance: should it disband, should it seek to maintain the status quo, or should it move toward enlarging and transforming its purpose and membership? The nascent EU was too weak to provide effective leadership alone. Consequently, the responsibility for ensuring security on the European continent devolved, for want of a seemingly better alternative, upon NATO. The countries of Central and Eastern Europe, and the Baltic states, now independent from the former Soviet Union, lobbied for admission to NATO and the EU. But the driving force that energized NATO and its prospective hopefuls came not from Europe but from the United States; the catalyst was not concern for security from any looming threat, but US domestic politics.

The fall of 1993 was a difficult time for Bill Clinton. The newly elected president was rebuffed by Congress in his intensive effort to have a national health plan passed, criticized for mishandling the involvement in Haiti and for equivocating on Bosnia, disturbed by the constitutional challenge to Russian President Boris Yeltsin and the ominous rise of a truculent ultra-nationalist Russian opposition, and urged by supporters to avail himself of a "peace dividend" by reducing America's defense expenditures in Europe. Simultaneously, the President was being urged to reformulate the objectives of NATO.

On an international level, intense political pressure was exercised as well. Post-Soviet Russia considered a post-Cold War NATO to be an affront and a threat. Yeltsin asserted that Russia would oppose NATO expansion unless the alliance were reformulated to include Russia. But in the fall of 1993, the Polish and Czech foreign ministers appealed to the NATO summit to send clear signals on enlargement and to commit to incorporating their countries into the alliance. Shortly afterward, eight more would-be aspirants, namely Estonia, Lithuania, Bulgaria, Slovakia, Hungary, Albania, and Latvia, also indicated their eagerness for NATO membership. Sensitive to appeals from their leaders, responsive to the concerns of Congressional leaders and lobbyists over what could transpire if the democratic experiment in Russia failed, and encouraged by West European leaders, to redefine NATO's purpose, Clinton was prodded to act.

On October 21, 1993, then Defense Secretary Les Aspin informally proposed NATO's expansion at a meeting of NATO defense ministers. Three months later, Clinton made it official. At a NATO summit meeting in Brussels on January 10, 1994, Clinton formally affirmed his commitment regarding NATO's future (Speech 3-1). The President praised the alliance and signaled his determination to strengthen it and extend its protective umbrella. He proposed the creation of a "Partnership for Peace" (PFP), which held out the prospect of NATO membership to the countries of Europe, including Russia and the other republics of the former Soviet Union. The timing and criteria for admission, however, were deliberately left ambiguous.

As originally envisaged, PFP was an invitation to prospective applicants to work with NATO for "transparency in national defense planning and budgeting processes," "ensuring democratic control of defense forces," "developing closer ties with NATO in order to undertake [joint] missions in the field of peacekeeping, search and rescue, humanitarian operations, and others as may subsequently be agreed," and fostering the training of "armed forces that are better able to operate with those of NATO."

In his speech to France's parliament on June 7, 1994, on the occasion of the fiftieth anniversary of the allied landings in France for the final assault on Nazi Germany during World War II, President Clinton reaffirmed America's intention to "remain engaged in Europe" and to work together with America's allies for a stronger and more relevant alliance (Speech 3-2). Clinton called for more active participation with NATO on the part of the EU and expressed satisfaction that over nineteen nations had already joined PFP. Indeed, on June 22, 1994, Russian Foreign Minister Andrei Kozyrev signed the PFP Framework Document in Brussels. At the time, he repeated the assumptions which were soon to create problems between NATO and Russia: namely, that NATO's initiative would involve treating the two former Cold War adversaries on an equal footing and that it would lead NATO to dovetail its activities with the Organization for Security and Cooperation in Europe (OSCE), the only all-European organization designed to promote security in which Russia is a full member.

By the end of 1994, enlargement completely overshadowed PFP's less ambitious menu of low-level cooperation in essentially military activities. PFP's purely military goals of participation, cooperation, confidence-building, and interoperability of forces were superseded by the political considerations and inherently contradictory strategic purposes of NATO enlargement: fostering security, promoting democracy, and dealing with Russia. Boris Yeltsin was less than satisfied with the PFP's vagueness concerning Russia's prospect for membership in an enlarged NATO, and warned Clinton that they were heading toward a "Cold Peace." But despite Yeltsin's initial dissatisfaction, Russia and the other former Soviet states (with the exception of Belarus and Tajikistan) joined PFP by the end of 1994, as did all the former Warsaw Pact members in Eastern Europe and the Northern European nations of Finland and Sweden.

With its embrace of NATO enlargement, the Clinton administration stressed the importance of NATO's role in post-Cold War Europe. Following the Republican Party's takeover of both Houses of Congress in the November 1994 mid-term elections, the administration adopted an even more activist stance in Europe to demonstrate its determination in the face of Russia's growing opposition to the new US policy. The ideological stimulus was supplied by strong advocates including Richard Holbrooke (at the time, US ambassador to Germany and the President's trouble shooter in Bosnia) and Madeleine Albright (then ambassador to the United Nations), think-tanks such as the RAND Corporation and the Brookings Institution, and a few prominent members of Congress such as Senator Richard Lugar and Senator Sam Nunn. Such advocates argued that NATO enlargement was necessary to promote stability in Europe, prevent any future revival of German-Russian rivalry in Central and Eastern Europe, and encourage a peaceful and sustained democratization. In this way, arms races could be avoided and economic development fostered.

On November 21, 1994, then Secretary of State Warren Christopher made clear in a statement the irrevocable course on which the Clinton administration had embarked: "NATO is and will remain the centerpiece of America's commitment to European security. But now our challenge is to extend the zone of security and stability that the Alliance has provided—to extend it across the continent to the east." This expression of intent largely dispelled the fog of ambivalence that had enveloped US policy. Whereas President Clinton himself had stated that NATO expansion "will not depend upon the appearance of a new threat in Europe," his principal adviser on Russian affairs and close friend, Deputy Secretary of State Strobe Talbott, cautioned that the expansion of NATO would be determined by the general security environment in Europe. However, once the President determined to press ahead with NATO enlargement, all equivocating interpretations disappeared. European allies were reassured, as were nations seeking NATO membership and domestic groups anxious over Washington's conflicting views.

In August 1995, Strobe Talbott, who had initially reacted coolly to enlargement because of its adverse consequences for US relations with Russia, gave (or was assigned the task of giving) an official response to the public criticism made by a blue-ribbon group of retired diplomats and military leaders. He argued that NATO enlargement should be undertaken for three basic reasons. The first of these was collective defense. Though acknowledging that the break-up of the Soviet Union and the dissolution of the Warsaw Pact had eliminated the threat that NATO had been originally created to counter during the Cold War, he nonetheless maintained that "new threats may arise that would require NATO to protect its members and to defer attack." The possible threat he saw, though nowhere on the horizon, was Russia. The second reason was the promotion of democracy. Admission to NATO would provide the countries of Central Europe and the former Soviet Union with substantial incentives to strengthen their democratic and legal institutions, ensure civilian command of their armed forces, liberalize their economies, and respect human rights, including the rights of minorities. The third reason given in support for NATO enlargement was regional peace and stability. In return for admission to NATO, new members would be expected to settle disputes peacefully and engage in peacekeeping operations.

The Partnership for Peace program continued to expand throughout 1995, as Austria, Belarus, Malta, and Macedonia joined. Non-NATO membership in the program rose to twenty-seven, Tajikistan being the only former Soviet Union republic not participating. NATO discussed the idea of enhancing PFP into "PFP Plus," which was aimed at creating a more meaningful military relationship with Russia. Many countries eagerly signed up for the Partnership for Peace program, but NATO put off inviting additional nations to join the alliance.

It was President Clinton who set the pace and determined the candidates for the first tranche. On October 22, 1996, in the final two weeks of a bitterly waged campaign for re-election, Clinton delivered a speech in Detroit, Michigan (Speech 3-3). Clinton announced his determination to admit the first group of countries in 1999 on "NATO's fiftieth anniversary and ten years after the fall of the Berlin Wall." The announcement was not anticipated by the US public or by the international community at large. Clearly, domestic considerations greatly influenced Clinton's decision to speak out as he did in Detroit, including the desire to attract support from the Central and Eastern European ethnic groups who were crucial to the electoral outcome in key Midwestern states. There was no prior consultation with Congress or with the European allies. Indeed, earlier in the year, Clinton had stated that there was no consensus to enlarge NATO, and that the NATO alliance did not wish to "draw a dividing line" in Europe after the Cold War. The politics of enlargement superseded the strategic rationale for PFP: NATO's rapid expansion to the east was to have far-reaching consequences for US-Russian relations.

Apart from the decision to announce the first tranche of NATO enlargement when he did, an allusion in Clinton's speech to expanded "missions beyond the territory of its members for the first time" was to prove momentous for NATO. Whether deliberate or inadvertent, this description of what NATO's enlargement signified clearly reflected Clinton's belief, expressed in the early part of his speech, that "America truly is the world's indispensable nation." It foreshadowed a greater embrace of "humanitarian intervention."

Soon after his re-election, Clinton obtained NATO's approval on December 10, 1996, for the timing of the first tranche: the NATO communiqué called for the convening of a summit meeting in Madrid on July 8 – 9, 1997, one aim of which was "inviting one or more countries which have expressed interest in joining the Alliance to begin accession negotiations." Accordingly, most observers concluded that NATO enlargement was a done deal. In May 1997, shortly before the scheduled NATO Summit, Clinton strengthened and developed his case for support of enlargement in a commencement address at West Point (Speech 3-4). In this speech, the President presented four concrete reasons for NATO to take in new members, in the context of which an enlarged NATO would serve to unify, rather than divide, Europe.

At the NATO Summit in July 1997, the sixteen NATO countries offered membership to Poland, Hungary, and the Czech Republic, notwithstanding strong Russian objections. Meanwhile, the Partnership for Peace program was bolstered in order to strengthen NATO links with nonmembers. In February 1998, on the eve of the US Senate's consideration of the admission of the three proposed new members, President Clinton spoke of the issues involved at the official ceremony transmitting the protocol of access to the Senate (Speech 3-5). On April 30, 1998, the Senate ratified the accession to NATO of the three East European states. After five years of intense political lobbying within the foreign policy community and with minimal public discussion, the Clinton administration had succeeded in expanding NATO's size and mission. Whether this first tranche was to be the last, or whether additional members (for example, the Baltic states, Slovenia, Romania) were to be admitted was yet to be decided. How this process eventuates will be a strong determinant in shaping the character of US relations with Russia.

In late April 1999, the leaders of the NATO member states and their PFP partners convened in Washington to commemorate the fiftieth anniversary of the alliance's founding, and the admission of its three new members. The celebratory occasion was, however, dampened by the crisis with Yugoslavia over the plight of the Albanians in the Serbian province of Kosovo. On March 24, President Clinton had announced NATO's decision to resort to force to compel Yugoslavia's President Slobodan Milosevic to comply with the alliance's demands. Against this background, his remarks at the NATO ceremony were sober and foreshadowed a new period of uncertainty in Europe (Speech 3-6).

By early June, Milosevic had been forced to accept NATO's basic demands. Despite its political and economic weakness, Russia played an important role in shaping the final outcome of the NATO-Serbian agreement, carrying on extensive negotiations with Milosevic and simultaneously bargaining with NATO to obtain concessions in return for Moscow's vote supporting the UN's participation in a post-Kosovo peace process. Russia's active role demonstrated that it still had diplomatic leverage, and that its cooperation still counted in any attempt to fashion long-term security in Europe. How an enlarged NATO deals with Russia will do much to shape the future of that security.

3-1 A New Security Structure for Europe

Remarks to the North Atlantic Council
Brussels, Belgium
January 10, 1994

... Each of us came here for the same compelling reason: the security of the North Atlantic region is vital to the security of the United States. The founders of this alliance created the greatest military alliance in history. It was a bold undertaking. I think all of us know that we have come together this week because history calls upon us to be equally bold once again in the aftermath of the Cold War. Now we no longer fear attack from a common enemy. But if our common adversary has vanished, we know our common dangers have not.

With the Cold War over, we must confront the destabilizing consequences of the unfreezing of history which the end of the Cold War has wrought. The threat to us now is not of advancing armies so much as of creeping instability. The best strategy against this threat is to integrate the former communist states into our fabric of liberal democracy, economic prosperity, and military cooperation. For our security in this generation will be shaped by whether reforms in these nations succeed in the face of their own very significant economic frustration, ethnic tensions, and intolerant nationalism.

The size of the reactionary vote in Russia's recent election reminds us again of the strength of democracy's opponents. The ongoing slaughter in Bosnia tallies the price when those opponents prevail. If we don't meet our new challenge, then most assuredly, we will once again, someday down the road, face our old challenges again. If democracy in the East fails, then violence and disruption from the East will once again harm us and other democracies.

I believe our generation's stewardship of this grand alliance, therefore, will most critically be judged by whether we succeed in integrating the nations to our east within the compass of Western security and Western values. For we've been granted an opportunity without precedent: We really have the chance to recast European security on historic new principles: the pursuit of economic and political freedom. And I would argue to you that we must work hard to succeed now, for this opportunity may not come to us again.

In effect, the world wonders now whether we have the foresight and the courage our predecessors had to act on our long-term interests. I'm confident that the steel in this alliance has not rusted. Our nations have proved that by joining together in the common effort in the Gulf war. We proved it anew this past year by working together, after seven long years of effort, in a spirit of compromise and harmony to reach a new GATT agreement. And now we must do it once again.

To seize the great opportunity before us I have proposed that we forge what we have all decided to call the Partnership For Peace, opened to all the former Communist states of the Warsaw Pact, along with other non-NATO states. The membership of the Partnership will plan and train and exercise together and work together on missions of common concern. They should be invited to work directly with NATO both here and in the coordination cell in Mons.

The Partnership will prepare the NATO alliance to undertake new tasks that the times impose upon us. The Combined Joint Task Force Headquarters we are creating will let us act both effectively and with dispatch in helping to make and keep the peace and in helping to head off some of the terrible problems we are now trying to solve today. We must also ready this alliance to meet new threats, notably from weapons of mass destruction and the means of delivering them.

Building on NATO's creation of the North Atlantic Cooperation Council two years ago, the Partnership For Peace sets in motion a process that leads to the enlargement of NATO. We began this alliance with twelve members. Today there are sixteen, and each one has strengthened the alliance.

Indeed, our treaty always looked to the addition of new members who shared the alliance's purposes and who could enlarge its orbit of democratic security. Thus, in leading us toward the addition of these Eastern states, the Partnership For Peace does not change NATO's original vision, it realizes that vision.

So let us say here to the people in Europe's east, we share with you a common destiny, and we are committed to your success. The democratic community has grown, and now it is time to begin welcoming these newcomers to our neighborhood.

As President Mitterrand said so eloquently, some of the newcomers want to be members of NATO right away, and some have expressed reservations about this concept of the Partnership For Peace. Some have asked me in my own country, "Well, is this just the best you can do? Is this sort of splitting the difference between doing nothing and full membership at least for the Visegrad states?" And to that, let me answer at least for my part an emphatic no, for many of the same reasons President Mitterrand has already outlined.

Why should we now draw a new line through Europe just a little further east? Why should we now do something which could foreclose the best possible future for Europe? The best possible future would be a democratic Russia committed to the security of all of its European neighbors. The best possible future would be a democratic Ukraine, a democratic government in every one of the newly independent states of the former Soviet Union, all committed to market cooperation, to common security, and to democratic ideals. We should not foreclose that possibility.

The Partnership For Peace, I would argue, gives us the best of both worlds. It enables us to prepare and to work toward the enlargement of NATO when other countries are capable of fulfilling their NATO responsibilities. It enables us to do it in a way that gives us the time to reach out to Russia and to these other nations of the former Soviet Union, which have been almost ignored through this entire debate by people around the world, in a way that leaves open the possibility of a future for Europe that totally breaks from the destructive past we have known.

So I say to you, I do not view this as some sort of half-hearted compromise. In substance, this is a good idea. It is the right thing to do at this moment in history. It leaves open the best possible future for Europe, and leaves us the means to settle for a future that is not the best but is much better than the past. And I would argue that is the course that we all ought to pursue.

I think we have to be clear, in doing it, about certain assumptions and consequences. First, if we move forward in this manner, we must reaffirm the bonds of our own alliance. America pledges its efforts in that common purpose. I pledge to maintain roughly 100,000 troops in Europe, consistent with the expressed wishes of our allies. The people of Europe can count on America to maintain this commitment.

Second, we have to recognize that this new security challenge requires a range of responses different from the ones of the past. That is why our administration has broken with previous American administrations in going beyond what others have done to support European efforts to advance their own security and interests. All of you have received our support in moving in ways beyond NATO. We supported the Maastricht Treaty. We support the commitment of the European Union to a common foreign and security policy. We support your efforts to refurbish the Western European Union so that it will assume a more vigorous role in keeping Europe secure. Consistent with that goal, we have proposed making NATO assets available to WEU operations in which NATO itself is not involved. While NATO must remain the linchpin of our security, all these efforts will show our people and our legislatures a renewed purpose in European institutions and a better balance of responsibilities within the transatlantic community.

Finally, in developing the Partnership For Peace, each of us must willingly assume the burdens to make that succeed. This must not be a gesture. It is a forum. It is not just a forum. This Partnership For Peace is also a military and security initiative, consistent with what NATO was established to achieve. There must be a somber appreciation that expanding our membership will mean extending commitments that must be supported by military strategies and postures. Adding new members entails not only hard decisions but hard resources. Today those resources are not great, but nonetheless, as the Secretary General told me in the meeting this morning, they must be forthcoming in order for this to be taken seriously by our allies and our friends who will immediately subscribe to the Partnership....

3-2 Reassuring Western Europe

Remarks to the French National Assembly
Paris, France
June 7, 1994

... After World War II, ... we reached out to rebuild our allies and our former enemies, Germany, Italy, and Japan, and to confront the threat of Soviet expansion and nuclear power. Together, we founded NATO, we launched the Marshall plan, the General Agreement on Tariffs and Trade, and other engines of economic development. And in one of history's great acts of reconciliation, France reached out to forge the Franco-German partnership, the foundation of unity and stability in modern Western Europe. Indeed, the members of the European Union have performed an act of political alchemy, a magical act that turned rubble into renewal, suspicion into security, enemies into allies....

Now we have arrived at this century's third moment of decision. The Cold War is over. Prague, Warsaw, Kiev, Riga, Moscow, and many others stand as democratic capitals, with leaders elected by the people. We are reducing nuclear stockpiles, and America and Russia no longer aim their nuclear missiles at each other. Yet once again, our work is far from finished. To secure this peace, we must set our sights on a strategic star. Here, where America and our allies fought so hard to save the world, let that star for both of us, for Americans and for Europeans alike, be the integration and strengthening of a broader Europe.

It is a mighty challenge. It will require resources. It will take years, even decades. It will require us to do what is very difficult for democracies, to unite our people when they do not feel themselves in imminent peril to confront more distant threats and to seize challenging and exciting opportunities. Yet, the hallowed gravestones we honored yesterday speak to us clearly. They define the price of failure in peacetime. They affirm the need for action now.

We can already see the grim alternative. Militant nationalism is on the rise, transforming the healthy pride of nations, tribes, religious and ethnic groups into cancerous prejudice, eating away at states and leaving their people addicted to the political painkillers of violence and demagoguery, and blaming their problems on others when they should be dedicated to the hard work of finding real answers to those problems in reconciliation, in power-sharing, in sustainable development. We see the signs of this disease from the purposeful slaughter in Bosnia to the random violence of skinheads in all our nations. We see it in the incendiary misuses of history and in the anti-Semitism and irredentism of some former Communist states. And beyond Europe, we see the dark future of these trends in mass slaughter, unbridled terrorism, devastating poverty, and total environmental and social disintegration.

Our transatlantic alliance clearly stands at a critical point. We must build the bonds among nations necessary for this time, just as we did after World War II. But we must do so at a time when our safety is not directly threatened, just as after World War I. The question for this generation of leaders is whether we have the will, the vision, and yes, the patience to do it.

Let me state clearly where the United States stands. America will remain engaged in Europe. The entire transatlantic alliance benefits when we, Europe and America, are both strong and engaged. America wishes a strong Europe, and Europe should wish a strong America, working together....

We also want Europe to be strong. That is why America supports Europe's own steps so far toward greater unity, the European Union, the Western European Union, and the development of a European defense identity. We now must pursue a shared strategy, to secure the peace of a broader Europe and its prosperity. That strategy depends upon integrating the entire continent through three sets of bonds: first, security cooperation; second, market economics; and third, democracy.

To start, we must remain strong and safe in an era that still has many dangers. To do so we must adapt our security institutions to meet new imperatives. America has reduced the size of its military presence in Europe, but we will maintain a strong force here. The EU, the WEU, the Conference on Security and Cooperation in Europe, and other organizations must all play a larger role. I was pleased that NATO recently approved an American proposal to allow its assets to be used by the WEU. To foster greater security cooperation all across Europe, we also need to adapt NATO to this new era.

At the NATO summit in January, we agreed to create the Partnership For Peace in order to foster security cooperation among NATO allies and the other states of Europe, both former Warsaw Pact countries, states of the former Soviet Union, and states not involved in NATO for other reasons. And just six months later, this Partnership For Peace is a reality. No less than nineteen nations have joined, and more are on the way. Russia has expressed an interest in joining.

The Partnership will conduct its first military exercises this fall. Imagine the transformation: Troops that once faced each other across the Iron Curtain will now work with each other across the plains of Europe.

We understand the historical anxieties of Central and Eastern Europe. The security of those states is important to our own security. And we are committed to NATO's expansion. At the same time, as long as we have the chance, the chance to create security cooperation everywhere in Europe, we should not abandon that possibility anywhere....

There is a language of democracy spoken among nations. It is expressed in the way we work out our differences, in the way we treat each other's citizens, in the way we honor each other's heritages. It is the language our two republics have spoken with each other for over 200 years. It is the language that the Western Allies spoke during the Second World War.

Now we have the opportunity to hear the language of democracy spoken across this entire continent. And if we can achieve that goal, we will have paid a great and lasting tribute to those from both our countries who fought and died for freedom fifty years ago....

3-3 Announcing NATO's First Tranche

Remarks at a Reelection Rally
Detroit, Michigan
October 22, 1996

... [I]n a world that is increasingly interconnected, we have to just sort of take down that artificial wall in our mind that this is completely a foreign policy issue and this is completely a domestic issue, because increasingly they impact one on the other. That is why I think, among other things, we have to resist those who believe that now that the Cold War is over the United States can completely return to focusing on problems within our borders and basically ignore those beyond our borders.

That escapism is not available to us because at the end of the Cold War, America truly is the world's indispensable nation. There are times when only America can make the difference between war and peace, between freedom and repression, between hope and fear. We cannot and should not try to be the world's policeman. But where our interests and values are clearly at stake, and where we can make a difference, we must act and lead....

Nowhere are our interests more engaged than in Europe. When Europe is at peace, our security is strengthened. When Europe prospers, so does America. We have a special bond because our Nation was formed from the hopes and dreams of those who came to our shores from across the Atlantic seeking religious freedom, fleeing persecution, looking for a better life. From the Pilgrims of 1620 to the Hungarian freedom fighters of 1956, whose struggle we commemorate tomorrow, they gave America the strength of diversity and the passion for freedom.

Remarkable generations of Americans invested in Europe's peace and freedom with their own sacrifice. They fought two World Wars. They had the vision to create NATO and the Marshall plan. The vigor of those institutions, the force of democracy, the determination of people to be free, all these helped to produce victory in the Cold War. But now that ... freedom has been won, it is this generation's responsibility to ensure that it will not be lost again, not ever.

President Reagan gave strength to those working to bring down the Iron Curtain. President Bush helped to reunify Germany. And now, for the very first time since nation-states first appeared in Europe, we have an opportunity to build a peaceful, undivided, and democratic continent. It has never happened before; it can be done now, a continent where democracy and free markets know no boundaries, but where nations can be assured that their borders will always be secure and their sovereignty and independence will always be respected.

In January 1994, during my first trip to Europe as President, I laid out a strategy for European integration: political integration around democracies, economic integration around free markets, security integration around military cooperation. I urged our enduring allies and new friends to build the bonds among our nations that are necessary for this time, through the European Union, through NATO, through the other institutions of a new Europe. I challenged all our people to summon the will and the resources to make this vision real.

The United States and Europe are answering that challenge. With our help, the forces of reform in Europe's newly free nations have laid the foundations of democracy. They have political parties and free elections, an independent media, civilian control of the military. We've helped them to develop successful market economies, and now are moving from aid to trade and investment.

Look at what has been achieved by our common efforts. In the seven years since the fall of the Berlin Wall, two-thirds of Russia's economy has moved from the heavy grip of the state into private hands. Poland has now one of the West's highest rates of growth. You're as likely to read about Poland on the business page as the front page today. The private sector produces half the national income of an independent Ukraine. From the Czech Republic to Hungary to Estonia, the same forces of freedom and free markets are creating bustling prosperity and hope for the future.

The bedrock of our common security remains NATO. When President Truman signed the North Atlantic Treaty forty-seven years ago, he expressed the goal of its founders plainly but powerfully: to preserve their present peaceful situation and to protect it in the future. All of us here today, every single one of us, are the beneficiaries of NATO's extraordinary success in doing just that.

NATO defended the West by deterring aggression. Even more, through NATO, Western Europe became a source of stability instead of hostility. France and Germany moved from conflict to cooperation. Democracy took permanent root in countries where fascism once ruled.

I came to office convinced that NATO can do for Europe's East what it did for Europe's West: prevent a return to local rivalries, strengthen democracy against future threats, and create the conditions for prosperity to flourish. That's why the United States has taken the lead in a three-part effort to build a new NATO for a new era: first, by adapting NATO with new capabilities for new missions; second, by opening its doors to Europe's emerging democracies; third, by building a strong and cooperative relationship between NATO and Russia.

To adapt NATO, we have taken on missions beyond the territory of its members for the first time and done so in cooperation with nonmember states, shifting our emphasis to smaller and more flexible forces prepared to provide for our defense but also trained and equipped for peacekeeping. We're setting up mobile headquarters to run these new missions more effectively and efficiently. We're giving our European allies a larger role within the alliance, while preserving NATO's vital core, which is an integrated command military structure....

But for NATO to fulfill its real promise of peace and democracy in Europe it will not be enough simply to take on new missions as the need arises. NATO must also take in new members, including those from among its former adversaries. It must reach out to all the new democracies in Central Europe, the Baltics, and the New Independent States of the former Soviet Union.

At the first NATO summit I attended in January of 1994, I proposed that NATO should enlarge—steadily, deliberately, openly. And our allies agreed. First, together, we created the Partnership For Peace as a path to full NATO membership for some and a strong and lasting link to the alliance for all. I think it would be fair to say that the Partnership For Peace has exceeded what even its most optimistic supporters predicted for it in the beginning. There are more than two dozen members now.

The more than two dozen members and the astonishing amount of cooperation and joint training and partnership that has developed as a result of this Partnership For Peace has made it something of significance—I believe enduring significance—beyond what we ever imagined when we started it. And the strategy is paying off. The prospect of membership in or partnership with NATO has given Europe's new democracies a strong incentive to continue to reform and to improve relations with their neighbors.

Through the Partnership For Peace, prospective new members are actually gaining the practical experience they need to join NATO. Thirteen partner nations are serving alongside NATO troops and helping to secure the peace in Bosnia. There are Polish and Czech combat battalions, Hungarian and Romanian engineering troops, soldiers from Ukraine and the Baltic States, forces from Sweden and Finland and a full Russian brigade.

Just seven years ago, these soldiers served on opposite sides of the Iron Curtain. Today, their teamwork with our troops and other European NATO allies is erasing the lines that once divided Europe while bringing an end to the bloodiest conflict in Europe since World War II.

We have kept NATO enlargement on track. Now it is time to take the next historic step forward. Last month, I called for a summit in the spring or early summer of next year to name the first group of future NATO members and to invite them to begin accession talks. Today I want to state America's goal. By 1999, NATO's fiftieth anniversary and ten years after the fall of the Berlin Wall, the first group of countries we invite to join should be full-fledged members of NATO.

I also pledged for my part, and I believe for NATO's part as well, that NATO's doors will not close behind its first new members. NATO should remain open to all of Europe's emerging democracies who are ready to shoulder the responsibilities of membership. No nation will be automatically excluded. No country outside NATO will have a veto. We will work to deepen our cooperation, meanwhile, with all the nations in the Partnership For Peace. A gray zone of insecurity must not reemerge in Europe.

Now, I want to say that as we go forward the American people should be aware that this plan is not free of costs. Peace and security are not available on the cheap. Enlargement will mean extending the most solemn security guarantee to our new allies. To be a NATO member means that all the other members make a commitment to treat an attack on one as an attack on all. But mark my words, if we fail to seize this historic opportunity to build a new NATO in a new Europe, if we allow the Iron Curtain to be replaced by a veil of indifference, we will pay a much higher price later on down the road. America will be stronger and safer if the democratic family continues to grow, if we bring to our ranks partners willing to share the risks and responsibilities of freedom.

By overwhelming majorities this summer, both Houses of Congress passed a NATO Enlargement Facilitation Act. I greatly appreciate this bipartisan support for our efforts to forge a broader alliance of prosperity, of security and, as the First Lady said in Prague on the last fourth of July, an alliance of values with Europe. I look forward to working with Congress to ratify the accession of new members, to provide the resources we need to meet this commitment, to secure the support of the American people. NATO enlargement is not directed against anyone. It will advance the security of everyone: NATO's old members, new members, and nonmembers alike.

I know that some in Russia still look at NATO through a Cold-War prism and, therefore, look at our proposals to expand it in a negative light. But I ask them to look again. We are building a new NATO, just as we support the Russian people in building a new Russia. By reducing rivalry and fear, by strengthening peace and cooperation, NATO will promote greater stability in Europe and Russia will be among the beneficiaries. Indeed, Russia has the best chance in history to help to build that peaceful and undivided Europe and to be an equal and respected and successful partner in that sort of future....

I wish every American could see our country as much of the world sees us. Our friends rely upon our engagement. Our adversaries respect our strength. When our family went to open the Olympics in Atlanta, I was so moved by the statements of young people from around the world about the efforts the United States had made to foster peace in Bosnia, peace in Northern Ireland, peace in the Middle East, things these young athletes felt personally because it was their lives, their future, and the children they still hope to have on the line.

As we enter the twenty-first century, we must make a commitment to remain true to the legacy of America's leadership, to make sure America remains the indispensable nation, not only for ourselves but for what we believe in and for all the people of the world. That is our burden. That is our opportunity. And it must be our future.

3-4 Justifying NATO Enlargement

Remarks at the US Military Academy
Commencement Ceremony
West Point, New York
May 31, 1997

... To build and secure a new Europe, peaceful, democratic, and undivided at last, there must be a new NATO, with new missions, new members, and new partners. We have been building that kind of NATO for the last three years with new partners in the Partnership For Peace and NATO's first out-of-area mission in Bosnia....

In a little more than a month, I will join with other NATO leaders in Madrid to invite the first of Europe's new democracies in Central Europe to join our alliance, with the consent of the Senate, by 1999, the fiftieth anniversary of NATO's founding.

I firmly believe NATO enlargement is in our national interests. But because it is not without cost and risk, it is appropriate to have an open, full, national discussion before proceeding. I want to further that discussion here today in no small measure because it is especially important to those of you in this class. For after all, as the sentinels of our security in the years ahead, your work will be easier and safer if we do the right thing, and riskier and much more difficult if we do not.

Europe's fate and America's future are joined. Twice in half a century, Americans have given their lives to defend liberty and peace in World Wars that began in Europe. And we have stayed in Europe in very large numbers for a long time throughout the Cold War. Taking wise steps now to strengthen our common security when we have the opportunity to do so, will help to build a future without the mistakes and the divisions of the past and will enable us to organize ourselves to meet the new security challenges of the new century. In this task, NATO should be our sharpest sword and strongest shield.

Some say we no longer need NATO because there is no powerful threat to our security now. I say there is no powerful threat in part because NATO is there. And enlargement will help make it stronger. I believe we should take in new members to NATO for four reasons.

First, it will strengthen our alliance in meeting the security challenges of the twenty-first century, addressing conflicts that threaten the common peace of all.

Consider Bosnia. Already the Czech Republic, Poland, Romania, the Baltic nations, and other Central European countries are contributing troops and bases to NATO's peacekeeping mission in Bosnia. We in the United States could not have deployed our troops to Bosnia as safely, smoothly, and swiftly as we did without the help of Hungary and our staging ground at Taszar, which I personally visited. The new democracies we invite to join NATO are ready and able to share the burdens of defending freedom in no small measure because they know the cost of losing freedom.

Second, NATO enlargement will help to secure the historic gains of democracy in Europe. NATO can do for Europe's East what it did for Europe's West at the end of World War II: provide a secure climate where freedom, democracy, and prosperity can flourish. Joining NATO once helped Italy, Germany, and Spain to consolidate their democracies. Now the opening of NATO's doors has led the Central European nations already—already—to deepen democratic reform, to strengthen civilian control of their military, to open their economies. Membership and its future prospect will give them the confidence to stay the course.

Third, enlarging NATO will encourage prospective members to resolve their differences peacefully. We see all over the world the terrible curse of people who are imprisoned by their own ethnic, regional, and nationalist hatreds, who rob themselves and their children of the lives they might have because of their primitive, destructive impulses that they cannot control.

When he signed the NATO treaty in 1949, President Truman said that if NATO had simply existed in 1914 or 1939, it would have prevented the World Wars that tore the world apart. The experience of the last fifty years supports that view. NATO helped to reconcile age-old adversaries like France and Germany, now fast friends and allies, and clearly has reduced tensions between Greece and Turkey over all these decades. Already the very prospect of NATO membership has helped to convince countries in Central Europe to settle more than half a dozen border and ethnic disputes, any one of which could have led to future conflicts. That, in turn, makes it less likely that you will ever be called to fight in another war across the Atlantic.

Fourth, enlarging NATO, along with its Partnership For Peace with many other nations and its special agreement with Russia and its soon-to-be-signed partnership with Ukraine, will erase the artificial line in Europe that Stalin drew and bring Europe together in security, not keep it apart in instability.

NATO expansion does not mean a differently divided Europe; it is part of unifying Europe. NATO's first members should not be its last. NATO's doors will remain open to all those willing and able to shoulder the responsibilities of membership, and we must continue to strengthen our partnerships with nonmembers.

Now, let me be clear to all of you: These benefits are not cost- or risk-free. Enlargement will require the United States to pay an estimated $200 million a year for the next decade. Our allies in Canada and Western Europe are prepared to do their part, so are NATO's new members, so must we.

More important, enlargement requires that we extend to new members our alliance's most solemn security pledge, to treat an attack against one as an attack against all. We have always made the pledge credible through the deployment of our troops and the deterrence of our nuclear weapons. In the years ahead, it means that you could be asked to put your lives on the line for a new NATO member, just as today you can be called upon to defend the freedom of our allies in Western Europe.

In leading NATO over the past three years to open its doors to Europe's new democracies, I weighed these costs very carefully. I concluded that the benefits of enlargement—strengthening NATO for the future, locking in democracy's gains in Central Europe, building stability across the Atlantic, uniting Europe, not dividing it—these gains decisively outweigh the burdens. The bottom line to me is clear: Expanding NATO will enhance our security. It is the right thing to do. We must not fail history's challenge at this moment to build a Europe peaceful, democratic, and undivided, allied with us to face the new security threats of the new century, a Europe that will avoid repeating the darkest moments of the twentieth century and fulfill the brilliant possibilities of the twenty-first....

3-5 Extending Membership to Poland, Hungary, and the Czech Republic

Remarks at a Ceremony Transmitting to the
United States Senate the Protocol of Access to NATO
for Poland, Hungary, and the Czech Republic
Washington DC
February 11, 1998

... [W]e come together not to sign another agreement to end a war, but instead to begin a new era of security and stability for America and for Europe. In just a moment I will transmit to the Senate for its advice and consent the documents that will add Poland, Hungary, and the Czech Republic to NATO. Their addition to the alliance is not only a pivotal event in the quest for freedom and security by their own people; it is also a major stride forward for America, for the alliance, and for the stability and unity of all Europe—a big part of our dream that we can in the twenty-first century create for the first time in all history a Europe that is free, at peace, and undivided.

As the Senate takes up consideration of these agreements, the question the members of the Senate must answer is, how does adding these states to NATO advance America's national security. I believe there are three compelling reasons. First, the alliance will make NATO stronger. The Cold War has passed, but dangers remain. Conflicts like the one in Bosnia, weapons of mass destruction, threats we cannot even predict today, require a NATO that is strong. A NATO that embraces Europe's new democracies will be more capable of carrying out the core mission of defending the territory of its members, as well as addressing new kinds of conflicts that threaten our common peace.

These three states will add some 200,000 troops to the alliance. A larger NATO will be a better deterrent against aggressors of the future. It will deepen the ranks of those who stand with us should deterrents fail. I am pleased that just last week sixty of America's top retired military leaders, including five former Chairmen of the Joint Chiefs of Staff, underscored that message when they said these three states will make NATO stronger. They are right and we have already seen the proof.

As we speak, Czech, Hungarian, and Polish troops are participating in NATO's peacekeeping effort in Bosnia. They served beside us in the Gulf War, where they made a significant contribution to our success. And they recognize the threat to the world posed today by Saddam Hussein and by his efforts to develop weapons of mass destruction. I am pleased that all three countries have announced that they are prepared to serve and support with us as appropriate should military action prove necessary.

We all hope we can avoid the use of force. But let's face it, in the end that is up to Saddam Hussein. He must let the weapons inspectors back with full and free access to all suspect sites. If he will not act, we must be prepared to do so.

The second reason NATO must grow is that it will make Europe more stable. NATO can do for Europe's east what it did for Europe's west after the Second World War: provide a secure climate in which democracy and prosperity can grow. Enlarging NATO will encourage prospective members to resolve their difference peacefully. We already see evidence of that. Already, the prospect of NATO membership has helped to convince countries in central Europe to improve ties with their neighbors, to settle border and ethnic disputes, any one of which could have led to a conflict. Enlargement, therefore, will make all of Europe more stable.

Finally, NATO's growth will erase the artificial line in Europe drawn by Joseph Stalin. Behind me is a picture of the wall that for so long represented the false and forced division of the European continent. It has been nearly ten years since that wall was torn down by brave people on both sides. Countries once confined by it now are truly free, with strong democracies, vibrant market economies, a proven track record of standing up for peace and security beyond their own borders. NATO cannot maintain the old Iron Curtain as its permanent eastern frontier. It must and can bring Europe together in security, not keep it apart in instability.

In the twentieth century, we have learned the hard way here in America just how vital Europe's security is to our own. Enlarging NATO will make us safer.

Our goal is and remains the creation of an undivided democratic and peaceful Europe for the first time in history. Bringing the three nations into the alliance will advance it; so will NATO's new Founding Act with Russia and the broad new relationship we are building with Moscow, helping us to move forward on arms control, building the peace in Bosnia, achieving progress on a wide range of issues; so will the Partnership for Peace, the Euro-Atlantic Partnership Council, the Charter with Ukraine and the Charter of Partnership I signed just last month with the presidents of the three Baltic states, and our Southeast Europe Action Plan, which I announced yesterday with President Stoyanav of Bulgaria.

Our effort to build a new Europe also depends upon keeping NATO's door open to other qualified European democracies. History teaches us that the realm of freedom in Europe has no fixed boundaries. The United States is determined that the visions of the past not circumscribe the boundaries of the future.... Now the decision rests in the hands of the Senate, and I believe it's in good hands....

... In the wake of the Cold War, some wondered whether our alliance faced a rising or a setting sun, whether it had just a brilliant past, or perhaps an even brighter future. With the step we take today, and the decision I am confident the Senate will take in the near future, I know that our historic partnership of nations is a rising sun, and that its ascendance will bring a more stable, more democratic, more peaceful, more unified future for all of us who live on both sides of the Atlantic....

3-6 Toward a Greater NATO in the Twenty-first Century

Remarks at the Close of the
NATO Fiftieth Anniversary Summit
Washington DC
April 25, 1999

... We came to this summit committed to chart a course for the NATO Alliance for the twenty-first century, one that embraces new members, new partners, and new missions. Here we committed NATO first to fulfill its mission of collective defense with the ability to meet new security threats; second, to remain open to new allies and to seek stronger partnership with nations all across Europe, central Asia, and obviously including Ukraine and Russia.

We've also reaffirmed our determination repeatedly to intensify our actions, military and economic, until we achieve our objectives in Kosovo. On this, the Alliance leaves Washington more united even than it was when we came here.

Meanwhile, we will stand by the neighboring countries that have accepted risks and hardship in support of this effort. If Mr. Milosevic threatens them for helping us, we will respond. And we will work to support democracy and development in the region, so that the forces pulling people together will be stronger than those pulling them apart, and all nations—including, someday, a democratic Serbia—can join the European mainstream.

What NATO did here this weekend was to reaffirm our commitment to a common future, rooted in common humanity. Standing against ethnic cleansing is both a moral imperative and a practical necessity, as the leaders of the frontline states, who have so much at stake in the outcome, made so clear to us.

Our vision of a Europe undivided, democratic, free, and at peace, depends upon our constructive commitment to the hundreds of thousands of poor refugees, so many men, women, and children, with no place else to turn, who have been made pawns in a power struggle. It depends upon our ability and our collective commitment after this crisis has past to help all the people of southeastern Europe build a better future....

... There has been this breathtaking explosion of freedom. But the old order has not yet been replaced by a new one that answers all the legitimate needs of people, not just for freedom but also for security and prosperity.

We must be committed to building that kind of future for the people of central Europe, for the people of southeastern Europe, and for our other partners, going all the way to the central Asian states. We cannot expect for people to stop being drawn back to old ways of organizing themselves, even profoundly destructive ways resting on ethnic and religious divisions, unless there is a far more powerful magnate out there before them.

And so we committed ourselves to building that kind of future for all of our allies in the twenty-first century. When all is said and done, I think people will look back on this summit, perhaps many years from now, and say, that was its lasting value. We looked to the future with a clear vision and made a commitment to build it....

4. Dealing with China: Friendly Competitor or Looming Adversary?

In a major foreign policy speech he delivered in Los Angeles on August 13, 1992, presidential candidate Bill Clinton criticized President George Bush for failing to stand up for American values "when China cracked down on pro-democracy demonstrators (in Tiananmen Square, Beijing, on June 3 – 4, 1989), exported advanced weapons to radical regimes, and suppressed Tibet," and for his signaling instead that he would do business as usual. As President, Clinton started out on a principled path, indifferent to Beijing's reactions. His first Secretary of State, Warren Christopher, on his first visit to the People's Republic of China (PRC) in March 1994, insisted that the PRC improve its human rights record and that there would be a linkage between improvement in this realm and expanded trade with America. However, Clinton quickly backed away from this stance as he came to appreciate the importance of long-term relations with China. Only two months after the Christopher trip, he embraced Bush's pragmatic approach, though with a better political gloss: "We are developing," Clinton explained, "a broader engagement with the People's Republic of China that will encompass both our economic and strategic interests. That policy is best reflected in our decision to delink China's Most-Favored-Nation status from its record on human rights" (Speech 4-1; see also the section on East Asia and the Pacific in Speech 1-4).

By the fall of 1994, Secretary of Defense William Perry's preferred focus on trying to establish a stable and comprehensive strategic relationship with the PRC took precedence over Christopher's advocacy of priority for human rights issues. After Perry's visit to Beijing in October 1994, no similarly high-level Chinese military delegation came to Washington until December 1996, the postponements arising out of tensions over Taiwan. But lower-level military contacts continued, signifying White House recognition of the influential role played by the military in China's evolving political system.

The Taiwan problem was an outgrowth of the Korean War of 1950 –
1953, and remains an unresolved political complication. Lying some 100
miles off China's southeast coast, Taiwan had been a backward province
of the Chinese empire. Japan seized it in 1895 and held on to the island
until 1945, when it reverted to China. When the Chinese Nationalist Kuo-
mintang (KMT) forces under Chiang Kai-shek, who had been allied to the
United States during World War II, were defeated in the summer of 1949
by the Communist armies led by Mao Zedong, their remnants fled to Taiwan. The KMT leadership hoped, somehow, to hold out, regroup, and return to fight the Communists on the mainland. Their assistance came,
providentially, when the pro-Moscow Communist North Korean army
invaded South Korea in June 1950. With PRC troops aiding North Korea
and US troops defending South Korea, the United States sought to contain
China. One measure was to interpose the Seventh Fleet to prevent the Chinese Communists from taking control of strategically situated Taiwan. In
this way, Washington became the island's protector-patron.

As long as the PRC was an ally of the Soviet Union and hostile to the
United States, Taiwan sheltered under Washington's nuclear umbrella: it
retained a seat in the United Nations and was recognized as the government of China. Starting in the late 1960s, it transformed itself into an economically productive and modern society and underwent a remarkable
democratization. When relations between the two colossi of world communism deteriorated in the 1960s, Washington sensed an opportunity to
weaken the Soviet Union, usher in a new era with China, and obtain the
PRC's assistance in helping to arrange a possible political settlement of
the Vietnam War. In mid-August 1971, Secretary of State Henry Kissinger
arrived secretly in Beijing and paved the way for President Richard
Nixon's visit in February 1972, in return for which the United States
"derecognized" Taiwan and acknowledged the PRC to be the rightful representative of China in the United Nations and other international organizations. During his visit, Nixon agreed to the carefully crafted Shanghai
communiqué of February 27, 1972: the Chinese side stated that the PRC
"is the sole legal government of China; Taiwan is a province of China...,
the liberation of Taiwan is China's internal affair in which no other country has the right to interfere; and all US forces and military installations
must be withdrawn from Taiwan." For its part, the US side acknowledged
"that all Chinese on either side of the Taiwan Strait maintain there is but
one China and that Taiwan is part of China," reaffirmed US interest in a
peaceful solution of the Taiwan question by the Chinese themselves, and
accepted the ultimate withdrawal of all US troops and installations. The
subtle differences in wording reflected substantive differences, which both
sides wanted to minimize on the Taiwan issue: how Taiwan would be integrated, when US troops would leave, and under what conditions.

By 1978, the deterioration in Soviet-American relations, coupled with steady improvement in Sino-American relations, prompted the Carter administration to expedite full and complete normalization: formal diplomatic relations between the United States and the People's Republic of China were established, effective January 1, 1979. Carter accepted Premier Deng Xiaoping's three conditions: termination of formal diplomatic ties with Taiwan; abrogation of the US-Taiwan mutual defense treaty, originally concluded in 1954; and the withdrawal of the remaining US forces on the island. In return Deng (who was China's strongman until his death in February 1997) agreed that the United States would establish an unofficial representation on Taiwan and that it could continue some kind of ongoing defensive arms sales.

Ever since the early 1950s, Congress has played an important role in shaping the contours of US-Taiwan and US-PRC relations. During the decades after the Korean War, Taiwan's cause was championed by a wide range of influential lobbying groups—economic, cultural, religious, anticommunist, and human rights groups whose interests cut across the political spectrum and were bolstered by Taiwan's democratization and flourishing market-oriented economy. These groups prevailed upon Congress to pass the Taiwan Relations Act (TRA) of April 10, 1979. In language stronger than President Carter had wished, the Act declared that the United States would "consider any effort to determine the future of Taiwan by other than peaceful means, including boycotts and embargoes, a threat to the peace of the Western Pacific area and of grave concern to the United States." By implying that the United States would take strong military measures to defend Taiwan from attack, the Act boosted morale on the island. Moreover, in calling on the administration to provide "such defense articles and defense services in such quantity as may be necessary to enable Taiwan to maintain a sufficient self-defense capability," it sustained the Taiwanese elites, at a time when Taiwan was forced to vacate membership in a host of international organizations and forums.

In 1982, the Reagan administration permitted Taiwan to continue to co-produce its F-5E fighter plane, and made allowance for extensive additions to its electronic equipment and future purchases that factored in inflation costs, but refused to sell more advanced models of military aircraft. Beijing criticized what it said were substantive departures from the Deng-Carter understanding. Whereas Reagan's aim was to sustain Taiwan's defense capability, his successor, George Bush, used China's 1989 crackdown on dissident pro-democracy elements as reason to upgrade the weapons sold to Taiwan. Openly abandoning the quantitative and qualitative limitations of the past, in 1992 he authorized the sale of 150 F-16s, an advanced high-performance fighter aircraft that unlike the F-5E, has an offensive capability. At upwards of $40 million per aircraft, Taiwan's purchases far exceeded any of the past. Bush's action not only signaled US displeasure to Beijing, it catered to the Taiwan lobby and mollified conservative elements in the Republican Party, with the approaching election in mind.

The Clinton administration has dealt with the Taiwan problem cautiously but flexibly. After more than a year of interagency assessment, it agreed in September 1994 to a change in the name of the "unofficial" Taiwan embassy office in Washington DC from Coordination Council for North American Affairs to Taipei Economic and Cultural Office; it also announced support for "Taiwan's membership in international organizations where statehood is not an issue" and for "opportunities for Taiwan's voice to be heard in organizations where it is denied membership." Thus, the Clinton administration seemed committed to promoting Taiwan's cause in the World Trade Organization (WTO) and in the Asia Pacific Economic Cooperation (APEC) venue, a loosely structured forum for discussion of broad economic issues.

Clinton's strategy of engagement and enlargement of relations with the PRC, increasingly backed by corporations interested in doing business in China, was crafted with consideration for the views of Congress, where the Republican Party had swept to a major victory in the November 1994 mid-term elections. In June 1995, faced with strong Congressional pressure, Clinton granted a visa for Taiwan's President Lee Teng-hui to attend his college reunion at Cornell University. This was an abrupt reversal of his assurance to Beijing several weeks earlier that he would not do so. Taiwan saw the visit as a diplomatic breakthrough; China was irate, questioning the administration's interest in improved relations. Almost immediately, "Beijing issued strong protests, suspended or canceled important bilateral dialogues, suspended important dialogues with Taiwan, and conducted provocative military exercises near Taiwan [a-series of missile tests off its northern coast]. It warned that a Taiwan move toward de jure independence would lead to a PRC invasion of Taiwan and a protracted Cold War with the United States."[1] Clinton tried to soothe Chinese sensibilities and restore planned meetings and negotiations. The PRC used its growing economic clout to attempt to influence key people in Congress, the media, and the business community.

Their efforts were eclipsed by a second crisis in the Taiwan Strait. In March 1996, amidst a presidential election campaign on Taiwan in which the pro-independence opposition Democratic Progressive Party (DDP) appeared to have a chance of winning, China mounted a more ominous display of military power than the previous summer's. Washington was concerned and sought to forestall any misperception of its commitment to Taiwan by deploying two aircraft carrier task force groups, without even notifying the Taiwan government. However, with the reelection of President Lee, whose policy was to maintain the status quo, tensions subsided and all parties again sought to restart their various bilateral negotiations.

The second Taiwan crisis over, Clinton reassured Beijing of Washington's acceptance that Taiwan was part of China. Realizing China's growing importance not just strategically but economically as well, and discerning less Congressional opposition to fostering cooperation with China, he addressed the future of the relationship. In a speech to the Pacific Basin Economic Council on May 20, 1996, Clinton emphasized anew the saliency of a strategic relationship with China, reaffirmed his commitment to economic engagement, and undertook to seek renewal of China's Most-Favored-Nation status (Speech 4-2).

In July 1996, NSC adviser Anthony Lake flew to Beijing, against the background of Congressional renewal of MFN status for China and quiet on the Taiwan front. Human rights issues remained unresolved, but Lake's talks proceeded amicably. On November 20, 1996, after President Clinton's reelection, Secretary of State Christopher made his second trip to China, and each side spoke of improved bilateral ties. At the same time, in Australia, President Clinton told the Parliament, "The United States has no interest in containing China. That is a negative strategy. What the United States wants is to sustain an engagement with China." When President Clinton and President Jiang Zemin met a few days later on November 24 at a session of APEC held in Manila, they agreed to reciprocal visits. Two weeks later, China's Defense Minister and a sizable delegation arrived in the United States to a friendly reception from the White House.

In March 1997, Vice-President Al Gore and Speaker of the House of Representatives Newt Gingrich paid visits to Beijing. In May, President Clinton made the case for MFN renewal. In June, Congress upheld another year's extension, and in July Great Britain returned Hong Kong to China, after 150 years of imperial rule. US-China relations were in a warming current.

On the eve of President Jiang Zemin's state visit to Washington at the end of October 1997, President Clinton made a major speech, his first devoted entirely to China, reviewing its importance to the United States (Speech 4-3). His elaboration of the strategy of engagement was his most concrete and compelling.

During a visit to China the following year, Clinton's message was the same, with no hint of troublesome days ahead for Sino-American relations as a result of allegations surfacing in Congress and the media of improper PRC behavior in the United States. Thus, in his speech to the National Geographic Society in Washington DC on June 11, 1998, two weeks before departing for China, President Clinton expressed no doubts, no reservations, no disappointments regarding dealings with China; the emphasis was on steady progress in all areas of interaction. Although his themes largely reprised those in his October 1997 speech and anticipated his talk in Beijing in late June, there were a few notable additions: Clinton praised China's progress in stopping the export of nuclear-missile technology, in combating organized crime and drug trafficking, and in discussing ways of protecting the environment; and, to reassure Congress, he spoke at length about human rights and the Defense Department's "strict safeguards" on any sales to China of equipment that could enhance its missile capability (Speech 4-4).

In Beijing, President Clinton lifted the veil of secrecy concerning repeated efforts to reassure China about US policy toward Taiwan. To the delight of his hosts, the dismay of Taiwan, and the anger of pro-Taiwan domestic critics of his China policy, in an interview in Shanghai on June 30, 1998, he said:

> I do believe that my coming here ... has helped to resolve some of the misunderstandings. I had a chance to reiterate our Taiwan policy, which is that we don't support independence for Taiwan, or two Chinas, or one Taiwan—one China. And we don't believe that Taiwan should be a member in any organization for which statehood is a requirement. So I think we have a consistent policy.

This statement of the administration's "three no's" policy toward Taiwan has been viewed by critics as an unnecessary deference to Beijing's position and a weakening of America's implicit guarantees to Taiwan. According to a prominent PRC specialist, the United States had privately agreed to the "three no's" formulation shortly after the 1996 Taiwan crisis, in order to reassure Beijing.[2] Allegedly, Clinton spelled out the three principles in a private letter to President Jiang Zemin, and reaffirmed them during Jiang's visit in October 1997. When Secretary of State Madeleine Albright visited Beijing in April 1998 to arrange for the President's June visit, she confirmed the policy. The net effect of Clinton's public declaration satisfied Beijing but exacerbated differences between the White House and the Congress on the Taiwan issue. Clinton's "three no's" policy eliminated the possibility, however remote, of an independent Taiwan as a "wild card" option in the complex diplomatic game: it went beyond the mere acknowledgment of "one China" and the 1994 statement of US opposition to Taiwan's right to be accredited to the UN and other international organizations where membership is based on statehood.[3]

Despite all efforts to normalize US-China relations, the future is indeterminate and fraught with danger. A fly in the ointment is the convincing evidence of China's meddling in American domestic politics. Its attempts to buy influence came to light during and after the 1996 presidential campaign. Several hundred thousand dollars in contributions funneled into Clinton's campaign were returned once the illegal source was revealed.

For its part, the Clinton administration's preoccupation with economically engaging China caused it to play loose with national security. One example of commercialism transcending prudent containment occurred in 1995 – 1996 when a small group of NSC advisers persuaded the President to override the State Department and ease controls on the sale of American space satellites to China. Pushing trade and business with China in the interest of breaking into new markets, the White House disregarded military judgments; and in the process of enhancing the economic component of national security in the post-Cold War era, it downgraded the military aspects. The Commerce Department was given authority that had heretofore resided with the State Department to make decisions on the sale and licensing of high-tech, dual-use equipment such as supercomputers and jet engines. The Pentagon was unhappy, but it carried little weight in inter-agency deliberations. This sale of previously classified advanced technology and equipment soon assumed enormous proportions, and machines intended for civilian use were indeed diverted by the Chinese to military factories. More than forty supercomputers have been sold to China, and as recently as late 1997 the Administration was seriously considering a large sale of nuclear technology. Deregulation and relaxation of export controls require rethinking.

Trade relations with China have been a problem for the Clinton administration. First, Clinton's belief that expanding trade would open markets and lead to a more democratic and cooperative China has not been fully borne out. Second, trade statistics show a huge growth in China's trade surplus on the balance-of-payments register, approaching in 1998 more than $50 billion a year; this represents an almost tenfold increase since Clinton took office. Despite warnings that such trade deficits cannot be sustained indefinitely, no effective counter-actions have as yet been taken. One bar to any meaningful action by the White House or the Congress is that the businesses most benefiting from trade with China are giant corporations that contribute to the coffers of both political parties; these corporations showed their political clout when in mid-April 1999 they pressured Clinton to reconsider his failure to endorse China's entry into the World Trade Organization. At the last minute, during Premier Zhu Rongji's visit in early April, President Clinton had backed away from supporting China's admission, allegedly because China's concessions did not go far enough, but mainly, it was widely believed, out of concern about Congressional anger over China's spying. A few days later, encouraged by corporate support, Clinton agreed to reopen discussions of WTO membership.

Nothing, however, is likely to prove as damaging to US-PRC relations as the indications of massive Chinese penetration of US security and theft of top-secret nuclear weapons data. Enough information about the preliminary findings of a Congressional investigation had leaked prior to Premier Zhu Rongji's arrival in Washington to prompt President Clinton to address the embarrassing revelations and try to put them in a broader and long-term context (Speech 4-5).

If NATO's inadvertent bombing of the Chinese Embassy in Belgrade on May 7, 1999, was a setback to Clinton's policy of engagement, the Report of the House Select Committee on US National Security and Military/Commercial Concerns with the People's Republic of China, made public on May 25, 1999, was a catastrophe. Known as the Cox Report (the Committee's chairman was Christopher Cox), it documents China's systematic policy of spying over the past twenty years. A few of the findings may be noted to give a sense of the profound effect that they will have on future American policy toward, and dealings with, the PRC:

1. PRC penetration of our national weapons laboratories spans at least the past several decades and almost certainly continues today.
2. The stolen information includes classified information on seven US thermonuclear warheads, including every currently deployed thermonuclear warhead in the US ballistic missile arsenal.
3. The Select Committee judges that elements of the stolen information on US thermonuclear warhead designs will assist the PRC in building its next generation of mobile ICBMs, which may be tested this year.
4. In the late 1990s, the PRC stole or illegally obtained US developmental and research technology that, if taken to successful conclusion, could be used to attack US satellites and submarines.
5. US policies relying on corporate self-policing to prevent technology loss have not worked.

A new and potentially destabilizing factor was added to the US-China and US-Taiwan relationships in mid-July 1999, when Taiwan's President Lee Teng-hui declared that Taiwan no longer felt bound by the long-accepted "one China" policy, and that henceforth Taiwan would treat all contacts with China as "state-to-state" relations. It was not known precisely what Lee meant by this; he did not elaborate. But Beijing immediately reacted, seeing the formulation as a challenge to the status quo and as a prelude to a Taiwan bid for independence. In view of the tensions between Beijing and Washington—over trade, the WTO, allegations of espionage, human rights, and the bombing of the Chinese Embassy in Belgrade during NATO's campaign against Serbia—the Chinese leadership grade during NATO's campaign against Serbia—the Chinese leadership was quick to see Lee's statement as a sign of ongoing US-Taiwan collusion to enhance Taiwan's international status. For its part, the Clinton administration reiterated its position that the relationship between China and Taiwan was a matter for the two parties to settle, peacefully, between themselves. And President Lee offered assurances that there is no change in his policy on reunification; he claimed merely to be expressing Taiwan's public mood.

Although the furor subsided, this "incident" (which may prove to be far more) demonstrates that foreign policy is in important measure the outcome of domestic politics. The 76-year-old President Lee was preparing for his expected retirement in the year 2000, when elections will be held in Taiwan. To ensure the election of his preferred successor and secure his own legacy, Lee shrewdly championed an issue that has wide popular appeal on Taiwan, the desire to function more independently in the international community. This comes at a time when existing tensions between China and the United States may force Washington, with its oft-repeated support for democratization and self-determination, to uphold Taiwan against any threat from China. New, hitherto unthinkable dilemmas may be in the offing for US leaders.

In a lecture sponsored by the Heritage Foundation in Washington DC some years ago, Henry Kissinger observed:

> I believe that, in Asia, stability requires a major effort of understanding between the United States and China and, therefore, I have opposed efforts to sanction China even on issues where I have agreed with the objectives of those who recommend the sanctions. It is extraordinarily important the United States and China find a way toward a serious political dialogue, which at this moment is not taking place adequately.

Strategic imperatives make US-China dialogue more relevant than ever.

Notes

1. Robert G. Sutter, "Domestic Politics and the US-China-Taiwan Triangle: The 1995-96 Taiwan Strait Conflict and Its Aftermath," in Robert S. Ross (ed.), *After the Cold War: Domestic Factors and US-China Relations* (Armonk NY: M.E. Sharpe, 1998), p. 82.

2. Jen Hui-wen, "Beijing Political Situation," Beijing, July 27, 1998, in Chinese, as translated by Foreign Broadcast Information Service-CHI-98-217.

3. Fan Wa Wong, "Taiwan Elites' Perspective on US-Taiwan Relations," unpublished manuscript, April 1999.

4-1 Call for Renewal of China's Most-Favored-Nation Status

Remarks at the Press Conference
Washington DC
May 26, 1994

… Our relationship with China is important to all Americans. We have significant interests in what happens there and what happens between us. China has an atomic arsenal and a vote and a veto in the UN Security Council. It is a major factor in Asian and global security. We share important interests, such as in a nuclear-free Korean Peninsula and in sustaining the global environment. China is also the world's fastest growing economy. Over $8 billion of United States exports to China last year supported over 150,000 American jobs.

I have received Secretary Christopher's letter recommending, as required by last year's Executive order, reporting to me on the conditions in that Executive order. He has reached a conclusion with which I agree, that the Chinese did not achieve overall significant progress in all the areas outlined in the Executive order relating to human rights, even though clearly there was progress made in important areas, including the resolution of all emigration cases, the establishment of a memorandum of understanding with regard to how prison labor issues would be resolved, the adherence to the Universal Declaration of Human Rights and other issues.

Nevertheless, serious human rights abuses continue in China, including the arrest and detention of those who peacefully voice their opinions and the repression of Tibet's religious and cultural traditions.

The question for us now is, given the fact that there has been some progress but that not all the requirements of the Executive order were met, how can we best advance the cause of human rights and the other profound interests the United States has in our relationship with China?

I have decided that the United States should renew most-favored-nation trading status toward China. This decision, I believe, offers us the best opportunity to lay the basis for long-term sustainable progress in human rights and for the advancement of our other interests with China.

Extending MFN will avoid isolating China and instead will permit us to engage the Chinese with not only economic contacts but with cultural, educational, and other contacts and with a continuing aggressive effort in human rights, an approach that I believe will make it more likely that China will play a responsible role, both at home and abroad.

I am moving, therefore, to delink human rights from the annual extension of most-favored-nation trading status for China. That linkage has been constructive during the past year. But I believe, based on our aggressive contacts with the Chinese in the past several months, that we have reached the end of the usefulness of that policy and it is time to take a new path toward the achievement of our constant objectives. We need to place our relationship into a larger and more productive framework.

In view of the continuing human rights abuses, I am extending the sanctions imposed by the United States as a result of the events in Tiananmen Square, and I am also banning the import of munitions, principally guns and ammunition from China. I am also pursuing a new and vigorous American program to support those in China working to advance the cause of human rights and democracy. This program will include increased broadcasts for Radio Free Asia and the Voice of America, increased support for nongovernmental organizations working on human rights in China, and the development with American business leaders of a voluntary set of principles for business activity in China.

I don't want to be misunderstood about this: China continues to commit very serious human rights abuses. Even as we engage the Chinese on military, political, and economic issues, we intend to stay engaged with those in China who suffer from human rights abuses. The United States must remain a champion of their liberties.

I believe the question, therefore, is not whether we continue to support human rights in China but how we can best support human rights in China and advance our other very significant issues and interests. I believe we can do it by engaging the Chinese....

4-2 Remarks by the President to the Pacific Basin Economic Council

Constitution Hall
Washington DC
May 20, 1996

... For nearly three decades the Pacific Basin Economic Council has stood on the cutting edge of trade, investment, and opportunity. Today, with nineteen member nations from Mexico to Malaysia, you're an integral part of this vibrant Asia-Pacific community. I am especially grateful for your active support of APEC....

The world has changed a lot since 1967, when PBEC was founded. Superpower confrontation has given way to growing cooperation. Freedom and democracy are on the march. Modern telecommunications have collapsed the distances between us. The new global economy is transforming the way we work and live, bringing tremendous opportunities for all our peoples. So many of these opportunities and some of our most significant challenges lie in the Asia-Pacific region.

Today half the people on our planet live in Asia. China alone is growing by the size of Canada every two years. Asia contains four of the seven largest militaries in the world, and two of its most dangerous flashpoints: the world's most heavily fortified border between North and South Korea, and the regional conflict in South Asia where India and Pakistan, two of America's friends, live on the edge of conflict or reconciliation. At the same time, the economies of East Asia have become the world's fastest growing, producing fully one-quarter of our planet's goods and services.

America has vital strategic and economic interests that affect the lives of each and every American citizen. We must remain an Asia-Pacific power. Disengagement from Asia, a region where we have fought three wars in this century, is simply not an option. It could spark a dangerous and destabilizing arms race that would profoundly alter the strategic landscape. It would weaken our power to deter states like North Korea that still can threaten the peace, and to take on problems, including global terrorism, organized crime, environmental threats, and drug trafficking in a region that produces 62 percent of the world's heroin.

Our leadership in Asia, therefore, is crucial to the security of our own people and to the future of the globe. It is also important to our future prosperity. The Asia-Pacific region is the largest consumer market in the world, accounting already for more than half of our trade and supporting millions of American jobs. By the year 2000 auto sales in Indonesia, Malaysia, and Thailand could equal our car sales to Canada and Mexico. Over the next ten years, Asian nations will invest more than $1 trillion in infrastructure projects alone. We can help to shape a region's open economic development, but if we sit on the sidelines we could watch our own prosperity decline.

When I took office, I had a vision of a Asia-Pacific community built on shared efforts, shared benefits, and shared destiny, a genuine partnership for greater security, freedom, and prosperity. Given all the currents of change in the region, I knew then and I know now the road will not be always even and smooth. But the strategy is sound, and we have moved forward steadily and surely toward our goal.

With both security and economic interests so deeply at stake, we have pursued from the outset an integrated policy, pursuing both fronts together, advancing on both fronts together. Though the end of the Cold War has lessened great power conflict in Asia and in Europe, in Asia, just as in Europe, a host of security challenges persist, from rising nationalism to nuclear proliferation, to drug trafficking, organized crime, and other problems.

To meet these tests in Europe we are adapting and expanding NATO, emphasizing the Partnership For Peace, including a new and more constructive relationship with Russia which is, or course, both a European and a Pacific nation and, therefore, must be a partner in making a stable and prosperous Asia Pacific future as well.

Asia has not evolved with similar unifying institutions, like NATO, so we are working with Asia to build new security structures, flexible enough to adapt to new threats, durable enough to defeat them. Each arrangement is like an overlapping plate of security armor, working individually and together to protect our interests and reinforce peace.

Our security strategy has four fundamental priorities: a continued American military commitment to the region, support for stronger security cooperation among Asian nations, leadership to combat the most serious threats, and support for democracy throughout the region. To pursue that strategy, we have updated and strengthened our formal alliances with Japan, Korea, the Philippines, Australia, and Thailand. We have reaffirmed our commitment to keep 100,000 troops in the region. Just a few weeks ago, we renewed our security alliance with Japan and moved to reduce the tensions related to our presence on Okinawa.

Today, that security relationship is stronger than ever. We have reached a series of security access agreements, magnifying the impact and deterrent effect of our forward deployed force. We have supported the ASEAN nations in building a new security alliance dialog in a region long fractured by distrust. We have launched new security initiatives such as the four-party talks President Kim and I proposed in an effort to bring a permanent peace to the Korean Peninsula.

With our South Korean allies, we stopped the North Korean nuclear threat that had been brewing since 1985 when North Korea began to build a plutonium production reactor. Through firmness and steadiness, we gained an agreement that has already halted and eventually will dismantle North Korea's nuclear weapons program. Today, a freeze is in place under strict international supervision. And last month, we began the canning of North Korea's spent fuel. One of the greatest potential threats to peace is, therefore, being diffused with American leadership....

When China expanded its military exercises in the Taiwan Strait, we made clear that any use of force against Taiwan would have grave consequences. The two carrier battle groups we sent to the area helped to defuse a dangerous situation and demonstrated to our allies our commitment to stability and peace in the region. In the long run we also strengthen security by deepening the roots of democracy in Asia.

Democratic nations, after all, are more likely to seek ways to settle conflicts peacefully, to join with us to conquer common threats, to respect the rights of their own people. Democracy and human rights are, I believe, universal human aspirations. We have only to look at South Korea, the Philippines, and Taiwan, the Cambodians who turned from bullets to ballots to build a democratic future, Burma's Aung San Suu Kyi, and other courageous leaders in the area....

Finally, let me turn to our relations with China, for they will shape all of our futures profoundly. How China defines itself and its greatness as a nation in the future and how our relationship with China evolves will have as great an impact on the lives of our own people and, indeed, on global peace and security, as that of any other relationship we have.

China is Asia's only declared nuclear weapons state, with the world's largest standing army. In less than two decades it may well be the world's largest economy. Its economic growth is bringing broader changes as steps toward freer enterprise fuel the hunger for a more free society. But the evolution underway in China is far from clearcut or complete. It is deep and profound, and today, China stands at a critical crossroads. Will it choose the course of openness and integration, or veer toward isolation and nationalism? Will it be a force for stability, or a force for disruption in the world? Our interests are directly at stake in promoting a secure, stable, open, and prosperous China, a China that embraces international non-proliferation, and trade rules, cooperates in regional and global security initiatives, and evolves toward greater respect for the basic rights of its own citizens.

Our engagement policy means using the best tools we have, incentives and disincentives alike, to advance core American interests. Engagement does not mean closing our eyes to the policies in China we oppose. We have serious and continuing concerns in areas like human rights, non-proliferation, and trade. When we disagree with China, we will continue to defend our interests and to assert our values. But by engaging China, we have achieved important benefits for our people and the rest of the world.

We worked closely with China to extend the nuclear nonproliferation treaty and to freeze North Korea's nuclear weapons program. We welcome China's constructive position regarding the proposed four-party talks for peace on the Korean Peninsula. We are working with China to conclude and to sign a comprehensive nuclear test ban treaty by September. And we are cooperating to combat threats like drug trafficking, alien smuggling and, increasingly, environmental decay.

Last week we reached an important understanding with China on nuclear exports. For the first time, China explicitly and publicly committed not to provide assistance to unsafeguarded nuclear programs in any country. China also agreed to hold consultations on export control policies and practices. We continue to have concerns about China's nuclear exports. This agreement provides a framework to help deal with those concerns.

Our economic engagement with China has also achieved real results. China's elimination of more than 1,000 quotas and licensing requirements has helped to fuel to rise of more than 200 percent in United States exports of telecommunications equipment since 1992. China has become our fastest growing export market, with exports up nearly 30 percent in 1995 alone.

Much remains to be done. Our bilateral trade deficit with China is too high, and China's trade barriers must come down. But the best way to address our trade problems is continue to work to open China's booming market by negotiating and enforcing good trade agreements. That is why we will use the full weight of our law to ensure that China meets its obligations to protect intellectual property. That is why we are insisting that China meet the same standard of openness applied to other countries seeking to enter the WTO—no more, no less. And that is why I have decided to extend unconditional most favored nation trade status to China.

Revoking MFN and, in effect, severing our economic ties to China, would drive us back into a period of mutual isolation and recrimination that would harm America's interests, not advance them. Rather than strengthening China's respect for human rights, it would lessen our contact with the Chinese people. Rather than limiting the spread of weapons of mass destruction, it would limit the prospect for future cooperation in this area. Rather than bringing stability to the region, it would increase instability, as the leaders of Hong Kong, Taiwan, and all the nations of the region have stated repeatedly. Rather than bolstering our economic interests, it would cede one of the fastest-growing markets to our competitors.

MFN renewal is not a referendum on all China's policies. It is a vote for America's interests. I will work with Congress in the weeks ahead to secure MFN renewal and to continue to advance our goal of a secure, stable, open, and prosperous China. This is a long-term endeavor, and we must be steady and firm.

Where we differ with China—and we will have our differences—we will continue to defend our interests. We will keep faith with those who stand for greater freedom and pluralism in China, as we did last month in cosponsoring a UN resolution condemning China's human rights practices. We will actively enforce US laws on unfair trade practices and nonproliferation. We will stand firm for a peaceful resolution of the Taiwan issue within the context of the one China policy, which has benefited the United States, China, and Taiwan for nearly two decades.

But we cannot walk backward into the future. We must not seek to isolate ourselves from China. We will engage with China, without illusion, to advance our interests in a more peaceful and prosperous world....

4-3 Speech by the President on the Eve of President Jiang Zemin's State Visit

Washington DC
October 24, 1997

... Next week, when President Jiang Zemin comes to Washington, it will be the first state visit by a Chinese leader to the United States for more than a decade. The visit gives us the opportunity and the responsibility to chart a course for the future that is more positive and more stable and, hopefully, more productive than our relations have been for the last few years.

China is a great country with a rich and proud history and a strong future. It will, for good or ill, play a very large role in shaping the twenty-first century in which the children in this audience today, children all across our country, all across China, and indeed all across the world, will live.

At the dawn of the new century, China stands at a crossroads. The direction China takes toward cooperation or conflict will profoundly affect Asia, America, and the world for decades. The emergence of a China as a power that is stable, open, and non-aggressive, that embraces free markets, political pluralism, and the rule of law, that works with us to build a secure international order, that kind of China, rather than a China turned inward and confrontational, is deeply in the interests of the American people.

Of course, China will choose its own destiny. Yet by working with China and expanding areas of cooperation, dealing forthrightly with our differences, we can advance fundamental American interests and values.

First, the United States has a profound interest in promoting a peaceful, prosperous, and stable world. Our task will be much easier if China is a part of that process, not only playing by the rules of international behavior but helping to write and enforce them.

China is a permanent member of the United Nations Security Council. Its support was crucial for peacekeeping efforts in Cambodia and building international mandates to reverse Iraq's aggression against Kuwait and restore democracy to Haiti. As a neighbor of India and Pakistan, China will influence whether these great democracies move toward responsible cooperation both with each other and with China.

From the Persian Gulf to the Caspian Sea, China's need for a reliable and efficient supply of energy to fuel its growth can make it a force for stability in these strategically critical regions. Next week, President Jiang and I will discuss our visions of the future and the kind of strategic relationship we must have to promote cooperation, not conflict.

Second, the United States has a profound interest in peace and stability in Asia. Three times this century, Americans have fought and died in Asian wars—37,000 Americans still patrol the Cold War's last frontier, on the Korean DMZ. Territorial disputes that could flare into crises affecting America require us to maintain a strong American security presence in Asia. We want China to be a powerful force for security and cooperation there.

China has helped us convince North Korea to freeze and ultimately end its dangerous nuclear program. Just imagine how much more dangerous that volatile peninsula would be today if North Korea, reeling from food shortages, with a million soldiers encamped 27 miles from Seoul, had continued this nuclear program. ...

Next week I'll discuss with President Jiang the steps we can take together to advance the peace process in Korea. We'll look at ways to strengthen our military-to-military contacts, decreasing the chances of miscalculation and broadening America's contacts with the next generation of China's military leaders. And I will reiterate to President Jiang America's continuing support for our one China policy, which has allowed democracy to flourish in Taiwan and Taiwan's relationship with the PRC to grow more stable and prosperous. The Taiwan question can only be settled by the Chinese themselves peacefully.

Third, the United States has a profound interest in keeping weapons of mass destruction and other sophisticated weaponry out of unstable regions and away from rogue states and terrorists. In the twenty-first century, many of the threats to our security will come not from great power conflict but from states that defy the international community and violent groups seeking to undermine peace, stability, and democracy. China is already a nuclear power with increasingly sophisticated industrial and technological capabilities. We need its help to prevent dangerous weapons from falling into the wrong hands.

For years, China stood outside the major international arms control regimes. Over the past decade, it has made important and welcome decisions to join the Nuclear Non-Proliferation Treaty, the Chemical Weapons Convention, the Biological Weapons Convention, and to respect key provisions of the Missile Technology Control Regime. Last year at the United Nations, I was proud to be the first world leader to sign the Comprehensive Test Ban Treaty. China's Foreign Minister was the second leader to do so.

China has lived up to its pledge not to assist unsafeguarded nuclear facilities in third countries, and it is developing a system of export controls to prevent the transfer or sale of technology for weapons of mass destruction.

But China still maintains some troubling weapons supply relationships. At the summit, I will discuss with President Jiang further steps we hope China will take to end or limit some of these supply relationships and to strengthen and broaden its export control system. And I will make the case to him that these steps are, first and foremost, in China's interest, because the spread of dangerous weapons and technology would increase instability near China's own borders.

Fourth, the United States has profound interest in fighting drug-trafficking and international organized crime. Increasingly, smugglers and criminals are taking advantage of China's vast territory and its borders with fifteen nations to move drugs and weapons, aliens, and the proceeds of illegal activities from one point in Asia to another or from Asia to Europe....

Fifth, the United States has a profound interest in making global trade and investment as free, fair, and open as possible. Over the past five years, trade has produced more than one-third of America's economic growth. If we are to continue generating good jobs and higher incomes in our country when we are just four percent of the world's population, we must continue to sell more to the other 96 percent. One of the best ways to do that is to bring China more fully into the world's trading system. With a quarter of the world's population and its fastest growing economy, China could and should be a magnet for our goods and services.

Even though American exports to China now are at an all-time high, so, too, is our trade deficit. In part, this is due to the strength of the American economy and to the fact that many products we used to buy in other Asian countries now are manufactured in China. But clearly, an important part of the problem remains lack of access to China's markets. We strongly support China's admission into the World Trade Organization. But in turn, China must dramatically improve access for foreign goods and services. We should be able to compete fully and fairly in China's marketplace, just as China competes in our own.

Tearing down trade barriers also is good for China and for the growth of China's neighbors and, therefore, for the stability and future of Asia. Next week, President Jiang and I will discuss steps China must take to join the WTO and assume its rightful place in the world economy.

Finally, the United States has a profound interest in ensuring that today's progress does not come at tomorrow's expense. Greenhouse gas emissions are leading to climate change. China is the fastest growing contributor to greenhouse gas emissions, and we are the biggest greenhouse gas emitter. Soon, however, China will overtake the United States and become the largest contributor. Already, pollution has made respiratory disease the number one health problem for China's people. Last March, when he visited China, Vice President Gore launched a joint forum with the Chinese on the environment and development so that we can work with China to pursue growth and protect the environment at the same time.

China has taken some important steps to deal with its need for more energy and cleaner air. Next week, President Jiang and I will talk about the next steps China can take to combat climate change. It is a global problem that must have a global solution that cannot come without China's participation as well. We also will talk about what American companies and technology can do to support China in its efforts to reduce air pollution and increase clean energy production.

Progress in each of these areas will draw China into the institutions and arrangements that are setting the ground rules for the twenty-first century, the security partnerships, the open trade arrangements, the arms control regime, the multinational coalitions against terrorism, crime, and drugs, the commitments to preserve the environment and to uphold human rights. This is our best hope, to secure our own interests and values and to advance China's in the historic transformation that began twenty-five years ago when China reopened to the world.

As we all know, the transformation already has produced truly impressive results. Twenty-five years ago, China stood apart from and closed to the international community. Now, China is a member of more than 1,000 international organizations, from the International Civil Aviation Organization to the International Fund for Agricultural Development. It has moved from the twenty-second largest trading nation to the eleventh. It is projected to become the second largest trader, after the United States, by 2020. And today, 40,000 young Chinese are studying here in the United States, with hundreds of thousands more living and learning in Europe, Asia, Africa, and Latin America.

China's economic transformation has been even more radical. Market reforms have spurred more than two decades of unprecedented growth, and the decision at the recently ended 15th Party Congress to sell off most all of China's big, state-owned industries promises to keep China moving toward a market economy.

The number of people living in poverty has dropped from 250 million to 58 million, even as China's population has increased by nearly 350 million. Per capital income in the cities has jumped 550 percent in just the past decade.

As China has opened its economy, its people have enjoyed greater freedom of movement and choice of employment, better schools and housing. Today, most Chinese enjoy a higher standard of living than at any time in China's modern history. But as China has opened economically, political reform has lagged behind.

Frustration in the West turned into condemnation after the terrible events in Tiananmen Square. Now, nearly a decade later, one of the great questions before the community of democracies is how to pursue the broad and complex range of our interests with China while urging and supporting China to move politically as well as economically into the twenty-first century. The great question for China is how to preserve stability, promote growth, and increase its influence in the world, while making room for the debate and the dissent that are a part of the fabric of all truly free and vibrant societies. The answer to those questions must begin with an understanding of the crossroads China has reached.

As China discards its old economic order, the scope and sweep of change has rekindled historic fears of chaos and disintegration. In return, Chinese leaders have worked hard to mobilize support, legitimize power, and hold the country together, which they see is essential to restoring the greatness of their nation and its rightful influence in the world. In the process, however, they have stifled political dissent to a degree and in ways that we believe are fundamentally wrong, even as freedom from want, freedom of movement, and local elections have increased.

This approach has caused problems within China and in its relationship to the United States. Chinese leaders believe it is necessary to hold the nation together, to keep it growing, to keep moving toward its destiny. But it will become increasingly difficult to maintain the closed political system in an ever-more open economy and society.

China's economic growth has made it more and more dependent on the outside world for investment, markets, and energy. Last year it was the second largest recipient of foreign direct investment in the world.

These linkages bring with them powerful forces for change. Computers and the Internet, fax machines and photocopiers, modems and satellites all increase the exposure to people, ideas, and the world beyond China's borders. The effect is only just beginning to be felt.

Today more than a billion Chinese have access to television, up from just 10 million two decades ago. Satellite dishes dot the landscape. They receive dozens of outside channels, including Chinese language services of CNN, Star TV, and Worldnet. Talk radio is increasingly popular and relatively unregulated in China's 1,000 radio stations. And 70 percent of China's students regularly listen to the Voice of America.

China's 2,200 newspapers, up from just 42 three decades ago, and more than 7,000 magazines and journals are more open in content. A decade ago, there were 50,000 mobile phones in China; now there are more than 7 million. The Internet already has 150,000 accounts in China, with more than a million expected to be on-line by the year 2000. The more ideas and information spread, the more people will expect to think for themselves, express their own opinions, and participate. And the more that happens, the harder it will be for their government to stand in their way.

Indeed, greater openness is profoundly in China's own interest. If welcomed, it will speed economic growth, enhance the world influence of China, and stabilize society. Without the full freedom to think, question, to create, China will be at a distinct disadvantage, competing with fully open societies in the information age where the greatest source of national wealth is what resides in the human mind.

China's creative potential is truly staggering. The largest population in the world is not yet among its top fifteen patent powers. In an era where these human resources are what really matters, a country that holds its people back cannot achieve its full potential.

Our belief that, over time, growing interdependence would have a liberalizing effect in China does not mean in the meantime we should or we can ignore abuses in China of human rights or religious freedom. Nor does it mean that there is nothing we can do to speed the process of liberalization....

Over the past year, our State Department's annual human rights report again pulled no punches on China. We cosponsored a resolution critical of China's human rights record in Geneva, even though many of our allies had abandoned the effort. We continue to speak against the arrest of dissidents and for a resumed dialog with the Dalai Lama, on behalf of the people and the distinct culture and unique identity of the people of Tibet, not their political independence but their uniqueness.

We established Radio Free Asia. We are working with Congress to expand its broadcast and to support civil society and the rule of law programs in China. We continue to pursue the problem of prison labor, and we regularly raise human rights in all our high-level meetings with the Chinese.

We do this in the hope of a dialog. And in dialog we must also admit that we in America are not blameless in our social fabric: Our crime rate is too high; too many of our children are still killed with guns; too many of our streets are still riddled with drugs. We have things to learn from other societies as well and problems we have to solve. And if we expect other people to listen to us about the problems they have, we must be prepared to listen to them about the problems we have.

This pragmatic policy of engagement, of expanding our areas of cooperation with China while confronting our differences openly and respectfully, this is the best way to advance our fundamental interests and our values and to promote a more open and free China.

I know there are those who disagree. They insist that China's interests and America's are inexorably in conflict. They do not believe the Chinese system will continue to evolve in a way that elevates not only human material condition but the human spirit. They, therefore, believe we should be working harder to contain or even to confront China before it becomes even stronger.

I believe this view is wrong. Isolation of China is unworkable, counterproductive, and potentially dangerous. Military, political, and economic measures to do such a thing would find little support among our allies around the world and, more importantly, even among Chinese themselves working for greater liberty. Isolation would encourage the Chinese to become hostile and to adopt policies of conflict with our own interests and values. It will eliminate, not facilitate, cooperation on weapons proliferation. It would hinder, not help, our efforts to foster stability in Asia. It would exacerbate, not ameliorate, the plight of dissidents. It would close off, not open up, one of the world's most important markets. It would make China less, not more, likely to play by the rules of international conduct and to be a part of an emerging international consensus.

As always, America must be prepared to live and flourish in a world in which we are at odds with China. But that is not the world we want. Our objective is not containment and conflict. It is cooperation. We will far better serve our interests and our principles if we work with a China that shares that objective with us.

Thirty years ago, President Richard Nixon, then a citizen campaigning for the job I now hold, called for a strategic change in our policy toward China. Taking the long view, he said, we simply cannot afford to leave China forever outside the family of nations. There is no place on this small planet for a billion of its potentially most able people to live in angry isolation.

Almost two decades ago, President Carter normalized relations with China, recognizing the wisdom of that statement. And over the past two and a half decades, as China has emerged from isolation, tensions with the West have decreased; cooperation has increased; prosperity has spread to more of China's people. The progress was a result of China's decision to play a more constructive role in the world and to open its economy. It was supported by a farsighted American policy that made clear to China we welcome its emergence as a great nation.

Now, America must stay on that course of engagement. By working with China and making our differences clear where necessary, we can advance our interests and our values and China's historic transformation into a nation whose greatness is defined as much by its future as its past.

Change may not come as quickly as we would like, but, as our interests are long-term, so must our policies be. We have an opportunity to build a new century in which China takes its rightful place as a full and strong partner in the community of nations, working with the United States to advance peace and prosperity, freedom and security for both our people and for all the world. We have to take that chance....

4-4 On US-China Relations in the Twenty-first Century

Speech to the National Geographic Society
Washington DC
June 11, 1998

... Let me say that, all of you know the dimensions, but I think it is worth repeating a few of the facts about China. It is already the world's most populous nation; it will increase by the size of America's current population every twenty years. Its vast territory borders fifteen countries. It has one of the fastest growing economies on Earth. It holds a permanent seat on the National Security Council of the United Nations. Over the past twenty-five years, it has entered a period of profound change, emerging from isolation, turning a closed economy into an engine for growth, increasing cooperation with the rest of the world, raising the standard of living for hundreds of millions of its citizens.

The role China chooses to play in preventing the spread of weapons of mass destruction or encouraging it, in combating or ignoring international crime and drug trafficking, in protecting or degrading the environment, in tearing down or building up trade barriers, in respecting or abusing human rights, in resolving difficult situations in Asia from the Indian subcontinent to the Korean Peninsula or aggravating them, the role China chooses to play will powerfully shape the next century.

A stable, open, prosperous China that assumes its responsibilities for building a more peaceful world is clearly and profoundly in our interests. On that point, all Americans agree. But as we all know, there is serious disagreement over how best to encourage the emergence of that kind of China and how to handle our differences, especially over human rights, in the meantime....

We have chosen a different course that I believe to be both principled and pragmatic, expanding our areas of cooperation with China while dealing forthrightly with our differences. This policy is supported by our key democratic allies in Asia: Japan, South Korea, Australia, Thailand, the Philippines. It has recently been publicly endorsed by a number of distin-

guished religious leaders, including Reverend Billy Graham and the Dalai
Lama. My trip has been recently supported by political opponents of the
current Chinese Government, including most recently, Wang Dan.

There is a reason for this. Seeking to isolate China is clearly unworkable. Even our friends and allies around the world do not support us—or
would not support us in that. We would succeed instead in isolating ourselves and our own policy.

Most important, choosing isolation over engagement would not make
the world safer. It would make it more dangerous. It would undermine
rather than strengthen our efforts to foster stability in Asia. It would eliminate, not facilitate cooperation on issues relating to weapons of mass destruction. It would hinder, not help the cause of democracy and human
rights in China. It would set back, not step up worldwide efforts to protect
the environment. It would cut off, not open up one of the world's most
important markets. It would encourage the Chinese to turn inward and to
act in opposition to our interests and values....

... [S]topping the spread of nuclear, chemical, and biological weapons is clearly one of our most urgent security challenges. As a nuclear
power with increasingly sophisticated industrial and technological capabilities, China can choose either to be a part of the problem or a part of the
solution.

For years, China stood outside the international arms control regimes.
In the last decade, it has joined the Nuclear Non-Proliferation Treaty, the
Chemical Weapons Convention, the Biological Weapons Convention, and
the Comprehensive Test Ban Treaty, each with clear rules, reporting requirements, and inspection systems. In the past, China has been a major
exporter of sophisticated weapons-related technologies. That is why in
virtually all our high-level contacts with China's leadership, and in my
summit meeting with President Jiang last October, nonproliferation has
been high on the agenda.

Had we been trying to isolate China rather than work with it, would
China have agreed to stop assistance to Iran for its nuclear program? To
terminate its assistance to unsafe, guarded nuclear facilities such as those
in Pakistan? To tighten its export control system, to sell no more anti-ship
cruise missiles to Iran? These vital decisions were all in our interests, and
they clearly were the fruit of our engagement.

I will continue to press China on proliferation. I will seek stronger
controls on the sale of missiles, missile technology, dual-use products, and
chemical and biological weapons. I will argue that it is in China's interest,
because the spread of weapons and technologies would increasingly destabilize areas near China's own borders.

... [T]he United States has a profound stake in combating international organized crime and drug trafficking. International criminal

syndicates threaten to undermine confidence in new but fragile market democracies. They bilk people out of billions of dollars and bring violence and despair to our schools and neighborhoods. These are problems from which none of us are isolated and which, as I said at the United Nations a few days ago, no nation is so big it can fight alone.

With a landmass spanning from Russia in the north to Vietnam and Thailand in the south, from India and Pakistan in the west to Korea and Japan in the east, China has become a transshipment point for drugs and the proceeds of illegal activities. Last month a special liaison group that President Jiang and I established brought together leading Chinese and American law enforcement officials to step up our cooperation against organized crime, alien smuggling, and counterfeiting. Next month the Drug Enforcement Agency of the United States will open an office in Beijing. Here, too, pursuing practical cooperation with China is making a difference for America's future.

... China and the United States share the same global environment, an interest in preserving it for this and future generations. China is experiencing an environmental crisis perhaps greater than any other nation in history at a comparable stage of its development. Every substantial body of water in China is polluted. In many places, water is in short supply. Respiratory illness is the number one health problem for China's people because of air pollution.

Early in the next century, China will surpass the United States as the world's largest emitter of greenhouse gases, which are dangerously warming our planet. This matters profoundly to the American people, because what comes out of a smokestack or goes into a river in China can do grievous harm beyond its borders. It is a fool's errand to believe that we can deal with our present and future global environmental challenges without strong cooperation with China....

... The question we Americans must answer is not whether we support human rights in China—surely, all of us do—but rather, what is the best way to advance them? By integrating China into the community of nations and the global economy, helping its leadership understand that greater freedom profoundly serves China's interests, and standing up for our principles, we can most effectively serve the cause of democracy and human rights within China.

Over time, the more we bring China into the world the more the world will bring freedom to China. China's remarkable economic growth is making China more and more dependent on other nations for investment, for markets, for energy, for ideas. These ties increase the need for the stronger rule of law, openness, and accountability. And they carry with them powerful agents of change: fax machines and photocopiers, computers, and the Internet....

The licensing of American commercial satellite launches on Chinese rockets was approved by President Reagan, begun by President Bush, continued under my administration, for the simple reason that the demand for American satellites far out-strips America's launch capacity, and because others, including Russian and European nations, can do this job at much less cost.

It is important for every American to understand that there are strict safeguards, including a Department of Defense plan for each launch, to prevent any assistance to China's missile programs. Licensing these launches allows us to meet the demand for American satellites and helps people on every continent share ideas, information, and images through television, cell phones, and pagers. In the case of China, the policy also furthers our efforts to stop the spread of missile technology by providing China incentives to observe nonproliferation agreements. This policy clearly has served our national interests.

Over time, I believe China's leaders must accept freedom's progress because China can only reach its full potential if its people are free to reach theirs.

In the information age, the wealth of any nation, including China's, lies in its people, in their capacity to create, to communicate, to innovate. The Chinese people must have the freedom to speak, to publish, to associate, to worship without fear of reprisal. Only then will China reach its full potential for growth and greatness.

I have told President Jiang that when it comes to human rights and religious freedom, China remains on the wrong side of history. Unlike some, I do not believe increased commercial dealings alone will inevitably lead to greater openness and freedom. We must work to speed history's course. Complacency or silence would run counter to everything we stand for as Americans. It would deny those fighting for human rights and religious freedom inside China the outside support that is a source of strength and comfort. Indeed, one of the most important benefits of our engagement with China is that it gives us an effective means to urge China's leaders publicly and privately to change course.

Our message remains strong and constant: Do not arrest people for their political beliefs; release those who are in jail for that reason; renounce coercive population control practices; resume your dialog with the Dalai Lama; allow people to worship when, where, and how they choose; and recognize that our relationship simply cannot reach its full potential so long as Chinese people are denied fundamental human rights....

Seeking to isolate China will not free one more political dissident, will not open one more church to those who wish to worship, will do nothing to encourage China to live by the laws it has written. Instead, it will limit our ability to advance human rights and religious and political freedom....

Protocol and honoring a nation's traditional practices should not be confused with principle. China's leaders, as I have repeatedly said, can only move beyond the events of June 1989, when they recognize the reality that what the Government did was wrong. Sooner or later they must do that. And perhaps even more important, they must change course on this fundamentally important issue.

In my meetings with President Jiang and other Chinese leaders and in my discussions with the Chinese people, I will press ahead on human rights and religious freedom, urging that China follow through on its intention to sign the Covenant on Civil and Political Rights, that it release more individuals in prison for expressing their opinions, that it take concrete steps to preserve Tibet's cultural, linguistic, and religious heritage.

We do not ignore the value of symbols. But in the end, if the choice is between making a symbolic point and making a real difference, I choose to make the difference. And when it comes to advancing human rights and religious freedom, dealing directly and speaking honestly to the Chinese is clearly the best way to make a difference....

4-5 Troublesome Times; Staying the Course

Speech at the United States Institute of Peace
Washington DC
April 7, 1999

In February I gave a speech in San Francisco about America's role in the century to come. We all know it's an extraordinary moment when there is no overriding threat to our security, when no great power need feel that any other is a military threat, when freedom is expanding, and open markets and technology are raising living standards on every continent, bringing the world closer together in countless ways (See Chapter 1, Speech 5)....

The United States, as the largest and strongest country in the world at this moment—largest in economic terms and military terms—has the unavoidable responsibility to lead in this increasingly interdependent world, to try to help meet the challenges of this new era.

Clearly, our first challenge is to build a more peaceful world, one that will apparently be dominated by ethnic and religious conflicts we once thought of—primitive but which Senator Moynihan, for example, has referred to now as postmodern. We know that we cannot stop all such conflicts. But when the harm is great and when our values and interests are at stake and when we have the means to make a difference, we should try.

That is what we and our NATO allies are doing in Kosovo, trying to end the horrible war there, trying to aid the struggling democracies of southeastern Europe, all of whom are threatened by the violence, the hatred, the human exodus President Milosevic's brutal campaign has unleashed. We are determined to stay united and to persist until we prevail....

The second challenge ... is that of bringing our former adversaries Russia and China into the international system as open, prosperous, and stable nations. Today I want to speak especially about our relationship with China, one that is being tested and hotly debated today as China's Premier, Zhu Rongji, travels to Washington....

For a long time, it seems to me, we have argued about China with competing caricatures. Is this a country to be engaged or isolated? Is this a country beyond our power to influence or a country that is ours to gain and ours to lose? Now we hear that China is a country to be feared. A growing number of people say that it is the next great threat to our security and our well-being.

What about this argument? Well, those who say it point out, factually, that if China's economy continues to grow on its present trajectory, it will be the world's largest in the next century. They argue, correctly, that the Chinese Government often defines its interests in ways sharply divergent from ours. They are concerned, rightly, by Chinese missiles aimed at Taiwan and at others. From this they conclude that China is or will be our enemy.

They claim it is building up its military machine for aggression and using the profits of our trade to pay for it. They urge us, therefore, to contain China, to deny it access to our markets, our technology, our investment, and to bolster the strength of our allies in Asia to counter the threat a strong China will pose in the twenty-first century. What about that scenario? Clearly, if it chooses to do so, China could pursue such a course, pouring much more of its wealth into military might and into traditional great power geopolitics. Of course, this would rob it of much of its future prosperity, and it is far from inevitable that China will choose this path. Therefore, I would argue that we should not make it more likely that China will choose this path by acting as if that decision has already been made.

I say this over and over again, but when I see this China debate in America, with people talking about how we've got to contain China, and they present a terrible threat to us in the future and it's inevitable and how awful it is, I remind people who work with us that the same kind of debate is going on in China, people saying, "The Americans do not want us to emerge. They do not want us to have our rightful position in the world. Their whole strategy is designed to keep us down on the farm."

And we have to follow a different course. We cannot afford caricatures. I believe we have to work for the better future that we want, even as we remain prepared for any outcome. This approach will clearly put us at odds with those who believe America must always have a great enemy. How can you be the great force for good in the world and justify all the things you do if you don't have a great enemy?

I don't believe that. I believe we have to work for the best but do it in a way that will never leave us unprepared in the event that our efforts do not succeed.

Among the first decisions I made in 1993 was to preserve the alliances that kept the peace during the Cold War. That meant in Asia, we kept 100,000 troops there and maintained robust alliances with Japan, Korea, Thailand, Australia, and the Philippines. We did this and have done it not to contain China or anyone else but to give confidence to all that the potential threats to Asia's security will remain just that, potential, and that America remains committed to being involved with Asia and to Asia's stability.

We've maintained our strong, unofficial ties to a democratic Taiwan while upholding our "one China" policy. We've encouraged both sides to resolve their differences peacefully and to have increased contact. We've made it clear that neither can count on our acceptance if it violates these principles.

We know that in the past decade, China has increased its deployment of missiles near Taiwan. When China tested some of those missiles in 1996, tensions grew in the Taiwan Strait. We demonstrated then, with the deployment of our carriers, that America will act to prevent a miscalculation there. Our interests lie in peace and stability in Taiwan and in China, in the strait and in the region, and in a peaceful resolution of the differences. We will do what is necessary to maintain our interests.

Now, we have known since the early 1980s that China has nuclear armed missiles capable of reaching the United States. Our defense posture has and will continue to take account of that reality. In part, because of our engagement, China has, at best, only marginally increased its deployed nuclear threat in the last fifteen years. By signing the Comprehensive Test Ban Treaty, China has accepted constraints on its ability to modernize its arsenal at a time when the nuclear balance remains overwhelmingly in our favor. China has fewer than two dozen long-range nuclear weapons today; we have over 6,000.

We are determined to prevent the diversion of technology and sensitive information to China. The restrictions we place on our exports to China are tougher than those applied to any other major exporting country in the world.

When we first learned, in 1995, that a compromise had occurred at our weapons labs, our first priority was to find the leak, to stop it, and to prevent further damage. When the Energy Department and the FBI discovered wider vulnerabilities, we launched a comprehensive effort to address them. Last year I issued a directive to dramatically strengthen security at the Energy labs. We have increased the Department's counterintelligence budget by fifteenfold since 1995.

But we need to be sure we're getting the job done. Last month I asked the President's Foreign Intelligence Advisory Board, an independent, bipartisan body chaired by former Senator Warren Rudman, to review the security threat and the adequacy of the measures we have taken to address it. It is vital that we meet this challenge with firmness and openness but without fear.

The issue is how to respond to this. I believe we should not look at China through rose-colored glasses, nor should we look through a glass darkly to see an image that distorts China's strength and ignores its complexities. We need to see China clearly, its progress and its problem, its system and its strains, its policies and its perceptions of us, of itself, of the world. Indeed, we should apply a bit of universal wisdom that China's late leader, Deng Xiaoping, used to preach, we should seek the truth from facts.

In the last twenty years, China has made incredible progress in building a new economy, lifting more than 200 million people out of absolute poverty. But consider this: Its working age population is increasing by more than 10 million people, the equivalent of the State of Illinois, every year. Tens of millions of Chinese families are migrating from the countryside, where they see no future, to the city where only some find work. Due in part to the Asian economic crisis, China's economic growth is slowing just when it needs to be rising to create jobs for the unemployed and to maintain support for economic reform.

For all the progress of China's reforms, private enterprise still accounts for less than 20 percent of the nonfarm economy. Much of China's landscape is still dominated by unprofitable polluting state industries. China state banks are still making massive loans to struggling state firms, the sector of the economy least likely to succeed. ...

China's biggest challenge in the coming years will be to maintain stability and growth at home by meeting, not stifling, the growing demands of its people for openness and accountability. It is easy for us to say; for them, it is a daunting task.

What does all this mean for us? Well, if we've learned anything in the last few years from Japan's long recession and Russia's current economic troubles, it is that the weaknesses of great nations can pose as big a challenge to America as their strengths. So as we focus on the potential challenge that a strong China could present to the United States in the future, let us not forget the risk of a weak China, beset by internal conflicts, social dislocation, and criminal activity, becoming a vast zone of instability in Asia.

Despite Beijing's best efforts to rein in these problems, we have seen the first danger signs: free-wheeling Chinese enterprises selling weapons abroad; the rise in China of organized crime; stirrings of ethnic tensions and rural unrest; the use of Chinese territory for heroin trafficking; and even piracy of ships at sea. In short, we're seeing in China the kinds of problems a society can face when it is moving away from the rule of fear but is not yet firmly rooted in the rule of law.

The solutions fundamentally lie in the choices China makes. But I think we would all agree, we have an interest in seeking to make a difference and in not pretending that the outcome is foreordained. We can't do that simply by confronting China or trying to contain her. We can only deal with the challenge if we continue a policy of principled, purposeful engagement with China's leaders and China's people.

Our long-term strategy must be to encourage the right kind of development in China; to help China grow at home into a strong, prosperous, and open society, coming together, not falling apart; to integrate China into the institutions that promote global norms on proliferation, trade, the environment, and human rights. We must build on opportunities for cooperation with China where we agree, even as we strongly defend our interests and values where we disagree. That is the purpose of engagement. Not to insulate our relationship from the consequences of Chinese actions but to use our relationship to influence China's actions in a way that advances our values and our interests....

China already has broad access to our markets, as you can see from any perusal of recent trade figures. If China accepts the responsibilities that come with WTO membership, that will give us broad access to China's markets, while accelerating its internal reforms and propelling it toward acceptance of the rule of law. The bottom line is this: If China is willing to play by the global rules of trade, it would be an inexplicable mistake for the United States to say no.

We have an interest as well in working with China to preserve the global environment. Toward the middle of the next century, China will surpass the United States as the world's largest emitter of greenhouse gases. At last year's summit in China, I made it clear there can be no meaningful solution to this problem unless China is a part of it. But I also emphasized, as I do over and over again, with sometimes mixed effect, that rapidly developing technologies now make it possible for China— indeed, for India, for any other developing economy—to be environmentally responsible without sacrificing economic growth.

That challenge is at the top of Vice President Gore's agenda on the forum on environment and development he shares with Premier Zhu. It will be meeting this week.

We have been encouraging the development of clean natural gas in China and cleaner technologies for burning coal. We've been working with China on a study of emissions trading, a tool that has cut pollution at low cost in the United States and which could do the same for China. In the information age, China need not, indeed, China will not be able to grow its economy by clinging to industrial age energy practices.

Finally, let me say we have an interest in encouraging China to respect the human rights of its people and to give them a chance to shape the political destiny of their country. This is an interest that cuts to the heart of our concerns about China's future.

The people-to-people ties have made it possible for over 100,000 Chinese students and scholars to study in America and thousands of American teachers and scholars—students—to go to China. They have enabled American nongovernmental organizations to help people in China set up NGO's of their own. They have allowed Americans to work with local governments, universities, and citizens' groups in China to save wetlands and forests, to manage urban growth, to support China's first private schools, to hook up schools to the Internet, to train journalists, to promote literacy for poor women, to make loans for Tibetan entrepreneurs, to begin countless projects that are sparking the growth of China's civil society. They have permitted Chinese lawyers, judges, and legal scholars to come to America to study our system.

Now, we don't assume for a moment that this kind of engagement alone can give rise to political reform in China, but despite the obstacles they face, the Chinese people clearly enjoy more freedom, in where they work and where they live and where they go, than they did a decade ago....

We will also urge China to embrace the International Covenant on Civil and Political Rights in word and in deed. We will keep pressing the Congress to fund programs that promote the rule of law in China. We will keep working to promote a dialog between China and the Dalai Lama and respect for Tibet's cultural and religious heritage.

But there is one thing that we will not do. We will not change our policy in a way that isolates China from the global forces that have begun to empower the Chinese people to change their society and build a better future, for that would leave the people of China with less access to information, less contact with the democratic world, and more resistance from their government to outside influence and ideas.

In all these areas, the debate China's policy has sparked in our country can be constructive by reminding us that we still face challenges in the world that require our vigilance. It can also remind the Chinese Government that the relationship between our two countries depends in large measure not only on the actions of the President and the executive branch but on the support of the American people and our Congress, which cannot be taken for granted.

But as the next Presidential election approaches, we cannot allow a healthy argument to lead us toward a campaign-driven Cold War with China, for that would have tragic consequences: an America driven by mistrust and bitter accusations; an end to diplomatic contact that has produced tangible gains for our people; a climate of mistrust that hurts Chinese-Americans and undermines the exchanges that are opening China to the world.

No one could possibly gain from that except for the most rigid, backward-looking elements in China itself. Remember what I said at the outset: The debate we're having about China today in the United States is mirrored by a debate going on in China about the United States. And we must be sensitive to how we handle this and responsible.

I know the vast majority of Americans and Members of Congress don't want this to happen. I will do everything in our power to see that it does not, so that we stay focused on our vital interests and the real challenges ahead.

We have much to be concerned about: There is North Korea, South Asia, the potential for tensions in the Taiwan Strait, and the South China Sea; there is the tragic plight of political prisoners; the possibility, also, that China will not realize its growth potential, that it will become unstable because of the distressed economy and angry people.

But we have every reason to approach our challenges with confidence and with patience. Our country, after all, now, is at the height of its power and the peak of its prosperity. Democratic values are ascendant throughout much of the world. And while we cannot know where China is heading for sure, the forces pulling China toward integration and openness are more powerful today than ever before. And these are the only forces that can make China a truly successful power, meeting the demands of its people and exercising appropriate and positive influence in the larger world in the twenty-first century.

Such a China would indeed be stronger, but it also would be more at peace with itself and at ease with its neighbors. It would be a good thing for the Chinese people and for the American people.

This has been the lodestar of our policy for the last six years—a goal that is consistent with our interests and that keeps faith with our values, an objective that we will continue to pursue, with your help and understanding, in the months and years ahead....

5. The United Nations and the United States: Rhetoric and Reality

Every American president since 1945 has expressed support for the United Nations, but has not seen fit to strengthen it institutionally, financially, or politically. In part, this is because initial US assumptions about the United Nations, founded by the victor nations of World War II, proved to be overly optimistic. Washington had assumed that the five permanent members of the Security Council would cooperate to preserve the peace. Instead, by 1946, the UN scene was permeated by the US-Soviet hostility. In great measure, it came to reflect the bipolar world that dominated international politics from 1945 to 1990. Another source of US disenchantment stemmed, paradoxically, from the organization's greater representativeness. By the 1960s, the mushrooming membership of newly independent Third World countries played an active political role that often conflicted with US interests and preferences, creating a tension between Washington and the collective security instrument it had helped to create.

Not until the Persian Gulf crisis (August 1990 – March 1991) did the UN Security Council function as its founders had envisaged. A reform-minded Soviet leader, Mikhail Gorbachev, was the key. Having determined on a course of improved relations with the West, he cooperated with the other permanent members of the Security Council to reverse Iraq's aggression against Kuwait, even though Iraq was an important Soviet client. Advocates of collective security believed the United Nations was poised to play the role intended, namely, to promote international peace and security.

No foreign policy option is more often mentioned than collective security—and none is more misunderstood or less frequently implemented. Like the term "the international community," it is more rhetoric than reality, more myth than instrumentality. Quite simply, collective security stipulates that in the event of an aggression against one member of the international community, all other members will immediately coalesce against the aggressor. It assumes that all states will be able to agree on who is the aggressor; that they will band together, irrespective of ideology, race, religion, economics, or ethnicity, in the common interest; and that once an aggressor has been thwarted, all such coalitions would disband. Further, it assumes a readiness to subsume one's own national interests, whatever they may be, in regard to the country held to be an aggressor, to the general will of the international community.

Despite its talk, the United States has been ambivalent about the collective security role of the United Nations. Apart from its distaste for the undercurrents of anti-Americanism periodically manifested in the UN General Assembly, the pressure from the less developed countries for more contributions to social, economic, and educational programs, and the bloated UN bureaucracies and their inefficient operations, Washington remains uneasy about the UN Security Council itself. Even when great power cooperation makes peacekeeping operations possible, the costs are considerable, and often encounter criticism in Congress. The United States, far from emerging as a leader on the crucial issue of financing and supporting UN peacekeeping operations, has shown itself a reluctant and laggard contributor. After the militarily successful UN-supported campaign to reverse Iraq's aggression, President Bush, in his final address to the General Assembly on September 21, 1992, called for the development of "enhanced peacekeeping capabilities" and a transformation of UN institutions. But he offered no proposals for financing and strengthening the UN's capacity to respond to situations deemed to threaten international peace and security. President Clinton, in his maiden speech to the UN General Assembly in September 1993, also spoke at great length on the importance of strengthening UN peacekeeping operations (Speech 1-2).

President Clinton's first jolt in foreign affairs came in the United Nations on the issue of Somalia. Every issue has a history. In the late 1980s, conflict among Somali clans had heated up. It intensified when the government of Siad Barre fell at the end of January 1991. The fighting worsened as drought spread throughout the country, placing more than 1.5 million people at risk of starvation. The UN Security Council passed a number of resolutions calling for an end to the fighting, clan reconciliation, and accelerated deliveries of food aid. In early December 1992, in accordance with a resolution authorizing member states to help establish "a secure environment" for humanitarian relief operations in Somalia, the Bush administration reversed its pre-election policy of no direct military involvement and sent 25,000 troops as part of a US-led multinational contingent that numbered about 38,000. By early 1993, the worst of the food crisis was over, but banditry and conditions of near anarchy were still widespread.

At this juncture, with strong US support, a unanimously approved UN Security Council Resolution 814 of March 26, 1993, raised the stakes from humanitarian relief to "rehabilitating" Somali political institutions and the economy "and promoting political settlement and national reconciliation." America's ambassador to the United Nations, Madeleine Albright, extolled the resolution as "an unprecedented enterprise aimed at nothing less than the restoration of an entire country as a proud, functioning and viable member of the community of nations." The estimated cost was put at $1.5 billion a year, a sum that was roughly half of the total 1993 UN budget for peacekeeping operations. Five months after the US-led multinational force had entered Somalia, the United Nations assumed control of the expanded mission, its first venture into nation building.

But building a civil society required resources beyond the UN's capability. The Somali port of Mogadishu became the site of urban warfare: in June, Pakistani peacekeepers were killed by forces of the warlord Mohamad Farah Aideed, and in August, four US soldiers were killed amidst the efforts to apprehend Aideed. Ambassador Albright spoke of the need "to stay the course and help lift the country ... from the category of a failed state into that of an emerging democracy." This rhetoric did not reflect the reality. In September, a US helicopter was downed and three more soldiers were lost. Congressional criticisms mounted, as did calls for a clarification of objectives not only in Somalia but in Bosnia as well. In early October, an American-initiated attempt to capture Aideed backfired, resulting in the death of eighteen US soldiers and dozens of wounded. The president of neighboring Eritrea derided the United States for acting "like Rambo." The administration's ambitious Somalia policy in shambles, a chastened President Clinton announced America's withdrawal (Speech 5-1). The impact of the debacle in Somalia was to restrain US policy involvement in Bosnia for the next two years.

Haiti offered a countering case for the administration's "assertive multilateralism." In September 1991, Haiti's President, Jean-Bertrand Aristide, was deposed in a military coup. The Western hemisphere's collective security organization, the Organization of American States (OAS), condemned the military's disruption of the democratic process, withheld diplomatic recognition, called for the island's economic and commercial isolation, and espoused "all measures necessary to protect and defend human rights in Haiti." Under the Clinton administration, measures to restore Aristide were accelerated by the OAS and the UN. On May 6, 1994, a complete embargo was imposed, and on July 31, 1994, the United Nations Security Council authorized the creation of a multinational force for Haiti, under US command. The putschists surrendered, and on September 19, a 20,000 troop force landed without incident. A confident Clinton spoke to the nation about the US involvement (Speech 5-2). Less than two weeks later, in his annual address to the UN General Assembly, Clinton used the success in Haiti to vindicate UN peacekeeping operations, reaffirm his pledge to meet US financial obligations to the United Nations, and propose a treaty to abolish antipersonnel land mines—his first innovative proposal (Speech 5-3). And on June 26, 1996, in San Francisco on the occasion of the fiftieth anniversary of the adoption of the UN Charter, the President defended the organization against congressional critics in sweeping and positive terms (Speech 5-4). In retrospect, this may have marked the apogee of his attachment to the United Nations.

The promise to meet US financial obligations to the United Nations was made often by President Clinton, but got derailed by domestic politics. In this respect, Congress may be considered to be as much at fault as the White House. However, in the final analysis, the President chose to appease domestic constituencies rather than fight to build a more effective United Nations organization that could rely on US support and financial resources. The politics of the dilemma are convoluted and intense.

The United States is assessed (a) 25 percent of the UN's regular budget, which Congress would like to have reduced to 20 percent; (b) 30.5 percent of the costs of peacekeeping operations, which Congress in 1994 unilaterally reduced to 25 percent, despite the UN's insistence that a nation's assessment can be changed only by mutual consent; and (c) a somewhat lesser assessment for the very small special budget financing the International Criminal Tribunals for the Former Yugoslavia and Rwanda, which are charged with investigating and prosecuting those responsible for genocide and gross violations of human rights in those regions. Over the years, US arrears have become an embarrassment. Indeed, in November 1996, the United States was voted off the General Assembly's Administrative and Budgetary Committee because of its nonpayment of dues, the first time it experienced such an indignity.

A hostile Republican-controlled Congress has insisted on major concessions as the price for paying the dues the United States owes. These concessions include a write-off of some arrears, credits for personnel and equipment contributed by the United States to peacekeeping operations, deeper UN budgetary and personnel cuts, and guarantees against the establishment of permanent standby UN forces to be used in emergencies. After extensive negotiations, a bipartisan agreement was cobbled together by Jesse Helms (R-NC), Chairman of the Senate Foreign Relations Committee, and Joseph Biden (D-DE), the ranking minority member on the committee, and a compromise agreement seemed imminent. However, at the last minute, a group of twenty-five Republicans attached an antiabortion rider to the measure, prohibiting US funds for international family planning groups that provide abortion services or that engage in any kind of advocacy about abortion. From that point on, stalemate prevailed, the President saying the anti-abortion provision went too far, and Senator Helms arguing that "with one stroke of his pen" the President could pay US arrears to the United Nations. Neither side would budge. In an op-ed piece in the *New York Times* on September 21, 1998, Senator Helms wrote:

> The original language—which was American policy under the Reagan and Bush Administrations, but later reversed by President Clinton—barred the use of Federal money by groups that perform abortions abroad. But that language is not what is in the bill now awaiting the President's signature. Last fall, in an effort to strike a deal, House leaders agreed to a watered-down restriction that does nothing more than ban the use of American tax dollars to lobby for changes in foreign abortion laws.

Unwilling to anger women's groups or other constituencies where the pro-choice issue looms large, the President persisted in his position. Meanwhile, as the indebtedness of the United States to the United Nations approached the $2 billion mark, resentment toward the United States was becoming more vocal and more open. Reforms undertaken by Kofi Annan, who succeeded Boutros Boutros-Ghali as UN Secretary-General in 1997, were largely ignored by the Congress, where pro-UN sentiment was even weaker than it had been at the start of the Clinton administration.

In the final years of his second term, President Clinton's annual speeches to the General Assembly had little impact. They were too general, too familiar, too geared to saying the usual thing—like his promise "to put the questions of debts and dues behind us once and for all"—rather than taking the necessary action (Speech 5-5). In 1998, on the occasion of the fiftieth anniversary of the Universal Declaration of Human Rights, the President devoted most of his UN address to the problems of terrorism, certainly a political-security staple on the agenda of many nations, but hardly a predominant worry of the UN's membership as a whole (Speech 5-6).

Notwithstanding its early rhetoric and good intentions, the Clinton administration's weak support of the United Nations extended to its peacekeeping operations. Despite a continuing UN presence in Haiti, little there has changed economically or politically since 1994. Cambodia may be viewed as a minor success story for the United Nations, in that the fighting has stopped, but democracy and economic development are distant hopes. The Somalia intervention was a failure. In early 1999, the UN Security Council terminated its operations in Angola: after five years and $4 billion, civil war and devastation continued unchecked. UN peacekeeping missions in Sierra Leone, the Central African Republic, and elsewhere in Africa faltered, as much because of tepid US support as because of the competing parties' lack of interest in UN mediation. Clinton's humanitarian interventions have been selective, and lack appeal outside of the small group of Western countries in the United Nations.

Another discouraging harbinger of future constraints on UN peacekeeping prospects was evident in China's use of the veto to terminate the peacekeeping contingent in Macedonia in retaliation for that country's establishing diplomatic relations with Taiwan, and in China's criticisms of NATO's war against Yugoslavia. Beijing, fearing possible UN interference in China's own domestic affairs, complained that the Security Council was ignored by NATO when it attacked Yugoslavia in late March 1999, purportedly to protect Muslim Albanians living in Yugoslavia's Kosovo province. The long-term effect of this US-led NATO operation may be the marginalization of the United Nations itself.

In an op-ed piece in the *New York Times* on May 27, 1999, former President Jimmy Carter lamented the downgrading of the UN Security Council by the United States. Alluding to NATO's attacks on targets in Kosovo and Serbia, and the US's "seriously flawed approach" to Iraq, Cuba, and the Sudan, as well, he noted:

> The approach the United States has taken recently has been to devise a solution that best suits its own purposes, recruit at least tacit support in whichever forum it can best influence, provide the dominant military force, present an ultimatum to recalcitrant parties and then take punitive action against the entire nation to force compliance.

Carter's critique stressed the Clinton administration's impatience with "patient negotiation," its bypassing of the UN Security Council, its seeming disdain for making use of other groups and organizations to jump start serious talks, and its indifference to serious conflicts in Africa. (For example, while NATO was bombing Serbia for its "ethnic cleansing" in Kosovo, Ethiopia summarily expelled 52,000 Eritreans. Washington and the media were silent.)

There is additional evidence that Clinton's policy in the United Nations has been ambivalent and ineffective. The President proposed a treaty to eliminate antipersonnel land mines, but was unable to obtain the US Senate's support for its ratification. He called on the United Nations to wage a war on drugs, but opted for appeasing Mexico, a major conduit of drugs into the United States, and did little to enlist more cooperation from Russia in interdicting drug trafficking across Eurasia. And although he has been an advocate of extending the rule of international law and the scope of human rights enforcement, Clinton refused, because of domestic opposition, to fight for the establishment of a permanent UN International

Criminal Court to prosecute war criminals. At the end of his term in office, he was a less staunch advocate of a strong United Nations than he had been at the beginning.

5-1 Explaining Somalia to the Congress

Message to Congress
The White House
October 13, 1993

In response to the request made by the House and Senate for certain information on our military operations in Somalia, I am pleased to forward the attached report.

In transmitting this report, I want to reiterate the points that I made on October 6 and to the American people in remarks on October 7. We went to Somalia on a humanitarian mission. We saved approximately a million lives that were at risk of starvation brought on by civil war that had degenerated into anarchy. We acted after 350,000 already had died.

Ours was a gesture of a great nation, carried out by thousands of American citizens, both military and civilian. We did not then, nor do we now plan to stay in that country. The United Nations agreed to assume our military mission and take on the additional political and rehabilitation activities required so that the famine and anarchy do not resume when the international presence departs.

For our part, we agreed with the United Nations to participate militarily with a much smaller US force for a period of time, to help the United Nations create a secure environment in which it could ensure the free flow of humanitarian relief. At the request of the United Nations and the United States, approximately thirty nations deployed over 20,000 troops as we reduced our military presence.

With the recent tragic casualties to American forces in Somalia, the American people want to know why we are there, what we are doing, why we cannot come home immediately, and when we will come home. Although the report answers those questions in detail, I want to repeat concisely my answers:

- We went to Somalia because without us a million people would have died. We, uniquely, were in a position to save them, and other nations were ready to share the burden after our initial action.

- What the United States is doing there is providing, for a limited period of time, logistics support and security so that the humanitarian and political efforts of the United Nations, relief organizations, and others can have a reasonable chance of success. The United Nations, in turn, has a longer term political, security, and relief mission designed to minimize the likelihood that famine and anarchy will return when the United Nations leaves. The US military mission is not now nor was it ever one of "nation building."

- We cannot leave immediately because the United Nations has not had an adequate chance to replace us, nor have the Somalis had a reasonable opportunity to end their strife. We want other nations to assume more of the burden of international peace. To have them do so, they must think that they can rely on our commitments when we make them. Moreover, having been brutally attacked, were American forces to leave now we would send a message to terrorists and other potential adversaries around the world that they can change our policies by killing our people. It would be open season on Americans.

- We will, however, leave no later than March 31, 1994, except for a few hundred support troops. That amount of time will permit the Somali people to make progress toward political reconciliation and allow the United States to fulfill our obligations properly, including the return of any Americans being detained. We went there for the right reasons and we will finish the job in the right way.

While US forces are there, they will be fully protected with appropriate American military capability.

Any Americans detained will be the subject of the most complete and thorough efforts of which this Government is capable, with the unrelenting goal of returning them home and returning them to health.

I want to thank all those who have expressed their support for this approach during the last week. At difficult times such as these, when we face international challenges, bipartisan unity among our two branches of government is vital.

5-2 Address to the Nation on Haiti

The White House
September 15, 1994

My fellow Americans, tonight I want to speak with you about why the United States is leading the international effort to restore democratic government in Haiti. Haiti's dictators, led by General Raoul Cedras, control the most violent regime in our hemisphere. For three years, they have rejected every peaceful solution that the international community has proposed. They have broken an agreement that they made to give up power. They have brutalized their people and destroyed their economy, and for three years we and other nations have worked exhaustively to find a diplomatic solution, only to have the dictators reject each one.

Now the United States must protect our interests, to stop the brutal atrocities that threaten tens of thousands of Haitians, to secure our borders and to preserve stability and promote democracy in our hemisphere and to uphold the reliability of the commitments we make and the commitments others make to us.

Earlier today, I ordered Secretary of Defense Perry to call up the military reserve personnel necessary to support United States troops in any action we might undertake in Haiti. I have also ordered two aircraft carriers, USS Eisenhower and the USS America into the region. ...

I want the American people to understand the background of the situation in Haiti, how what has happened there affects our national security interests and why I believe we must act now. Nearly 200 years ago, the Haitian people rose up out of slavery and declared their independence. Unfortunately, the promise of liberty was quickly snuffed out, and ever since, Haiti has known more suffering and repression than freedom. In our time, as democracy has spread throughout our hemisphere. Haiti has been left behind.

Then, just four years ago, the Haitian people held the first free and fair elections since their independence. They elected a parliament and a new President, Father Jean-Bertrand Aristide, a Catholic priest who received almost 70 percent of the vote. But eight months later, Haitian dreams of democracy became a nightmare of bloodshed.

General Raoul Cedras led a military coup that overthrew President Aristide, the man who had appointed Cedras to lead the army. Resistors were beaten and murdered. The dictators launched a horrible intimidation campaign of rape, torture, and mutilation. People starved; children died; thousands of Haitians fled their country, heading to the United States across dangerous seas. At that time, President Bush declared the situation posed, and I quote, "an unusual and extraordinary threat to the national security, foreign policy, and economy of the United States."

Cedras and his armed thugs have conducted a reign of terror, executing children, raping women, killing priests. As the dictators have grown more desperate, the atrocities have grown ever more brutal. Recent news reports have documented the slaying of Haitian orphans by the nation's deadly police thugs....

Let me be clear: General Cedras and his accomplices alone are responsible for this suffering and terrible human tragedy. It is their actions that have isolated Haiti.

Neither the international community nor the United States has sought a confrontation. For nearly three years we've worked hard on diplomatic efforts. The United Nations, the Organization of American States, the Caribbean community, the six Central American Presidents all have sought a peaceful end to this crisis. We have tried everything: persuasion and negotiation, mediation and condemnation. Emissaries were dispatched to Port-au-Prince and were turned away.

The United Nations labored for months to reach an agreement acceptable to all parties. Then last year, General Cedras himself came here to the United States and signed an agreement on Governors Island in New York in which he pledged to give up power, along with the other dictators.

But when the day came for the plan to take effect, the dictators refused to leave and instead increased the brutality they are using to cling to power. Even then, the nations of the world continued to seek a peaceful solution while strengthening the embargo we had imposed. We sent massive amounts of humanitarian aid, food for a million Haitians, and medicine to try to help the ordinary Haitian people as the dictators continued to loot the economy. Then this summer, they threw out the international observers who had blown the whistle on the regime's human rights atrocities.

In response to that action, in July the United Nations Security Council approved a resolution that authorizes the use of all necessary means, including force, to remove the Haitian dictators from power and restore democratic government. Still, we continue to seek a peaceful solution, but the dictators would not even meet with the United Nations Special Envoy. In the face of this continued defiance and with atrocities rising, the United States has agreed to lead a multinational force to carry out the will of the United Nations....

I know that the United States cannot, indeed, we should not be the world's policemen. And I know that this is a time with the Cold War over that so many Americans are reluctant to commit military resources and our personnel beyond our borders. But when brutality occurs close to our shores, it affects our national interests. And we have a responsibility to act.

Thousands of Haitians have already fled toward the United States, risking their lives to escape the reign of terror. As long as Cedras rules, Haitians will continue to seek sanctuary in our Nation. This year, in less than two months, more than 21,000 Haitians were rescued at sea by our Coast Guard and Navy. Today, more than 14,000 refugees are living at our naval base in Guantanamo. The American people have already expended almost $200 million to support them, to maintain the economic embargo, and the prospect of millions and millions more being spent every month for an indefinite period of time loom ahead unless we act.

Three hundred thousand more Haitians, 5 percent of their entire population, are in hiding in their own country. If we don't act, they could be the next wave of refugees at our door. We will continue to face the threat of a mass exodus of refugees and its constant threat to stability in our region and control of our borders.

No American should be surprised at the recent tide of migrants seeking refuge from on our shores comes from Haiti and from Cuba. After all, they're the only nations left in the Western Hemisphere where democratic government is denied, the only countries where dictators have managed to hold back the wave of democracy and progress that has swept over our entire region, and that our own government has so actively promoted and supported for years.

Today, thirty-three of the thirty-five countries in the Americas have democratically elected leaders. And Haiti is the only nation in our hemisphere where the people actually elected their own government and chose democracy, only to have tyrants steal it away.

There's no question that the Haitian people want to embrace democracy; we know it because they went to the ballot box and told the world. History has taught us that preserving democracy in our own hemisphere strengthens America's security and prosperity. Democracies here are more likely to keep the peace and to stabilize our region. They're more likely to create free markets and economic opportunity, and to become strong, reliable trading partners. And they're more likely to provide their own people with the opportunities that will encourage them to stay in their nation and to build their own futures.

Restoring Haiti's democratic government will help lead to more stability and prosperity in our region, just as our actions in Panama and Grenada did. Beyond the human rights violations, the immigration problems, the importance of democracy, the United States also has strong interests in not letting dictators, especially in our own region, break their word to the United States and the United Nations....

In Haiti, we have a case in which the right is clear, in which the country in question is nearby, in which our own interests are plain, in which the mission is achievable and limited, and in which the nations of the world stand with us. We must act.

Our mission in Haiti, as it was in Panama and Grenada, will be limited and specific. Our plan to remove the dictators will follow two phases. First, it will remove dictators from power and restore Haiti's legitimate, democratically elected government. We will train a civilian-controlled Haitian security force that will protect the people rather than repress them. During this period, police monitors from all around the world will work with the authorities to maximize basic security and civil order and minimize retribution....

Then, in the second phase, a much smaller US force will join forces from other members of the United Nations. And their mission will leave Haiti after elections are held next year and a new Haitian takes office in early 1996.

Tonight, I can announce that President Aristide has pledged to step down when his term ends, in accordance with the constitution he has sworn to uphold. He has committed himself to promote reconciliation among all Haitians and to set an historic example by peacefully transferring power to a duly elected successor. He knows, as we know, that when you start a democracy, the most important election is the second election.

President Aristide has told me that he will consider his mission fulfilled not when he regains office but when he leaves office to the next democratically elected President of Haiti. He has pledged to honor the Haitian voters who put their faith in the ballot box.

In closing, let me say that I know the American people are rightfully concerned whenever our soldiers are put at risk. Our volunteer military is the world's finest, and its leaders have worked hard to minimize risks to all our forces. But the risks are there, and we must be prepared for that....

5-3 Reaffirming Multilateralism

Address to the United Nations General Assembly
New York, New York
September 26, 1994

... Working together increases the impact and the legitimacy of each of our actions, and sharing the burdens lessons everyone's load. We have no desire to be the world's policemen, but we will do what we can to help civil societies emerge from the ashes of repression, to sustain fragile democracies and to add more free markets to the world and, of course, to restrain the destructive forces that threaten us all....

A coalition for democracy—it's good for America. Democracies, after all, are more likely to be stable, less likely to wage war. They strengthen civil society. They can provide people with the economic and political opportunities to build their futures in their own homes, not to flee their borders.

Our efforts to help build more democracies will make us all more secure, more prosperous, and more successful as we try to make this era of terrific change our friend and not our enemy.

In our Nation, as in all of your nations, there are many people who are understandably reluctant to undertake these efforts, because often the distances are great or the cultures are different. There are good reasons for the caution that people feel. Often, the chances of success or the costs are unclear. And of course, in every common endeavor there is always the potential for failure and often the risk of loss of life. And yet our people, as we have seen in the remarkable global response to the terrible crisis in Rwanda, genuinely want to help their neighbors around the world and want to make some effort in our common cause.

We have seen that progress can be made as well. The problem is deciding when we must respond and how we shall overcome our reluctance. This will never be easy; there are no simple formulas. All of us will make these decisions, in part, based on the distance of the problem from our shores or the interests of our Nation or the difference we think we can make or the cost required or the threat to our own citizens in the endeavor. Hard questions will remain and cannot be erased by some simple formula.

But we should have the confidence that these efforts can succeed, whether they are efforts to keep people alive in the face of terrible tragedy, as in Rwanda, or our efforts to avert a tragedy, as in the Horn of Africa, or our efforts to support processes that are literally changing the future of millions. History is on our side....

And today I am proposing a first step toward the eventual elimination of a less-visible but still deadly threat: the world's 85 million antipersonnel land mines, one for every fifty people on the face of the Earth. I ask all nations to join with us and conclude an agreement to reduce the number and availability of those mines. Ridding the world of those often hidden weapons will help to save the lives of tens of thousands of men and women and innocent children in the years to come....

Here, at the United Nations, we must develop a concrete plan to meet the challenges of the next fifty years, even as we celebrate the last fifty years. I believe we should declare next year's fiftieth anniversary not just a year of celebration, but a year of renewal. We call on the Secretary General to name a working group so that, by the time we meet next year, we will have a concrete action plan to revitalize the UN's obligations to address the security, economic, and political challenges ahead, obligations we must all be willing to assume.

Our objectives should include ready, efficient, and capable UN peacekeeping forces. And I am happy to report that as I pledged to you last year, and thanks to the support in the United States Congress, $1.2 billion is now available from the United States for this critical account.

We must also pledge to keep UN reform moving forward, so that we do more with less. And we must improve our ability to respond to urgent needs. Let me suggest that it is time for the members of this Assembly to consider seriously President Menem's suggestion for the creation of a civilian rapid response capability for humanitarian crises.

And let us not lose sight of the special role that development and democracy can play in preventing conflicts once peace has been established.

Never before has the United Nations been in a better position to achieve the democratic goals of our Founders. The end of the Cold War has freed us from decades of paralyzing divisions, and we all know that multilateral cooperation is not only necessary to address the new threats we face but possible to succeed.

The efforts we have taken together in Haiti are a prime example. Under the sponsorship of the United Nations, American troops, now being joined by the personnel of an ever-growing international coalition of over two dozen nations, are giving the people of Haiti their chance at freedom. Creative diplomacy, the influence of economic power, the credible threat of military force, all have contributed to this moment of opportunity.

Essential civil order will be restored. Human rights violations will be curbed. The first refugees are returning within hours on this day. The military leaders will step down; the democratic government will be restored. President Aristide will return. The multinational mission will turn its responsibilities over to the United Nations mission, which will remain in Haiti throughout 1995 until a new President is elected. During this time, a multinational development effort will make available more than $1 billion to begin helping the Haitians rebuild their country....

The situation in Bosnia, to that extent, has improved. But in recent weeks, the situation around Sarajevo has deteriorated substantially, and Sarajevo once again faces the prospect of strangulation. A new resolve by the United Nations to enforce its resolutions is now necessary to save Sarajevo. And NATO stands ready to act.

The situation in Bosnia is yet another reminder of the greatest irony of this century we are leaving: This century so full of hope and opportunity and achievement has also been an age of deep destruction and despair....

5-4 In Defense of the United Nations

San Francisco, California
June 26, 1995

The 800 delegates from fifty nations who came here fifty years ago to lift the world from the ashes of war and bring life to the dreams of peacemakers included both giants of diplomacy and untested leaders of infant nations. They were separated by tradition, race and language, sharing only a vision of a better, safer future. On this day fifty years ago, the dreams President Roosevelt did not live to see of a democratic organization of the world was launched.

The Charter the delegates signed reflected the harsh lessons of their experience; the experience of the thirties, in which the world watched and reacted too slowly to fascist aggression, bringing millions sacrificed on the battlefields and millions more murdered in the death chambers.

Those who had gone through this and the Second World War knew that celebrating victory was not enough; that merely punishing the enemy was self-defeating; that instead the world needed an effective and permanent system to promote peace and freedom for everyone....

Just months before his death, President Roosevelt said, "We have learned that we cannot live alone at peace, that our own well-being is dependent on the well-being of other nations far away." Today, more than ever, those words ring true. Yet some here in our own country, where the United Nations was founded, dismissed Roosevelt's wisdom. Some of them acknowledge that the United States must play a strong role overseas, but refuse to supply the nonmilitary resources our nation needs to carry on its responsibilities. Others believe that outside our border America should only act alone.

Well, of course, the United States must be prepared to act alone when necessary, but we dare not ignore the benefits that coalitions bring to this nation. We dare not reject decades of bipartisan wisdom. We dare not reject decades of bipartisan support for international cooperation. Those who

155

would do so, these new isolationists, dismiss fifty years of hard evidence.

In those years we've seen the United Nations compile a remarkable record of progress that advances our nation's interest and, indeed, the interest of people everywhere. From President Truman in Korea to President Bush in the Persian Gulf, America has built United Nations' military coalitions to contain aggressors. UN forces also often pick up where United States' troops have taken the lead.

As the Secretary of State said, we saw it just yesterday, when Haiti held parliamentary and local elections with the help of UN personnel. We saw the UN work in partnership with the United States and the people of Haiti, as they labor to create a democracy. And they have now been given a second chance to renew that promise.

On every continent the United Nations has played a vital role in making people more free and more secure. For decades, the UN fought to isolate South Africa, as that regime perpetuated apartheid. Last year, under the watchful eyes of UN observers, millions of South Africans who had been disenfranchised for life cast their first votes for freedom.

In Namibia, Mozambique, and soon we hope in Angola, the United Nations is helping people to bury decades of civil strife and turn their energies into building new democratic nations. In Cambodia, where a brutal regime left more than 1 million dead in the Killing Fields, the UN helped hundreds of thousands of refugees return to their native land, and stood watch over democratic elections that brought 90 percent of the people to the polls. In El Salvador, the UN brokered an end to twelve years of bloody civil war, and stayed on to help reform the army and bring justice to the citizens and open the doors of democracy.

From the Persian Gulf to the Caribbean, UN economic and political sanctions have proved to be a valuable means short of military action to isolate regimes and to make aggressors and terrorists pay at least a price for their actions: In Iraq, to help stop that nation from developing weapons of mass destruction, or threatening its neighbors again. In the Balkans, to isolate aggressors; in North Africa, to pressure Libya to turn over for trial those indicted in the bombing of Pan Am flight 103.

The record of the United Nations includes a proud battle for child survival, and against human suffering and disease of all kinds. Every year UNICEF oral vaccines save the lives of 3 million children. Last year alone the World Food Program, using the contributions of many governments including our own, fed 57 million hungry people. The World Health Organization has eliminated small pox for the face of the Earth, and is making great strides in its campaign to eliminate polio by the year 2000. It has helped to contain fatal diseases like the Ebola virus that could have threatened an entire continent....

But now the end of the Cold War, the strong trend toward democratic ideals among all nations, the emergence of so many problems that can best be met by collective action, all these things enable the United Nations at this fifty-year point finally to fulfill the promise of its founders.

But if we want the UN to do so, we must face the fact that for all its successes and all its possibilities, it does not work as well as it should. The United Nations must be reformed. In this age of relentless change, successful governments and corporations are constantly reducing their bureaucracies, setting clearer priorities, focusing on targeted results.

In the United States we have eliminated hundreds of programs, thousands of regulations. We're reducing our government to its smallest size since President Kennedy served here, while increasing our efforts in areas most critical to our future. The UN must take similar steps.

Over the years it has grown too bloated, too often encouraging duplication, and spending resources on meetings rather than results. As its board of directors, all of us—we, the member states—must create a UN that is more flexible, that operates more rapidly, that wastes less and produces more, and most importantly, that inspires confidence among our governments and our people.

In the last few years we have seen some good reforms—a new oversight office to hold down costs, a new system to review personnel, a start toward modernization and privatization. But we must do more.

The United Nations supports the proposal of the President of the General Assembly, Mr. Essyi, who spoke so eloquently here earlier this morning, to prepare a blueprint for renewing the UN and to approve it before the 50th General Assembly finishes its work next fall.

We must consider major structural changes. The United Nations simply does not need a separate agency with its own acronym, stationary and bureaucracy for every problem. The new UN must peel off what doesn't work and get behind what will.

We must also realize, in particular, the limits to peacekeeping and not ask the Blue Helmets to undertake missions they cannot be expected to handle. Peacekeeping can only succeed when the parties to a conflict understand they cannot profit from war. We have too often asked our peacekeepers to work miracles while denying them the military and political support required, and the modern command-and-control systems they need to do their job as safely and effectively as possible. Today's UN must be ready to handle tomorrow's challenges. Those of us who most respect the UN must lead the charge of reform.

Not all the critics of today's United Nations are isolationists. Many are supporters who gladly would pay for the UN's essential work if they were convinced their money was being well-spent. But I pledge to all of you, as we work together to improve the United Nations, I will continue to work to see that the United States takes the lead in paying its fair share of our common load.

Meanwhile, we must all remember that the United Nations is a reflection of the world it represents. Therefore, it will remain far from perfect. It will not be able to solve all problems. But even those it cannot solve, it may well be able to limit in terms of the scope and reach of the problem, and it may well be able to limit the loss of human life until the time for solution comes.

So just as withdrawing from the world is impossible, turning our backs on the UN is no solution. It would be shortsighted and self-destructive. It would strengthen the forces of global disintegration. It would threaten the security, the interest and the values of the American people. So I say especially to the opponents of the United Nations here in the United States, turning our back on the UN and going it alone will lead to far more economic, political and military burdens on our people in the future and would ignore the lessons of our own history.

Instead, on this fiftieth anniversary of the charter signing, let us renew our vow to live together as good neighbors. And let us agree on a new United Nations agenda to increase confidence and ensure support for the United Nations, and to advance peace and prosperity for the next fifty years.

First and foremost, the UN must strengthen its efforts to isolate states and people who traffic in terror, and support those who continue to take risks for peace in the face of violence....

Where nations and groups honestly seek to reform, to change, to move away from the killing of innocents, we should support them. But when they are unrepentant in the delivery of death, we should stand tall against them. My friends, there is no easy way around the hard question: If nations and groups are not willing to move away from the delivery of death, we should put aside short-term profits for the people in our countries to stop, stop, stop their conduct.

Second, the UN must continue our efforts to stem the proliferation of weapons of mass destruction. There are some things nations can do on their own. The US and Russia today are destroying our nuclear arsenals rapidly. But the UN must also play a role. We were honored to help secure an indefinite extension of the Nuclear Non-Proliferation Treaty under UN auspices....

We rely on UN agencies to monitor nations bent on acquiring nuclear capabilities. We must work together on the Chemical Weapons Convention. We must strengthen our common efforts to fight biological weapons. We must do everything we can to limit the spread of fissile materials. We must work on conventional weapons like the land mines that are the curse of children the world over. And we must complete a comprehensive nuclear test ban treaty.

Third, we must support through the United Nations the fight against manmade and natural forces of disintegration, from crime syndicates and drug cartels, to new diseases and disappearing forests. These enemies are elusive; they cross borders at will. Nations can and must oppose them alone. But we know, and the Cairo Conference reaffirmed, that the most effective opposition requires strong international cooperation and mutual support.

Fourth, we must reaffirm our commitment to strengthen UN peacekeeping as an important tool for deterring, containing and ending violent conflict. The UN can never be an absolute guarantor of peace, but it can reduce human suffering and advance the odds of peace.

... Fifth, we must continue what is too often the least noticed of the UN's missions: its unmatched efforts on the front lines of the battle for child survival and against disease and human suffering.

And finally, let us vow to make the United Nations an increasing strong voice for the protection of fundamental human dignity and human rights. After all, they were at the core of the founding of this great organization....

5-5 The United Nations' Role in the New Global Era

Speech at the Fifty-second Session of the
United Nations General Assembly
New York, New York
September 22, 1997

... In the twenty-first century, our security will be challenged increasingly by interconnected groups that traffic in terror, organized crime, and drug smuggling. Already these international crime and drug syndicates drain up to $750 billion a year from legitimate economies. That sum exceeds the combined GNP of more than half the nations in this room. These groups threaten to undermine confidence in fragile new democracies and market economies that so many of you are working so hard to see endure.

Two years ago, I called upon all the members of this Assembly to join in the fight against these forces. I applaud the UN's recent resolution calling on its members to join the major international antiterrorism conventions, making clear the emerging international consensus that terrorism is always a crime and never a justifiable political act. As more countries sign on, terrorists will have fewer places to run or hide.

I also applaud the steps that members are taking to implement the declaration on crime and public security that the United States proposed two years ago, calling for increased cooperation to strengthen every citizen's right to basic safety, through cooperation on extradition and asset forfeiture, shutting down gray markets for guns and false documents, attacking corruption, and bringing higher standards to law enforcement in new democracies.

The spread of these global criminal syndicates also has made all the more urgent our common quest to eliminate weapons of mass destruction. We cannot allow them to fall or to remain in the wrong hands. Here, too, the United Nations must lead, and it has, from UNSCOM in Iraq to the International Atomic Energy Agency, now the most expansive global system ever devised to police arms control agreements.

When we met here last year, I was honored to be the first of 146 leaders to sign the comprehensive test ban treaty, our commitment to end all nuclear tests for all time, the longest sought, hardest fought prize in the history of arms control. It will help to prevent the nuclear powers from developing more advanced and more dangerous weapons. It will limit the possibilities for other states to acquire such devices. I am pleased to announce that today I am sending this crucial treaty to the United States Senate for ratification. Our common goal should be to enter the CTBT into force as soon as possible, and I ask for all of you to support that goal.

The United Nations' second core mission must be to defend and extend universal human rights and to help democracy's remarkable gains endure. Fifty years ago, the UN's Universal Declaration of Human Rights stated the international community's conviction that people everywhere have the right to be treated with dignity, to give voice to their opinions, to choose their leaders; that these rights are universal, not American rights, not Western rights, not rights for the developed world only but rights inherent in the humanity of people everywhere.

Over the past decade, these rights have become a reality for more people than ever from Asia to Africa, from Europe to the Americas. In a world that links rich and poor, North and South, city and countryside, in an electronic network of shared images in real time, the more these universal rights take hold, the more people who do not enjoy them will demand them.

Armed with photocopiers and fax machines, e-mail and the Internet, supported by an increasingly important community of nongovernmental organizations, they will make their demands known, spreading the spirit of freedom, which as the history of the last ten years has shown us, ultimately will prevail.

The United Nations must be prepared to respond not only by setting standards but by implementing them. To deter abuses, we should strengthen the UN's field operations and early warning systems. To strengthen democratic institutions, the best guarantors of human rights, we must pursue programs to help new legal, parliamentary, and electoral institutions get off the ground. To punish those responsible for crimes against humanity and to promote justice so that peace endures, we must maintain our strong support for the UN's war crime tribunals and truth commissions. And before the century ends, we should establish a permanent international court to prosecute the most serious violations of humanitarian law....

On every previous occasion I have addressed this Assembly, the issue of our country's dues has brought the commitment of the United States to the United Nations into question. The United States was a founder of the UN. We are proud to be its host. We believe in its ideals. We continue to be, as we have been, its largest contributor. We are committed to seeing the United Nations succeed in the twenty-first century.

This year, for the first time since I have been President, we have an opportunity to put the questions of debts and dues behind us once and for all and to put the United Nations on a sounder financial footing for the future. I have made it a priority to work with our Congress on comprehensive legislation that would allow us to pay off the bulk of our arrears and assure full financing of America's assessment in the years ahead. Our Congress' actions to solve this problem reflects a strong bipartisan commitment to the United Nations and to America's role within it.

At the same time, we look to member states to adopt a more equitable scale of assessment. Let me say that we also strongly support expanding the Security Council to give more countries a voice in the most important work of the UN. In more equitably sharing responsibility for its successes, we can make the UN stronger and more democratic than it is today. I ask the General Assembly to act on these proposals this year so that we can move forward together....

5-6 Human Rights in Contemporary Perspective

Remarks to the Opening Session of the Fifty-third
United Nations General Assembly
New York, New York
September 21, 1998

We celebrate the fiftieth anniversary of the Universal Declaration of Human Rights, with those rights more widely embraced than ever before. On every continent, people are leading lives of integrity and self-respect, and a great deal of credit for that belongs to the United Nations.

Still, as every person in this room knows, the promise of our time is attended by perils. Global economic turmoil today threatens to undermine confidence in free markets and democracy. Those of us who benefit particularly from this economy have a special responsibility to do more to minimize the turmoil and extend the benefits of global markets to all citizens. And the United States is determined to do that.

We still are bedeviled by ethnic, racial, religious, and tribal hatreds; by the spread of weapons of mass destruction; by the almost frantic effort of too many states to acquire such weapons. And despite all efforts to contain it, terrorism is not fading away with the end of the twentieth century. It is a continuing defiance of Article 3 of the Universal Declaration of Human Rights, which says, and I quote, "Everyone has the right to life, liberty, and security of person."

Here at the UN, at international summits around the world, and on many occasions in the United States, I have had the opportunity to address this subject in detail, to describe what we have done, what we are doing, and what we must yet do to combat terror. Today I would like to talk to you about why all nations must put the fight against terrorism at the top of our agenda....

First, terrorism has a new face in the 1990s. Today, terrorists take advantage of greater openness and the explosion of information and weapons technology. The new technologies of terror and their increasing availability, along with the increasing mobility of terrorists, raise chilling prospects of vulnerability to chemical, biological, and other kinds of attacks, bringing each of us into the category of possible victim. This is a threat to all humankind....

We must also acknowledge that there are economic sources of this rage as well. Poverty, inequality, masses of disenfranchised young people are fertile fields for the siren call of the terrorists and their claims of advancing social justice. But deprivation cannot justify destruction, nor can inequity ever atone for murder. The killing of innocents is not a social program.

Nevertheless, our resolute opposition to terrorism does not mean we can ever be indifferent to the conditions that foster it. The most recent UN human development report suggests the gulf is widening between the world's haves and have-nots. We must work harder to treat the sources of despair before they turn into the poison of hatred. Dr. Martin Luther King once wrote that the only revolutionary is a man who has nothing to lose. We must show people they have everything to gain by embracing cooperation and renouncing violence. This is not simply an American or a Western responsibility; it is the world's responsibility....

If terrorism is at the top of the American agenda—and should be at the top of the world's agenda—what, then, are the concrete steps we can take together to protect our common destiny? What are our common obligations? At least, I believe, they are these: to give terrorists no support, no sanctuary, no financial assistance; to bring pressure on states that do; to act together to step up extradition and prosecution; to sign the global anti-terror conventions; to strengthen the biological weapons and chemical conventions; to enforce the Chemical Weapons Convention; to promote stronger domestic laws and control the manufacture and export of explosives; to raise international standards for airport security; to combat the conditions that spread violence and despair....

But no matter how much each of us does alone, our progress will be limited without our common efforts. We also will do our part to address the sources of despair and alienation through the Agency for International Development in Africa, in Asia, in Latin America, in Eastern Europe, in Haiti, and elsewhere. We will continue our strong support for the UN development program, the UN High Commissioners for Human Rights and Refugees, UNICEF, the World Bank, the World Food Program. We also recognize the critical role these agencies play and the importance of all countries, including the United States, in paying their fair share.

In closing, let me urge all of us to think in new terms on terrorism, to see it not as a clash of cultures or political action by other means, or a divine calling, but a clash between the forces of the past and the forces of the future, between those who tear down and those who build up, between hope and fear, chaos and community....

6. Transitions and Nationalism in the Former Yugoslavia

The end of the Cold War eroded the basic international stability that had been the hallmark of the bipolar world dominated by the United States and the Soviet Union. Ethnic nationalism, which had long been suppressed by strong, centralized, imperial-minded ruling elites, became a palpably potent force for unruly, often violent change. Unscrupulous leaders manipulated ethno-nationalist sentiments, memories, and ambitions to acquire or keep power. Violence was seen as a necessary instrument to achieve political goals.

Although ethno-nationalist tensions had long been apparent, in the post-1990 period they greatly intensified. In the Middle East, Turkey and Iraq suppressed their rebellious Kurdish minorities; the Sudan's Muslim Arabs of the north waged a war of attrition against the Christian and animist Blacks of the south; and Israelis and Palestinians contended for territory. In Africa south of the Sahara, a genocidal struggle raged between the Hutus and the Tutsis of Rwanda and Burundi, and spilled over into the Congo; in post-apartheid South Africa there was a struggle for power, mainly between the Xhosa (who control the ruling African National Congress) and the Zulus; and in Ethiopia, the Eritrean minority was expelled. In South Asia, ethno-nationalist conflicts divided the Sinhalese and the Tamils in Sri Lanka, the Pathans and Tajiks in Afghanistan, the Sindis and Punjabis in Pakistan, and a dozen major ethnic groups in India. And in the former Soviet Union, Armenians fought Azeris, Russians fought Chechens, and much of Central Asia seemed on the brink of open conflict.

During the Cold War, when the Soviet Union was the unmistakable threat to US national interests, Washington maintained its distance from most ethno-nationalist conflicts, the exceptions being the Arab-Israeli and Palestinian-Israeli conflicts. In the post-Cold War period, the United States has also become deeply enmeshed in conflicts stemming from the splitting apart of the former Yugoslavia.

In the early 1990s, three federal states—Yugoslavia, the Soviet Union, and Czechoslovakia—fell victims to ethnic nationalism. In the former Soviet Union, the transition from communism to nationalism was remarkably peaceful: although Moscow lost 25 percent of its territory and almost 40 percent of its population, it allowed the secession of fourteen non-Russian union-republics to proceed without challenge. Lingering disputes abound, but they for the most part remain dormant. In the case of Czechoslovakia, the Czechs and the Slovaks divorced peacefully in 1993. In the former Yugoslavia ethnic nationalism has brought a decade of war and violence, with no real peace in prospect; Russia, too, is facing violent separatist rebellions in its Caucasus regions of Chechnya and Dagestan.

Yugoslavia disintegrated when four of its six constituent republics—Croatia, Slovenia, Macedonia, and Bosnia-Herzegovina—declared their independence; Serbia and Montenegro stayed united in a truncated country they continued to call "Yugoslavia"—the land of the South Slavs. When it was created at the end of World War I out of the ruins of the Austro-Hungarian Empire, the Yugoslav state epitomized the prevailing belief in liberal nationalism, which assumed that ethno-linguistic unity would make for political cohesion. But such a notion has been shown to be flawed—in Ireland, India, Lebanon, Iraq, and the former Soviet Union. In addition to a common language, also important for fostering national integration are a common religion, cultural affinity, a shared historical memory, and effective political leadership and institutions—none of which were present in the Yugoslav republic of Bosnia-Herzegovina (commonly referred to as Bosnia).

War broke out in Bosnia in the spring of 1992 and was waged with much cruelty. Ethnically, the approximately 3.6 million people of Bosnia are either Serbs or Croats. There is no Bosnian ethnic group or language. In 1945, in the communist state that Marshal (Josip Broz) Tito established on the territory of prewar Yugoslavia, he redrew the internal boundaries to weaken the influence of the Serbs, who made up about 50 percent of the country's population. By creating six constituent republics, he ensured that the Serbs would end up as minorities in republics other than Serbia. To advance this process of ethnic dispersion and equalization, Tito conferred ethnic status on the approximately 40 percent of Bosnia's population who identified their religion as Muslim. As long as Yugoslavia remained one country, this political manipulation to minimize Serb influence did no harm. That changed once the population of Bosnia was given the option of remaining part of Yugoslavia or becoming independent in a 1992 referendum. Then, most Bosnian Muslims joined with the Bosnian Croats, who are Roman Catholic and represented about 20 percent of the population, to outvote the Bosnian Serbs, a little over 30 percent of the population, who are Eastern Orthodox and who sought to remain part of Yugoslavia.

One need not delve any further back into history than to World War II to find the deeply imbedded and tangled roots of Serb-Croat-Muslim hostility. In 1941 and after, most Serbs resisted the German and Italian occupiers, while most Croats and Muslims supported the Nazis and under their patronage proceeded to kill hundreds of thousands of Serbs. The Serbs determined never again to live under Croat or Muslim rule. When the great powers, with Germany in the lead, extended recognition to the first two seceding republics, Slovenia and Croatia, thereby foreclosing the possibility of Yugoslavia's continuing as one country, they opened the Pandora's box of self-determination. Serbia's President Slobodan Milosevic, Croatia's President Franjo Tudjman, and Bosnia's President Alija Izetbegovic, became the flag-bearers of separatist nationalism and harsh dictatorship.

The US approach to Bosnia was criticized from the very beginning. The Bush administration was faulted for permitting Germany to set policy for NATO and meekly following suit, and for extending recognition to the separating republics, instead of using US influence and prestige to push for negotiation of a confederation, along the lines of Switzerland. In their defense, Bush officials maintained that the follow-the-West Europeans option made sense in 1991 – 1992, overwhelmed as the administration was by the problems posed by Iraq in the aftermath of the Gulf War and by managing the nuclear-political relationship with the Soviet Union and its successor, the Russian Federation.

The Clinton administration, too, has been criticized for slighting opportunities to shape a peaceful outcome. Early on, it brushed aside a peace plan for Bosnia crafted by former Secretary of State Cyrus Vance and former British Foreign Secretary David Owen. The key provisions called for the division of Bosnia into ten separate, ethnically homogenous (relatively speaking) cantons, with Sarajevo as the capital of the loose confederation; they drew on the Swiss model and on the de facto shifts caused by the ongoing fighting, which had already uprooted 500,000 people. Nor was the inexperienced Clinton White House willing to risk criticism by agreeing to a threefold partition of Bosnia into separate states—Serb, Croat, and Muslim. It insisted on adhering to the principle it had advocated during the election, namely, a multiethnic, multireligious democratic Bosnia. And, like his predecessor, Clinton was not willing to commit American ground troops to stop the fighting.

Clinton followed Bush's lead in supporting the United Nations Protection Force (UNPROFOR) that was established in March 1992 to operate in Croatia but then was given the added responsibility for facilitating the delivery of humanitarian assistance to Bosnia. In October 1992 the

United Nations added a "no-fly zone" over Bosnia, to safeguard the food deliveries, and in May 1993 it declared Sarajevo and five other Muslim enclaves "safe areas" under UN protection. The fighting continued, the refugee count mounted, and the savagery spread. Throughout 1993 and 1994, the Clinton administration, though deploring the violence and calling on the parties to join at the conference table, undertook no major initiatives.

However, by the spring of 1995, stung by criticism that his policy was confused and cowardly, and warned that a Serb victory might require the insertion of US troops to help extract UN forces, Clinton adopted measures, some of them covert, which had Congressional support. These included equipping and training Croatian forces, turning a blind eye to Iranian arms supplied to the Bosnian Muslims, and ordering the US Navy not to uphold the UN arms embargo on ships heading for Croatian ports. A dramatic shift in Clinton's policy came when aerial evidence and interviewing in the field showed that after the Bosnian Serbs had seized the UN-designated "safe area" of Srebenica in July 1995, they murdered upwards of 6,000 Muslim males of military age. In early August, Secretary of State Albright showed intelligence photos of the graves to the UN Security Council.

As so often happens, facts on the battlefield affect the dynamics of diplomacy. In mid-August, the US-equipped and trained Croatian army launched an offensive that retook the Krajina region of southwestern Croatia from the Croatian Serbs, who had set up an independent "mini-republic" there in 1992 with the aid of the Bosnian Serbs. Croatia's President Tudjman used the stunning military victory to expel some 250,000 Serbs. That is an "ethnic cleansing" that no one talks of reversing. In late August—early September 1995, US and NATO aircraft bombed Bosnian Serb strongholds and troop deployments. Simultaneously pushing for a political settlement, Washington dealt directly with Yugoslavia's President Milosevic, persuading him to use his influence with the Bosnian Serb leadership to agree to a settlement. The key elements of the plan were announced on September 5, serious negotiations started in early November, and on November 21 an exultant President Clinton announced that an agreement had been fashioned at Dayton (Ohio) to end the fighting in Bosnia. On November 27, he spoke to the nation of the results of Dayton Accords and what they meant for the United States (Speech 6-1). Bosnia would remain a single state with its present borders, as a federation composed of two "entities"—a Bosnian Federation of Muslims and Croats occupying 51 percent of the territory, and a Serb Republic holding 49 percent. Sarajevo, the capital, would remain undivided. To enforce the settlement, a NATO-dominated International Protection Force (IFOR) of

60,000 heavily armed troops, 20,000 of whom were American, took over responsibility for Bosnia from the lightly armed UN contingent of peace-keepers. To obtain Congress's support, President Clinton said that US troops would be deployed for only about eighteen months and that the estimated cost to the United States would not be more than $1 billion to $1.5 billion per year.

One year later, the fighting had ended, but Bosnia remained deeply divided in its Serb, Croat, and Muslim areas. Few refugees returned to villages controlled by another ethnic group, and economic conditions discouraged EU subsidies and foreign investment. On November 15, 1996, soon after his reelection, Clinton admitted that his earlier deadline for the withdrawal of US troops had been overly optimistic, and he asked Congress and the American people to be patient a bit longer (Speech 6-2).

After still another year, on December 18, 1997, the President admitted the obvious—that American troops would not be withdrawn in June 1998, as had been scheduled. Speaking with reporters afterward, he responded candidly to criticisms, acknowledging that American forces might be required in Bosnia for the indefinite future (Speech 6-3).

The high expectations for the Dayton accords have been steadily diminished, and American troops in Bosnia have no exit in prospect. The costs are double the original estimate of no more than $1.5 billion a year. In the Muslim-Croat part of Bosnia, which was supposed to set the standard, community-building, common institutions, and free movement of population are overshadowed by separateness and ethnic exclusivity. Sarajevo, a former symbol of a multiethnic, multireligious Bosnia, has become mainly Muslim. Elections have put hardline representatives of each ethnic group in control. And few refugees have been able to return to their homes, notwithstanding the goal of permitting people to move freely throughout Bosnia. If it turns out to be the case in Bosnia that ethnic separatism is the price of a stable settlement, how much more likely is it to be true of Kosovo?

In the struggle to empower the Serbs of Bosnia to unite with Yugoslavia, Milosevic exploited Serb nationalism and long sense of victimization. Memories of Bosnian Croats and Muslims willingly joining with Nazi Germany and Fascist Italy to kill more than 1 million Serbs during World War II were catalysts for popular support for "ethnic cleansing." But the aim of a "Greater Serbia" was stymied by US and West European opposition.

As the uneasy status quo imposed by NATO settled over Bosnia in late 1995, Yugoslavia (now reduced to Serbia and the small Serb-populated republic of Montenegro) looked to settle its problems in the province of Kosovo. Kosovo is deeply imbedded in the historical memory and psychology of the Serbs. After 1389, when the Kingdom of Serbia fell to the expanding Ottoman Empire, Kosovo's population became increasingly Albanian and Muslim in character, even as the specific boundary of the area was altered over time. After the Balkan Wars of 1912 – 1913 and World War I (1914 – 1918), Serbia regained possession of Kosovo; in 1919, a new country was established, initially known as the Kingdom of the Serbs, Croats, and Slovenes: in 1929, renamed Yugoslavia.

A circular region about sixty miles in diameter, bordering Albania, Macedonia, Montenegro, and the rest of Serbia, Kosovo was becoming a serious problem for Yugoslavia in the decades after World War II as a consequence of a demographic shift, the Albanian birth rate being the highest in Europe. In recognition of the Muslim Albanians' growing majority in the province, in 1974 Yugoslav President Tito accorded it the status of an autonomous province. However, in 1987, seven years after Tito's death, Slobodan Milosevic, a rising Serb politician, became a hero to all nationalist-minded Serbs when he visited the historic battlefield of Kosovo Polje (Field) and told the Serbs, "you need not be afraid any longer. No one will beat you again." Two years later, on the occasion of the 600th anniversary of the Serb defeat at the hands of the Ottoman Turks in the Battle of Kosovo, he returned as President of the Yugoslav Republic of Serbia and gave a rousing speech to a gathering of almost a million Serbs at a rally in Kosovo Field. By this time, Serbs were less than 10 percent of the population in the province and in the process of being systematically pushed out by the Albanians. Soon afterward, Milosevic ended Kosovo's autonomy and instituted a harsh crackdown on the Albanian population there.

Overnight, Milosevic's brand of populist, anti-Albanian, anti-Muslim nationalism took hold and quickly brought him almost total power. Terminating Kosovo's autonomy, he placed all political, military, and legal institutions in the hands of Serbs, and squeezed the Albanians out of political life. The Albanians of Kosovo, now referred to as "Kosovars," developed parallel institutions, including an underground parliament and constitution, and on July 2, 1990, declared their independence. These claims, asserted relatively peacefully under the leadership of Ibrahim Rugova, were just ignored. In December 1992, President Bush warned Milosevic against resorting to violence in Kosovo, a sentiment echoed by President Clinton early in his administration.

As long as Bosnia was an active military theatre, Milosevic kept a low profile in Kosovo. Indeed, in 1996, shortly after Dayton had seemingly settled the Bosnian crisis, Milosevic and Rugova signed an agreement designed to bring Albanian students back into the classroom in government-run school buildings; and in Belgrade, the press speculated on a solution based on partition of the province, as suggested by, among others, Dr. Alexander Despic, President of the influential Serbian Academy of Arts and Sciences. Despic argued that unless the Serbs untangled the demographic and political knot in Kosovo, in less than two generations the Muslim Albanians would outnumber the Serbs in Serbia. But martial law took its toll in Kosovo, politicizing the population, weakening Rugova's position, and hardening Milosevic's reliance on force.

A political crisis in neighboring Albania in early 1997 resulted in the overthrow of its government, emptying of the prisons, and looting of the weapons depots. New recruits and modern weapons poured into Kosovo, greatly strengthening the Kosovo Liberation Army (KLA), a group that had started an armed insurgency against the Serbs in the early 1990s and rejected Rugova's nonviolent approach. As recently as 1997, the US State Department labeled the KLA a terrorist organization with ties to organized crime and drug trafficking. But deteriorating conditions—Serbia's expulsion of thousands of Albanians, intensifying clashes between Serbs and Albanians, villages burned, human rights violated on a massive scale, and starvation looming—led Washington to a more benign view of the KLA. The spillover of fleeing Kosovars into Macedonia and Albania further inflamed ethnic tensions and threatened to destabilize the region even more.

In October 1998, the United States helped negotiate a ceasefire in Kosovo. Within weeks, however, the KLA exploited the US-brokered arrangement, moving into areas from which Serb forces had withdrawn as part of their compliance. In December, the murder of Serb policemen triggered a new round of escalating violence.

Differences beset the NATO alliance. France wanted any military action against Serbia to bear a United Nations Security Council imprimatur; but the United States objected, arguing that NATO should be prepared to act independently of the UN, especially since Washington worried that Russia would use its veto to frustrate any crackdown on Serbia, a fellow Slavic country. In a low-key Saturday morning radio talk, the President, on December 13, 1998, tested the political waters, announcing that he was prepared to send 4,000 troops to Kosovo as part of a NATO peacekeeping force, if necessary (Speech 6-4). The media reported that his announcement was timed to strengthen Secretary of State Albright's position in the peace negotiations underway in Rambouillet, outside of Paris. On January 30, 1999, deeply concerned by the rising tide of refugees and Milosevic's obduracy, NATO members authorized air strikes against Serbian military targets, if Belgrade did not restore autonomy to Kosovo. On March 19, 1999, at his first press conference in nine months, Clinton spoke about Kosovo and alerted public opinion to what might happen.

On March 24, 1999, no doubt to Milosevic's surprise, Clinton unleashed NATO's air power (mostly American planes); in a statement to the
nation, he spoke of the historical, moral, and diplomatic considerations
that guided his decision (Speech 6-5). As NATO's war went on day after
day, week after week, month after month in the face of stubborn Serbian
resistance, no doubt to Clinton's surprise, the stated aim of protecting the
Kosovars took second place to the aim of destroying Serbia's military and
civilian infrastructure and capability.

On May 7, 1999, President Clinton said he thought that the solution
worked out for Bosnia would be applicable to Kosovo, but in blurring the
differences between "peace" and "no-war," Clinton was underestimating
the consequences of unforeseen developments. Indeed, on that very day,
NATO planes mistakenly bombed the Chinese Embassy in Belgrade,
evoking sharp criticisms from Beijing of America's hegemonistic ambitions, all-too-free recourse to military means to get its way, and failure to
bring the matter first to the UN Security Council. America went to war to
forestall a humanitarian catastrophe, but NATO's bombing may have
brought about the very thing it sought to prevent. Clinton's March 24
speech has been debated in regard to the accuracy of its rendition of history and its alleged "lessons for the future," and he has been criticized for
waging a war without Congress's approval.

On June 10, 1999, President Clinton reported to the nation that "the
Serb army and police are withdrawing from Kosovo ... we have achieved a
victory for a safer world, for our democratic values and for a stronger
America" (Speech 6-6). He went on to explain "why we fought, what we
achieved, and what we have to do now to advance the peace...."

Critics remained unconvinced. They continue to believe that the war
was avoidable. They contend that the United States could have fashioned a
political settlement by working through the UN Security Council in
March, as it was, in the final analysis, required to do in June, in order to
obtain the diplomatic legitimation to accompany its triumph on the battlefield; that a willingness to accept Serbian sovereignty over Kosovo at
Rambouillet in March, as the United Nations did in June, might have led
Milosevic to grant the Kosovars official autonomy; and that Clinton's recourse to NATO and a unilateralist policy was reinforced by his belief in
the US role as "the indispensable nation," which demonstrated just how
far he had departed from his early commitment to multilateralism and constructive engagement.

The final outcome of the Kosovo crisis, like that of the Bosnian crisis, will take time to become clear. Western leaders will have to put the
Balkans back together and repair relationships with Russia and China. Rebuilding what has been destroyed may prove more difficult than defeating

Slobodan Milovevic's Serbia. The nineteenth-century Prussian military strategist Karl von Clausewitz warned of the need always to take account of the unpredictable that occurs in "the fog of war," and to remember that "war can never be separated from political intercourse, and if, in the consideration of the matter, this occurs anywhere, all the threads of the different relations are in a certain sense broken, and we have before us a senseless thing without an object."

6-1 The Dayton Accords: Imposing Peace for Bosnia

The White House
November 27, 1995

... Last week, the warring factions in Bosnia reached a peace agreement, as a result of our efforts in Dayton, Ohio, and the support of our European and Russian partners. Tonight, I want to speak with you about implementing the Bosnian peace agreement, and why our values and interests as Americans require that we participate.

Let me say at the outset, America's role will not be about fighting a war. It will be about helping the people of Bosnia to secure their own peace agreement. Our mission will be limited, focused, and under the command of an American general.

In fulfilling this mission, we will have the chance to help stop the killing of innocent civilians, especially children, and at the same time, to bring stability to Central Europe, a region of the world that is vital to our national interests. It is the right thing to do....

As the Cold War gives way to the global village, our leadership is needed more than ever because problems that start beyond our borders can quickly become problems within them. We're all vulnerable to the organized forces of intolerance and destruction; terrorism; ethnic, religious and regional rivalries; the spread of organized crime and weapons of mass destruction and drug trafficking. Just as surely as fascism and communism, these forces also threaten freedom and democracy, peace and prosperity. And they, too, demand American leadership.

But nowhere has the argument for our leadership been more clearly justified than in the struggle to stop or prevent war and civil violence. From Iraq to Haiti, from South Africa to Korea, from the Middle East to Northern Ireland, we have stood up for peace and freedom because it's in our interest to do so and because it is the right thing to do.

Now, that doesn't mean we can solve every problem. My duty as President is to match the demands for American leadership to our strategic interest and to our ability to make a difference. America cannot and must not be the world's policeman. We cannot stop all war for all time, but we can stop some wars. We cannot save all women and all children, but we can save many of them. We can't do everything, but we must do what we can.

There are times and places where our leadership can mean the difference between peace and war, and where we can defend our fundamental values as a people and serve our most basic, strategic interests. My fellow Americans, in this new era there are still times when America and America alone can and should make the difference for peace.

The terrible war in Bosnia is such a case. Nowhere today is the need for American leadership more stark or more immediate than in Bosnia. For nearly four years a terrible war has torn Bosnia apart. Horrors we prayed had been banished from Europe forever have been seared into our minds again: skeletal prisoners caged behind barbed-wire fences; women and girls raped as a tool of war; defenseless men and boys shot down into mass graves, evoking visions of World War II concentration camps; and endless lines of refugees marching toward a future of despair.

When I took office, some were urging immediate intervention in the conflict. I decided that American ground troops should not fight a war in Bosnia because the United States could not force peace on Bosnia's warring ethnic groups, the Serbs, Croats, and Muslims. Instead, America has worked with our European allies in searching for peace, stopping the war from spreading, and easing the suffering of the Bosnian people.

We imposed tough economic sanctions on Serbia. We used our air power to conduct the longest humanitarian airlift in history and to enforce a no-fly zone that took the war out of the skies. We helped to make peace between two of the three warring parties, the Muslims and the Croats. But as the months of war turned into years, it became clear that Europe alone could not end the conflict.

This summer, Bosnian Serb shelling once again turned Bosnia's playgrounds and marketplaces into killing fields. In response, the United States led NATO's heavy and continuous air strikes, many of them flown by skilled and brave American pilots. Those air strikes, together with the renewed determination of our European partners and the Bosnian and Croat gains on the battlefield convinced the Serbs, finally, to start thinking about making peace.

At the same time, the United States initiated an intensive diplomatic effort that forged a Bosnia-wide cease-fire and got the parties to agree to the basic principles of peace....

Finally, just three weeks ago, the Muslims, Croats, and Serbs came to Dayton, Ohio, in America's heartland, to negotiate a settlement. There, exhausted by war, they made a commitment to peace. They agreed to put down their guns, to preserve Bosnia as a single state, to investigate and prosecute war criminals, to protect the human rights of all citizens, to try to build a peaceful, democratic future. And they asked for America's help as they implement this peace agreement.

America has a responsibility to answer that request, to help to turn this moment of hope into an enduring reality. To do that, troops from our country and around the world would go into Bosnia to give them the confidence and support they need to implement their peace plan. I refuse to send American troops to fight a war in Bosnia, but I believe we must help to secure the Bosnian peace.

I want you to know tonight what is at stake, exactly what our troops will be asked to accomplish, and why we must carry out our responsibility to help implement the peace agreement. Implementing the agreement in Bosnia can end the terrible suffering of the people, the warfare, the mass executions, the ethnic cleansing, the campaigns of rape and terror. Let us never forget a quarter of a million men, women, and children have been shelled, shot, and tortured to death. Two million people, half of the population, were forced from their homes and into a miserable life as refugees. And these faceless numbers hide millions of real personal tragedies. For each of the war's victims was a mother or daughter, a father or son, a brother or sister.

Now the war is over. American leadership created the chance to build a peace and stop the suffering. Securing peace in Bosnia will also help to build a free and stable Europe. Bosnia lies at the very heart of Europe, next-door to many of its fragile new democracies and some of our closest allies. Generations of Americans have understood that Europe's freedom and Europe's stability is vital to our own national security. That's why we fought two wars in Europe. That's why we launched the Marshall Plan to restore Europe. That's why we created NATO and waged the Cold War. And that's why we must help the nations of Europe to end their worst nightmare since World War II, now.

The only force capable of getting this job done is NATO, the powerful, military alliance of democracies that has guaranteed our security for half a century now. And as NATO's leader and the primary broker of the peace agreement, the United States must be an essential part of the mission. If we're not there, NATO will not be there; the peace will collapse; the war will reignite; the slaughter of innocents will begin again. A conflict that already has claimed so many victims could spread like poison throughout the region, eat away at Europe's stability, and erode our partnership with our European allies.

And America's commitment to leadership will be questioned if we refuse to participate in implementing a peace agreement we brokered right here in the United States, especially since the Presidents of Bosnia, Croatia, and Serbia all asked us to participate and all pledged their best efforts to the security of our troops.

When America's partnerships are weak and our leadership is in doubt, it undermines our ability to secure our interests and to convince others to work with us. If we do maintain our partnerships and our leadership, we need not act alone. As we saw in the Gulf War and in Haiti, many other nations who share our goals will also share our burdens. But when America does not lead, the consequences can be very grave, not only for others but eventually for us as well.

As I speak to you, NATO is completing its planning for IFOR, an international force for peace in Bosnia of about 60,000 troops. Already, more than twenty-five other nations, including our major NATO allies, have pledged to take part. They will contribute about two-thirds of the total implementation force, some 40,000 troops. The United States would contribute the rest, about 20,000 soldiers.

Later this week, the final NATO plan will be submitted to me for review and approval. Let me make clear what I expect it to include, and what it must include, for me to give final approval to the participation of our Armed Forces.

First, the mission will be precisely defined with clear, realistic goals that can be achieved in a definite period of time. Our troops will make sure that each side withdraws its forces behind the frontlines and keeps them there. They will maintain the cease-fire to prevent the war from accidentally starting again. These efforts, in turn, will help to create a secure environment, so that the people of Bosnia can return to their homes, vote in free elections, and begin to rebuild their lives.

Our Joint Chiefs of Staff have concluded that this mission should and will take about one year.

Second, the risks to our troops will be minimized. American troops will take their orders from the American general who commands NATO. They will be heavily armed and thoroughly trained. By making an overwhelming show of force, they will lessen the need to use force. But unlike the UN forces, they will have the authority to respond immediately, and the training and the equipment to respond with overwhelming force to any threat to their own safety or any violations of the military provisions of the peace agreement.

If the NATO plan meets with my approval I will immediately send it to Congress and request its support. I will also authorize the participation of a small number of American troops in a NATO advance mission that will lay the groundwork for IFOR, starting sometime next week. They will establish headquarters and set up the sophisticated communication systems that must be in place before NATO can send in its troops, tanks, and trucks to Bosnia.

The implementation force itself would begin deploying in Bosnia in the days following the formal signature of the peace agreement in mid-December. The international community will help to implement arms control provisions of the agreement so that future hostilities are less likely and armaments are limited, while the world community, the United States and others, will also make sure that the Bosnian Federation has the means to defend itself once IFOR withdraws. IFOR will not be a part of this effort. Civilian agencies from around the world will begin a separate program of humanitarian relief and reconstruction, principally paid for by our European allies and other interested countries. This effort is also absolutely essential to making the peace endure. It will bring the people of Bosnia the food, shelter, clothing, and medicine so many have been denied for so long. It will help them to rebuild—to rebuild their roads and schools, their power plants and hospitals, their factories and shops. It will reunite children with their parents and families with their homes. It will allow the Bosnians freely to choose their own leaders. It will give all the people of Bosnia a much greater stake in peace than war, so that peace takes on a life and a logic of its own.

In Bosnia we can and will succeed because our mission is clear and limited, and our troops are strong and very well-prepared. But my fellow Americans, no deployment of American troops is risk-free, and this one may well involve casualties. There may be accidents in the field or incidents with people who have not given up their hatred. I will take every measure possible to minimize these risks, but we must be prepared for that possibility.

As President my most difficult duty is to put the men and women who volunteer to serve our Nation in harm's way when our interests and values demand it. I assume full responsibility for any harm that may come to them. But anyone contemplating any action that would endanger our troops should know this: America protects its own. Anyone—anyone who takes on our troops will suffer the consequences. We will fight fire with fire and then some.

After so much bloodshed and loss, after so many outrageous acts of inhuman brutality, it will take an extraordinary effort of will for the people of Bosnia to pull themselves from their past and start building a future of peace. But with our leadership and the commitment of our allies, the people of Bosnia can have the chance to decide their future in peace. They have a chance to remind the world that just a few short years ago the mosques and churches of Sarajevo were a shining symbol of multiethnic tolerance, that Bosnia once found unity in its diversity. Indeed, the cemetery in the center of the city was just a few short years ago a magnificent stadium which hosted the Olympics, our universal symbol of peace and harmony. Bosnia can be that kind of place again. We must not turn our backs on Bosnia now.

And so I ask all Americans, and I ask every Member of Congress, Democrat and Republican alike, to make the choice for peace. In the choice between peace and war, America must choose peace.

My fellow Americans, I ask you to think just for a moment about this century that is drawing to close and the new one that will soon begin. Because previous generations of Americans stood up for freedom and because we continue to do so, the American people are more secure and more prosperous. And all around the world, more people than ever before live in freedom. More people than ever before are treated with dignity. More people than ever before can hope to build a better life. That is what America's leadership is all about.

We know that these are the blessings of freedom. And America has always been freedom's greatest champion. If we continue to do everything we can to share these blessings with people around the world, if we continue to be leaders for peace, then the next century can be the greatest time our Nation has ever known.

A few weeks ago, I was privileged to spend some time with His Holiness, Pope John Paul II, when he came to America. At the very end of our meeting, the Pope looked at me and said, "I have lived through most of this century. I remember that it began with a war in Sarajevo. Mr. President, you must not let it end with a war in Sarajevo." In Bosnia, this terrible war has challenged our interests and troubled our souls. Thankfully, we can do something about it. I say again, our mission will be clear, limited, and achievable....

6-2 Reconstructing Bosnia: A Longer Term Process

The White House
November 15, 1996

... One year ago in Dayton, the leaders of Bosnia, Croatia, and Serbia turned from the horror of war to the promise of peace. Their historic decision came after nearly four years of horrible bloodshed, the bloodiest conflict Europe has seen since World War II, after a quarter million deaths, after 2 million people were made refugees, after countless atrocities that shocked the conscience of the world.

When the Balkan leaders chose peace, I asked the American people to help them by supporting the participation of our troops in a NATO-led implementation force to secure the Dayton Agreement. I promised that the mission would be carefully defined with clear and realistic goals. I said it would be completed in about a year.

IFOR has succeeded beyond our expectations. As a result, its mission will end as planned on December 20, and every single item on IFOR's military checklist has been accomplished. It has maintained the cease-fire and separated the parties along a new demilitarized zone. It has monitored the placement of thousands of heavy weapons in holding areas, overseen a massive troop demobilization and the transfer of hundreds of square miles of territory from one side to another, and allowed the people of Bosnia to vote in free national elections.

That has been a remarkable achievement. In the process we have seen how important and effective the NATO Alliance remains. And we have seen the possibilities for cooperation with Russia and the other members of the Partnership For Peace. Today, the Bosnian people are far better off than they were a year ago; their prospects for a future of peace and freedom are much brighter.

Already, the change in the day-to-day lives of the people there is dramatic: marketplaces are full of life, not death; more people have roofs over their head, food on their tables, heat and hot water. The routines of normal life—going to work, coming home from school—are slowly becoming a reality. Bosnia's bitter harvest of hatred, however, has not yet disappeared. For the last twelve months, the killing has stopped, and with time, the habits of peace can take hold. This success we owe to IFOR. But its achievements on the military side have not been matched, despite all our efforts, by similar progress on the civilian side. Quite frankly, rebuilding the fabric of Bosnia's economic and political life is taking longer than anticipated.

Economic activity is only just resuming. Its pace must be quickened and its reach extended. The Presidency, the Parliament, the constitutional court, created by the elections, are still in their infancy. They need time to work. Civilian police forces must be better trained. We must complete training and equipping the Bosnian Federation military so that a stable balance of power can take hold and renewed aggression is less likely. And municipal elections remain to be organized and held. Let me emphasize that the Bosnian people, with the help of international civilian groups, will be responsible for all this work. But for a time, they will need the stability and the confidence that only an outside security force can provide.

NATO has been studying options to give them the help that time will provide by providing a new security presence in Bosnia when IFOR withdraws. That study is now complete. I have carefully reviewed its options, and I have decided to instruct the United States representative to NATO to inform our allies that, in principle, the United States will take part in a follow-on force in Bosnia.

For my agreement in principle to become a commitment, however, I must be satisfied that the final recommendation NATO adopts and the operational plan it develops are clear, limited, and achievable. The new mission's focus should be to prevent a resumption of hostilities so that economic reconstruction and political reconciliation can accelerate. That will require a strong but limited military presence in Bosnia, able to respond quickly and decisively to any violations of the cease-fire.

The new mission will be more limited than IFOR and will require fewer troops. It will not face the fundamental military challenge of separating two hostile armies, because IFOR has accomplished that task. It will be charged with working to maintain the stability that IFOR created. It will discourage the parties from taking up arms again, while encouraging them to resume full responsibility for their own security as quickly as possible.

IFOR plowed the field in which the seeds of peace have been planted. This new mission will provide the climate for them to take root and the time to begin growing.

Our military planners have concluded that this new mission will require fewer than half the number of troops we contributed to IFOR, about 8,500. There will be an American commander and tough rules of engagement. Every six months we will review whether the stability can be maintained with fewer forces. By the end of 1997, we expect to draw down to a much smaller deterrent force, about half the initial size, and we will propose to our NATO Allies that by June of 1998 the mission's work should be done, and the forces should be able to withdraw.

The United States cannot and should not try to solve every problem in the world, but where our interests are clear and our values are at stake, where we can make a difference, we must act, and we must lead. Clearly, Bosnia is such an example. Every American should be proud of the difference the United States has already made in Bosnia, ending a terrible slaughter, saving thousands of lives, securing countless futures. We have a responsibility to see that commitment through, to give the peace America helped to make in Bosnia a chance to grow strong, self-sufficient, and lasting....

6-3 The Case for the Long Haul in Bosnia

The White House
December 18, 1997

I want to speak with you today about the progress we have made toward a lasting peace in Bosnia and the challenges that still must be faced in order to finish the job.

For nearly four years, Bosnia was the battleground for the bloodiest war in Europe since World War II. The conflict killed or wounded one out of every ten Bosnians. It drove half the country's people from their homes, left nine out of ten of them unemployed....

We helped Bosnians to put in place national democratic institutions, including a Presidency, a Parliament, a Supreme Court, and hold peaceful and free elections for all levels of government, with turnouts exceeding 70 percent. We've begun to restore normal life, repairing roads and schools, electricity and water, heat and sewage, doubling economic output, quadrupling wages. Unemployment in the Bosnian-Croat Federation has been cut from 90 percent to 50 percent.

We're helping the Bosnians to provide for their own security, training ethnically integrated police forces in the Federation, taking the first steps toward a professional democratic police force in the Serb Republic. We've helped to turn the media from an instrument of war into a force for peace, stifling the inflammatory radio and television broadcasts that helped to fuel the conflict. And we've provided a secure environment for 350,000 displaced persons to return to their homes, while bringing 22 war criminals to justice. Just a few hours ago, SFOR captured and transported to The Hague two more war crimes suspects.

The progress is unmistakable, but it is not yet irreversible. Bosnia has been at peace only half as long as it was at war. It remains poised on a tightrope, moving toward a better future but not at the point yet of a self-sustaining peace. To get there, the people of Bosnia still need a safety net and a helping hand that only the international community, including the United States, can provide.

Our assistance must be twofold. First we must intensify our civilian and economic engagement. As a result of the progress we've achieved in recent months, we know where to focus our efforts. Civilian and voluntary agencies working with Bosnian authorities must help to do the following things: first, deepen and spread economic opportunity while rooting out corruption; second, reform, retrain, and re-equip the police; third, restructure of the state-run media to meet international standards of objectivity and access and establish alternative independent media; fourth, help more refugees return home; and fifth, make indicted war criminals answer for their crimes, both as a matter of justice and because they are stumbling blocks to lasting stability.

The second thing we must do is to continue to provide an international military presence that will enable these efforts to proceed in an atmosphere of confidence. Our progress in Bosnia to date would not have been possible without the secure environment created first by IFOR, now by SFOR. They've allowed dozens of civilian agencies and literally hundreds of voluntary agencies to do their job in security, laying the foundation for a self-sustaining peace.

In authorizing American troops to take part in the SFOR mission, I said the mission would end in eighteen months, in June of 1998. It was my expectation that by that time we would have rebuilt enough of Bosnia's economic and political life to continue the work without continuing outside military support. But following intensive consultations with my national security and military advisers, with our NATO allies, and with leaders from both parties in Congress, it has become clear that the progress we've seen in Bosnia, in order for it to continue, a follow-on military force led by NATO will be necessary after SFOR ends. America is a leader of NATO, and America should participate in that force.

Therefore, I have instructed our representatives in NATO to inform our allies that, in principle, the United States will take part in a security presence in Bosnia when SFOR withdraws this summer. The agreement in principle will become a commitment only when I have approved the action plan NATO's military authorities will develop and present early next year after careful study of all the options. The details of that plan, including the mission's specific objectives, its size, and its duration, must be agreed to by all NATO allies.

Without prejudging the details, let me make clear the key criteria the plan must meet for me to approve United States participation: First, the mission must be achievable and tied to concrete benchmarks, not a deadline. We should have clear objectives that when set—when met will create a self-sustaining, secure environment and allow us to remove our troops.

Second, the force must be able to protect itself. Over two years we have steadily decreased the number of our troops in Bosnia from about 27,000 Americans in IFOR in 1996 to 8,500 in SFOR today. I hope the follow-on force will be smaller, but I will insist it be sufficient in number and in equipment to achieve its mission and to protect itself in safety.

Third, the United States must retain command. Time and again, events have proven that American leadership is crucial to decisive collective action.

Fourth, our European allies must assume their share of responsibility. Now Europe and our other partners are already doing a great deal, providing three times as many troops as we are, five times as much economic assistance, nine times as many international police, ten times as many refugees have been received by them. And while Bosnia is a challenge to American interests and values, the longer term and fundamental challenge is to make Bosnia a genuine part of Europe, and we hope the Europeans will do more.

Fifth, the cost must be manageable.

And sixth and finally, the plan must have substantial support from Congress and the American people. I have been pleased by the spirit and the substance of our consultations with leading members of both parties. As we develop the details of the new NATO mission, these consultations must and will continue....

Now, some say a lasting peace in Bosnia is impossible and, therefore, we should end our efforts now, in June, and/or allow the country to be partitioned along ethnic lines. I believe they're profoundly wrong. A full and fair reading of Bosnia's history and an honest assessment of the progress of the last twenty-three months simply refutes the proposition that the Dayton peace agreement cannot work. But if we pull out before the job is done, Bosnia almost certainly will fall back into violence, chaos, and, ultimately, a war every bit as bloody as the one that was stopped.

And partition is not a good alternative. It would sanction the horrors of ethnic cleansing and send the wrong signal to extremists everywhere. At best, partition would require a peacekeeping force to patrol a volatile border for years to come. More likely it would set the stage also for renewed conflict.

A lasting peace is possible, along the lines of the Dayton peace agreement. For decades, Muslim Croats and Serbs lived together, worked together, raised their families together. Thanks to the investments of America and others in Bosnia over the past two years, they have begun again to lead more normal lives.

Ultimately, Bosnia's future is in the hands of its own people. But we can help them make it a future of peace. We should finish the job we began for the sake of that future and in the service of our own interests and values....

Questions and Answers

Q. Mr. President, a number of Americans are understandably going to be concerned about an open-ended US military commitment to Bosnia. Can you at least assure the American people that by the time you leave office, a little more than three years from now, those American troops will be out of Bosnia?

A. ... [W]e don't believe the peace is self-sustaining. I think the responsible thing for me to do, since I do not believe we can meet the eighteen-month deadline, and no one I know now believes that, is to say to the American people what the benchmarks are.

What are the benchmarks? Let's talk about that. Can they be achieved in the near-term? I believe they can. Do I think we should have a permanent presence in Bosnia? No. I don't believe this is like Germany after World War II or in the Cold War or Korea after the Korean War. This is not what I'm suggesting here....

... But I will say again, I understand your job is try to get a deadline nailed down, but we tried it in this SFOR period, and it turned out we were wrong. I am not suggesting a permanent presence in Bosnia. I am suggesting that it's a more honest thing to do to say what our objectives are and that these objectives should be pursued, and they can be pursued at an affordable cost with fair burden-sharing with the Europeans. If that can be done, we should pursue them....

Q. Mr. President, sir, one of the benchmarks you listed was the willingness of the political parties there really to work toward progress. Does that not make us hostages of those political figures there, particularly those who don't want progress? They can simply undermine the attempt to reach that benchmark and keep US troops there forever.

A. Well, let me—I don't think I was clear about that. What I mean is the willingness of the political parties—or whether they're willing or not, our capacity to stop them from, in effect, perverting the state-run media and using them as an instrument of violence and suppression. I don't think it's necessary for us to stay until everybody wants to go have tea together at four o'clock in the afternoon in a civil environment. I think it's—I do think that there are—and again let me say, we will make public a final set of benchmarks before we go forward with this, and our allies have to work on this. I'm just telling you what my thoughts are....

Q. Just to wrap up this by asking you the question that a lot of Republican critics of yours are suggesting that your credibility was undermined on Bosnia by imposing these two deadlines which you failed to meet, and knowing that some of your own advisers at the time were saying, "Don't give these deadlines because they're unrealistic; the job can't be done within a year or within eighteen months....

A. Well, first of all, let me say, I have a fundamentally different view of the first deadline. I mean, we did—the mission I defined for IFOR was achieved, and it was achieved before a year was out. And I was—it's not worth going through and rewriting history there about who said what at the time. I did think that in eighteen months—I honestly believed in 18 months we could get this done at the time I said it. And it wasn't—I wasn't right, which is why I don't want to make that error again.

Now, having acknowledged the error I made, let's look at what we were right about. Let's flip this around before we get too much into who was right about what happened after eighteen months.

What has happened? With the leadership of the United States, NATO and its allies, including Russia, working side by side, ended almost overnight and with virtually no bloodshed the worst war in Europe since World War II. We have seen democratic elections with 70 percent participation take place; hundreds of thousands of people have been able to go home under circumstances that were difficult, to say the least; economic growth has resumed; infrastructure has been rebuilt; the conditions of normal life have come back for tens of thousands, hundreds of thousands of people.

So if I take the hit for being wrong about the timetable, I would like some acknowledgement that in the larger issue here, the United States and its allies were right to undertake this mission and that the results of the mission have been very, very good. They have justified the effort. And the cost of the mission in lives and treasure to the United States and to its allies has been much lower than even the most ardent supporters of the mission thought that it would be.

So I think—I don't mind taking a hit for being wrong about the timetable. But after the hit is dished out, I would like the larger truth looked at. That is, did we do the right thing? Was it in our interests? Did it further our values? Are the American people less likely to be drawn into some other conflict in Europe ten, twenty, thirty years from now where the costs could be far greater if we make this work? I think they are....

6-4 Why Kosovo Matters

The White House
December 13, 1998

This week, the warring parties in Kosovo have been meeting at a fourteenth century castle in France in search of a twenty-first century peace. They've come together because of the determination of the United States, our European allies and Russia to help end Kosovo's bloodshed and build a peaceful future there.

Today I want to speak to you about why peace in Kosovo is important to America. World War II taught us that America could never be secure if Europe's future was in doubt. We and our allies formed NATO after the war, and together we deterred aggression, secured Europe, and eventually made possible the victory of freedom all across the European continent.

In this decade, violent ethnic conflicts in the former Yugoslavia have threatened Europe's stability and future. For four years, Bosnia was the site of Europe's bloodiest war in half a century. With American leadership and that of our allies, we worked to end the war and moved the Bosnian people toward reconciliation and democracy. Now, as the peace takes hold, we've been steadily bringing our troops home.

But Bosnia taught us a lesson. In this volatile region, violence we fail to oppose leads to even greater violence we will have to oppose later, at a greater cost. We must heed that lesson in Kosovo. In 1989, Serbia stripped away Kosovo's autonomy. A year ago, Serbian forces launched a brutal crackdown against Kosovo's ethnic Albanians. Fighting and atrocities intensified, and hundreds of thousands of people were driven from their homes.

Last fall, using diplomacy backed by the threat of NATO force, we averted a humanitarian crisis and slowed the fighting. But now it's clear that only a strong peace agreement can end it. America has a national interest in achieving this peace. If the conflict persists, there likely will be a tremendous loss of life and a massive refugee crisis in the middle of Europe.

There is a serious risk the hostilities would spread to the neighboring new democracies of Albina and Macedonia and re-ignite the conflict in Bosnia we worked so hard to stop. It could even involve our NATO allies, Greece and Turkey. If we wait until casualties mount and war spreads, any effort to stop it will come at a higher price under more dangerous conditions.

The time to stop the war is right now. With our NATO allies and Russia, we have offered a comprehensive plan to restore peace and return self-government to Kosovo. NATO has authorized air strikes if Serbia fails to comply with its previous commitment to withdraw forces and fails to support a peace accord. At the same time, we've made it clear to the Kosovo Albanians that if they reject our plan or continue to wage ware, they will not have our support.

There are serious obstacles to overcome at the current talks. It is increasingly clear that this effort can only succeed if it includes a NATO-led peace implementation force that gives both sides the confidence to lay down their arms. It's also clear that if there is a real peace, American participation in the force can provide such confidence, particularly for Kosovo's Albanians. For them, as for so many people around the world, America symbolizes hope and resolve.

Europeans would provide the great bulk of any NATO force, roughly 85 percent. Our share would amount to a little less than 4,000 personnel. Now, a final decision on troops, which I will make in close consultation with Congress, will depend upon the parties reaching a strong peace agreement. It must provide for an immediate cease-fire, rapid withdrawal of most Serbian security forces, and demilitarization of the insurgents. The parties must agree to the NATO force and demonstrate that they are ready to implement the agreement. NATO's mission must be well-defined, with a clear and realistic strategy to allow us to bring our forces home when their work is done.

Any time we send troops, we must be mindful of the risks. But if these conditions are met, if there is an effective agreement and a clear plan, I believe America should contribute to securing peace for Kosovo. And I look forward to working with Congress in making this final decision. America cannot be everywhere or do everything overseas, but we must act when important interest are at stake and we can make a difference. Peace in Kosovo clearly is important to the United States. And with bipartisan support in Congress and the backing of the American people, we can make a difference....

6-5 America's War on Serbia (Yugoslavia)

Statement to the Nation
The White House
March 24, 1999

My fellow Americans, today our Armed Forces joined our NATO allies in airstrikes against Serbian forces responsible for the brutality in Kosovo. We have acted with resolve for several reasons.

We act to protect thousands of innocent people in Kosovo from a mounting military offensive. We act to prevent a wider war, to diffuse a powder keg at the heart of Europe that has exploded twice before in this century with catastrophic results. And we act to stand united with our allies for peace. By acting now, we are upholding our values, protecting our interests, and advancing the cause of peace.

Tonight I want to speak to you about the tragedy in Kosovo and why it matters to America that we work with our allies to end it. First, let me explain what it is we are responding to. Kosovo is a province of Serbia, in the middle of southeastern Europe, about 160 miles east of Italy. That's less than the distance between Washington and New York and only about 70 miles north of Greece. Its people are mostly ethnic Albanian and mostly Muslim.

In 1989 Serbia's leader, Slobodan Milosevic, the same leader who started the wars in Bosnia and Croatia and moved against Slovenia in the last decade, stripped Kosovo of the constitutional autonomy its people enjoyed, thus denying them their right to speak their language, run their schools, shape their daily lives. For years, Kosovars struggled peacefully to get their rights back. When President Milosevic sent his troops and police to crush them, the struggle grew violent.

Last fall our diplomacy, backed by the threat of force from our NATO alliance, stopped the fighting for a while and rescued tens of thousands of people from freezing and starvation in the hills where they had fled to save their lives. And last month, with our allies and Russia, we proposed a peace agreement to end the fighting for good. The Kosovar leaders signed that agreement last week. Even though it does not give them all they want, even though their people were still being savaged, they saw that a just peace is better than a long and unwinnable war.

The Serbian leaders, on the other hand, refused even to discuss key elements of the peace agreement. As the Kosovars were saying yes to peace, Serbia stationed 40,000 troops in and around Kosovo in preparation for a major offensive—and in clear violation of the commitments they had made.

Ending this tragedy is a moral imperative. It is also important to America's national interest. Take a look at this map. Kosovo is a small place, but it sits on a major fault line between Europe, Asia, and the Middle East, at the meeting place of Islam and both the Western and Orthodox branches of Christianity. To the south are our allies, Greece and Turkey; to the north, our new democratic allies in central Europe. And all around Kosovo there are other small countries struggling with their own economic and political challenges, countries that could be overwhelmed by a large, new wave of refugees from Kosovo. All the ingredients for a major war are there: ancient grievances, struggling democracies, and in the center of it all a dictator in Serbia who has done nothing since the Cold War ended but start new wars and pour gasoline on the flames of ethnic and religious division.

Sarajevo, the capital of neighboring Bosnia, is where World War I began. World War II and the Holocaust engulfed this region. In both wars, Europe was slow to recognize the dangers, and the United States waited even longer to enter the conflicts. Just imagine if leaders back then had acted wisely and early enough, how many lives could have been saved, how many Americans would not have had to die.

We learned some of the same lessons in Bosnia just a few years ago. The world did not act early enough to stop that war, either. And let's not forget what happened: innocent people herded into concentration camps, children gunned down by snipers on their way to school, soccer fields and parks turned into cemeteries, a quarter of a million people killed, not because of anything they have done but because of who they were. Two million Bosnians became refugees. This was genocide in the heart of Europe, not in 1945 but in 1995; not in some grainy newsreel from our parents' and grandparents' time but in our own time, testing our humanity and our resolve.

At the time, many people believed nothing could be done to end the bloodshed in Bosnia. They said, "Well, that's just the way those people in the Balkans are." But when we and our allies joined with courageous Bosnians to stand up to the aggressors, we helped to end the war. We learned that in the Balkans, inaction in the face of brutality simply invites more brutality, but firmness can stop armies and save lives. We must apply that lesson in Kosovo before what happened in Bosnia happens there, too.

Over the last few months we have done everything we possibly could to solve this problem peacefully. Secretary Albright has worked tirelessly for a negotiated agreement. Mr. Milosevic has refused....

Today we and our eighteen NATO allies agreed to do what we said we would do, what we must do to restore the peace. Our mission is clear: to demonstrate the seriousness of NATO's purpose so that the Serbian leaders understand the imperative of reversing course; to deter an even bloodier offensive against innocent civilians in Kosovo and, if necessary, to seriously damage the Serbian military's capacity to harm the people of Kosovo. In short, if President Milosevic will not make peace, we will limit his ability to make war.

Now, I want to be clear with you, there are risks in this military action, risks to our pilots and the people on the ground. Serbia's air defenses are strong. It could decide to intensify its assault on Kosovo or to seek to harm us or our allies elsewhere. If it does, we will deliver a forceful response.

Hopefully, Mr. Milosevic will realize his present course is self-destructive and unsustainable. If he decides to accept the peace agreement and demilitarize Kosovo, NATO has agreed to help to implement it with a peacekeeping force. If NATO is invited to do so, our troops should take part in that mission to keep the peace. But I do not intend to put our troops in Kosovo to fight a war.

Do our interests in Kosovo justify the dangers to our Armed Forces? I've thought long and hard about that question. I am convinced that the dangers of acting are far outweighed by the dangers of not acting—dangers to defenseless people and to our national interests. If we and our allies were to allow this war to continue with no response, President Milosevic would read our hesitation as a license to kill. There would be many more massacres, tens of thousands more refugees, more victims crying out for revenge.

Right now our firmness is the only hope the people of Kosovo have to be able to live in their own country without having to fear for their own lives. Remember: We asked them to accept peace, and they did. We asked them to promise to lay down their arms, and they agreed. We pledged that we, the United States and the other eighteen nations of NATO, would stick by them if they did the right thing. We cannot let them down now.

Imagine what would happen if we and our allies instead decided just to look the other way, as these people were massacred on NATO's doorstep. That would discredit NATO, the cornerstone on which our security has rested for fifty years now.

We must also remember that this is a conflict with no natural national boundaries. Let me ask you to look again at a map. The red dots are towns the Serbs have attacked. The arrows show the movement of refugees north, east, and south. Already, this movement is threatening the young democracy in Macedonia, which has its own Albanian minority and a Turkish minority. Already, Serbian forces have made forays into Albania from which Kosovars have drawn support. Albania has a Greek minority. Let a fire burn here in this area, and the flames will spread. Eventually, key US allies could be drawn into a wider conflict, a war we would be forced to confront later, only at far greater risk and greater cost.

I have a responsibility as President to deal with problems such as this before they do permanent harm to our national interests. America has a responsibility to stand with our allies when they are trying to save innocent lives and preserve peace, freedom, and stability in Europe. That is what we are doing in Kosovo.

If we've learned anything from the century drawing to a close, it is that if America is going to be prosperous and secure, we need a Europe that is prosperous, secure, undivided, and free. We need a Europe that is coming together, not falling apart, a Europe that shares our values and shares the burdens of leadership. That is the foundation on which the security of our children will depend.

That is why I have supported the political and economic unification of Europe. That is why we brought Poland, Hungary, and the Czech Republic into NATO, and redefined its missions, and reached out to Russia and Ukraine for new partnerships....

6-6 Building Peace in the Balkans

Address to the Nation on Kosovo Agreement
Washington DC
June 10, 1999

My fellow Americans, tonight for the first time in seventy-nine days, the skies over Yugoslavia are silent. The Serb army and police are withdrawing from Kosovo. The 1 million men, women, and children driven from their land are preparing to return home. The demands of an outraged and united international community have been met.

I can report to the American people that we have achieved a victory for a safer world, for our democratic values, and for a stronger America. Our pilots have returned to base. The airstrikes have been suspended. Aggression against an innocent people has been contained and is being turned back.

When I ordered our Armed Forces into combat, we had three clear goals: to enable the Kosovar people, the victims of some of the most vicious atrocities in Europe since the Second World War, to return to their homes with safety and self-government; to require Serbian forces responsible for those atrocities to leave Kosovo; and to deploy an international security force, with NATO at its core, to protect all the people of that troubled land, Serbs and Albanians, alike. Those goals will be achieved. A necessary conflict has been brought to a just and honorable conclusion.

The result will be security and dignity for the people of Kosovo, achieved by an alliance that stood together in purpose and resolve, assisted by the diplomatic efforts of Russia. This victory brings a new hope that when a people are singled out for destruction because of their heritage and religious faith and we can do something about it, the world will not look the other way....

I want to speak with you for a few moments tonight about why we fought, what we achieved, and what we have to do now to advance the peace, and together with the people of the Balkans, forge a future of freedom, progress, and harmony.

We should remember that the violence we responded to in Kosovo was the culmination of a ten-year campaign by Slobodan Milosevic, the leader of Serbia, to exploit ethnic and religious differences in order to impose his will on the lands of the former Yugoslavia. That's what he tried to do in Croatia and in Bosnia, and now in Kosovo....

For these atrocities, Mr. Milosevic and his top aides have been indicted by the International War Crimes Tribunal for war crimes and crimes against humanity. I will never forget the Kosovar refugees I recently met. Some of them could barely talk about what they had been through. All they had left was hope that the world would not turn its back.

When our diplomatic efforts to avert this horror were rebuffed and the violence mounted, we and our Allies chose to act. Mr. Milosevic continued to do terrible things to the people of Kosovo, but we were determined to turn him back. Our firmness finally has brought an end to a vicious campaign of ethnic cleansing, and we acted early enough to reverse it, to enable the Kosovars to go home.

When they do, they will be safe. They will be able to reopen their schools, speak their language, practice their religion, choose their leaders, and shape their destiny....

NATO has achieved this success as a united alliance, ably led by Secretary General Solana and General Clark. Nineteen democracies came together and stayed together through the stiffest military challenge in NATO's fifty-year history.

We also preserved our critically important partnership with Russia, thanks to President Yeltsin, who opposed our military effort but supported diplomacy to end the conflict on terms that met our conditions. I'm grateful to Russian envoy Chernomyrdin and Finnish President Ahtisaari for their work, and to Vice President Gore for the key role he played in putting their partnership together. Now, I hope Russian troops will join us in the force that will keep the peace in Kosovo, just as they have in Bosnia.

Finally, we have averted the wider war this conflict might well have sparked. The countries of southeastern Europe backed the NATO campaign, helped the refugees, and showed the world there is more compassion than cruelty in this troubled region. This victory makes it all the more likely that they will choose a future of democracy, fair treatment of minorities, and peace.

Now we're entering a new phase, building that peace, and there are formidable challenges. First, we must be sure the Serbian authorities meet their commitments. We are prepared to resume our military campaign should they fail to do so. Next, we must get the Kosovar refugees home safely; mine fields will have to be cleared; homes destroyed by Serb forces will have to be rebuilt; homeless people in need of food and medicine will have to get them; the fate of the missing will have to be determined; the Kosovar Liberation Army will have to demilitarize, as it has agreed to do. And we in the peacekeeping force will have to ensure that Kosovo is a safe place to live for all its citizens, ethnic Serbs as well as ethnic Albanians.

For these things to happen, security must be established. To that end, some 50,000 troops from almost 30 countries will deploy to Kosovo. Our European Allies will provide the vast majority of them; America will contribute about 7,000. We are grateful that during NATO's air campaign we did not lose a single serviceman in combat. But this next phase also will be dangerous. Bitter memories will still be fresh, and there may well be casualties. So we have made sure that the force going into Kosovo will have NATO command and control and rules of engagement set by NATO. It will have the means and the mandate to protect itself while doing its job.

In the meantime, the United Nations will organize a civilian administration while preparing the Kosovars to govern and police themselves. As local institutions take hold, NATO will be able to turn over increasing responsibility to them and draw down its forces.

A third challenge will be to put in place a plan for lasting peace and stability in Kosovo and through all the Balkans. For that to happen, the European Union and the United States must plan for tomorrow, not just today. We must help to give the democracies of southeastern Europe a path to a prosperous, shared future, a unifying magnet more powerful than the pull of hatred and destruction that has threatened to tear them apart. Our European partners must provide most of the resources for this effort, but it is in America's interest to do our part, as well. A final challenge will be to encourage Serbia to join its neighbors in this historic journey to a peaceful, democratic, united Europe.

I want to say a few words to the Serbian people tonight. I know that you, too, have suffered in Mr. Milosevic's wars. You should know that your leaders could have kept Kosovo as a part of your country without driving a single Kosovar family from its home, without killing a single adult or child, without inviting a single NATO bomb to fall on your country. You endured seventy-nine days of bombing, not to keep Kosovo a province of Serbia, but simply because Mr. Milosevic was determined to eliminate Kosovar Albanians from Kosovo, dead or alive.

As long as he remains in power, as long as your nation is ruled by an indicted war criminal, we will provide no support for the reconstruction of Serbia. But we are ready to provide humanitarian aid now and to help to build a better future for Serbia, too, when its Government represents tolerance and freedom, not repression and terror....

7. Continuing the American Legacy in the Middle East

The United States first became strategically and politically involved in the Middle East at the end of World War II. A financially strapped Great Britain was no longer able to afford large-scale military deployments in the Middle East, Greece was threatened by Communist subversion, and the Soviet Union was trying to extract territorial concessions from Turkey and Iran. These developments prompted the enunciation of the Truman Doctrine in March 1947 and US military involvement in the Eastern Mediterranean and the Persian Gulf region, previously the imperial preserves of Britain and France. The United States undertook to guarantee the territorial integrity of Turkey and Iran against possible attack by the USSR. The strategic purpose was to prevent the expansion of Soviet power; this remained the driving force behind US foreign policy until the end of the Cold War in 1991.

Washington's support for the partition of Palestine by the United Nations in November 1947 and its recognition of Israel on May 15, 1948, slowly led to a deepening US involvement in Arab-Israeli disputes. Throughout the period between 1949 and 1967, the United States attempted to remain on the fence as it sought to come to terms with Arab nationalism. But even President Dwight D. Eisenhower's rescue of Egypt's leader, Gamal Abdel Nasser, from combined British, French, and Israeli efforts to topple him in the fall of 1956, failed to elicit friendship from Nasser or from any other radical Arab nationalist leader.

After the June 1967 Arab-Israeli War, US-Soviet rivalry in the Middle East intensified and transformed the Arab-Israeli conflict from a troublesome regional conflict into a dangerous one with global implications. As Egypt, Syria, Iraq, and other "front-line" Arab states turned to the Soviet Union for arms and advisers, US policy took a decidedly pro-Israeli shift. President Lyndon B. Johnson, who was preoccupied with the

500,000 American troops fighting in Vietnam, saw Israel as an asset, not a problem. In view of the extensive Soviet military presence, he believed Israel was entitled to retain captured Arab territories, to ensure its security pending an overall peace settlement and to help it deter any Syrian move against Jordan and Saudi Arabia. Moreover, Johnson opened the American arms tap. For the first time, the United States became Israel's primary source for modern weapons.

After the October 1973 Middle East war, the US position in the Middle East was enormously enhanced. Paradoxically, although an intervention by Moscow had saved Egypt and Syria from another defeat and enabled them to garner a political triumph of sorts, no sooner had the fighting stopped than Egypt turned to Washington, not Moscow. And whereas in 1967, the Arab states had broken off diplomatic relations with the United States even though it had not aided Israel, in 1973 they restored diplomatic ties despite Washington's significant support of Israel during the fighting.

Then-Secretary of State Henry Kissinger succeeded in fashioning a disengagement agreement between Egypt and Israel and between Syria and Israel without Soviet participation, much to Moscow's annoyance. In the process, US leaders came to realize that, although military power mattered a great deal, Israel was in no position to impose a political settlement on the Arabs, and that only the United States could serve as the "honest broker" between the regional adversaries.

New presidents often try to make their mark in the Middle East arena, which holds a continuing attraction for the American public. A major example of this occurred in 1977, when President Jimmy Carter joined with Soviet leader Leonid Brezhnev in calling for the convening of a peace conference in Geneva without first obtaining the approval of the regional parties. The initiative failed, in large measure because Egypt mistrusted the Soviet Union. Egyptian President Anwar Sadat (who came to office on Nasser's death at the end of September 1970), however, unexpectedly announced a willingness to go to Jerusalem to reach a peace agreement with Israel. On November 19, 1977, his dramatic move set in motion developments that led, with invaluable assistance from President Carter, to the signing of an Egyptian-Israeli peace treaty on March 26, 1979. The challenge was to extend the peacemaking process.

After the 1991 Gulf War, the peace process was given new impetus with the convening of a conference in Madrid in October by US President George Bush and Soviet President Mikhail Gorbachev. The Madrid Conference involved face-to-face talks between Israel and all the key parties to the Arab-Israeli conflict, including Syria and the Palestinians. The Bush administration, which had a checkered and at times difficult relationship with Israeli Prime Minister Yitzhak Shamir, pushed the peace process, in large measure because of promises made to Egypt, Syria, Jordan, and Saudi Arabia for their support in the Gulf War against Iraq. At the Madrid Conference, the negotiations were organized along three tracks: The first focused on bilateral negotiations between Israel and its neighbors—Syria, Jordan, and Lebanon. The second brought Israel and the Palestinians together, but was hampered by Israel's unwillingness to deal directly with the Palestinian Liberation Organization (PLO) and its head, Yasir Arafat. And the third track sought progress on functional issues such as economic cooperation, water, and refugees. There were no breakthroughs during the last year of the Bush administration or of the Shamir government, which, as matters eventuated, was defeated in the June 1992 election, and succeeded by a Labor government under the leadership of Yitzhak Rabin.

Though new to Arab-Israeli issues, having visited Israel only once, in 1981, President Clinton expressed interest in trying to jump start the peace process. Following Clinton's lead, and, perhaps, having in mind the success of the Carter administration in which he had served, Warren Christopher made his first trip abroad as Secretary of State to the Middle East, meeting with Syrian President Hafez Asad for what was to be the first of more than twenty times during the next four years. But it was as a result of the hitherto secret negotiations that had taken place between the Israelis and the PLO in Olso, through Norwegian intermediaries, that the United States once again became the hub of the peace process. The Oslo negotiations outflanked parallel ones that Israel and the Palestinians had been conducting under US auspices at Madrid. During the summer of 1993, Rabin and Arafat reached an agreement on what came to be known as the Declaration of Principles.

Both parties welcomed US involvement. On September 13, 1993, with President Clinton officiating on the White House lawn, Prime Minister Rabin and Chairman Arafat signed the Declaration of Principles and shook hands. Israel accepted the PLO as the legitimate representative of the Palestinians and the PLO recognized the State of Israel.

The accord was the most significant breakthrough in the peace process since the US-brokered peace between Israel and Egypt in 1979. At the signing ceremony, Clinton signified his eagerness to play a central role in moving the negotiations forward and finding a way to a lasting Arab-Israeli settlement (Speech 7-1). Generally known as the Oslo Accord, the Declaration of Principles stipulated:

- A five-year interim period of Palestinian self-rule, during which permanent status issues such as Jerusalem, Jewish settlements, and permanent borders, were to be excluded from discussion.
- Israeli retention of the sole responsibility for security along international borders and crossing points to Egypt and Jordan.

- Israeli responsibility for the overall security of Israelis and Israeli settlements, and of the freedom of movement on roads in the West Bank and Gaza.
- Immediate self-rule for Palestinians in the Gaza Strip and the West Bank City of Jericho.
- For the remaining Palestinians in the West Bank, responsibility for education, health, social welfare, direct taxation, and tourism to be transferred to Palestinian representatives.
- Calls for the election of a Palestinian Council and the establishment of a Palestinian police force.
- Permanent status negotiations to begin no later than the third year of the interim accord (May 1996).

To nudge Rabin and Arafat to rapid implementation of the Declaration of Principles, Clinton held out tempting benefits: for Israel, financial assistance to cover the expenses of redeploying troops from Gaza and Jericho (on the West Bank), assurances of continuing foreign aid at existing levels, and a promise of access to advanced combat aircraft—the F-15E's; for Arafat, financial help and the US commitment to press Israel on rapid implementation of the Oslo Accord. However, the details were not worked out until May 1994. By July, sufficient agreement was reached for Israel to turn over the Gaza strip and the city of Jericho to the Palestinian Authority (PA), as Arafat's interim government was known.

A major development in the Arab-Israeli peace process took place in July 1994. Israel and Jordan signed an agreement in Washington that led to their signing a formal peace treaty on October 26, 1994, with President Clinton in attendance at the site on the Israeli-Jordanian border. On the eve of the historic occasion, the President commended the two parties, hailed the move as an important step toward peace in the region, and promised that "the United States would stand shoulder-to-shoulder with those who are taking risks for peace" (Speech 7-2).

With the signing of the Israeli-Jordanian peace treaty, Clinton's prestige as a peacemaker soared. When Rabin visited Washington in late November 1994, Clinton was generous: he approved export licenses for the purchase of two supercomputers, reaffirmed his intentions to support Israel's $3 billion a year aid package, and even went so far as to hold out the prospect of providing US troops to serve as a peacekeeping contingent on the Golan Heights, should Israel and Syria conclude a peace agreement.

In late January 1995, however, terrorism once again, as so often in the past, temporarily derailed the peace process. Relations between Israel and the Palestinian Authority deteriorated, when a series of suicidal car bombings took a heavy toll on Israeli civilians. Arafat disclaimed any advance knowledge of the events, but the Israeli public was not convinced that he was serious about cracking down on the militants of Hamas and

Islamic Jihad, two Palestinian fundamentalist groups bitterly opposed to any accommodation with Israel. Increasingly, the demand grew in both constituencies—Israeli and Palestinian—for more concessions by the other side.

On May 7, 1995, in a speech to the American Israel Public Affairs Committee, a leading pro-Israel interest group, the President gave a far-ranging condemnation of terrorism and its patrons (Speech 7-3). Clearly worried about obstacles to further advances in Israeli-Palestinian relations, he spoke strongly of his enduring commitment to Israel's security and sought to reassure the Israeli public, as well as American supporters of Israel, on that score.

On November 4, 1995, Prime Minister Rabin was assassinated by an Israeli religious zealot. Pending new Israeli elections, Shimon Peres became the interim prime minister. The agreements that Rabin and Arafat had reached a month earlier calling for further Israeli withdrawals in the West Bank were put on hold until the new elections.

Acts of terrorism continued to frustrate Israeli-Palestinian negotiations. A cycle of violence took a heavy toll of civilians. For example, after the murder in the Gaza Strip of Yahya Ayyash, the man believed to have been the mastermind behind suicide bombings against Israelis, Hamas vowed revenge. On February 25, 1996, Palestinian terrorists killed twenty-six people in separate attacks in Jerusalem and Ashkelon. Several days later, Hamas offered to halt attacks against Israeli civilians in exchange for the release of Palestinian prisoners. On March 3, a bomb exploded on a bus in Jerusalem, killing eighteen civilians and the suicide bomber. A day later, another suicide bomber killed a dozen people and wounded almost a hundred at a busy Tel Aviv shopping mall.

In response to these disruptive and potentially destabilizing events, President Clinton and Israeli Prime Minister Shimon Peres signed a US-Israel Counter-terrorism Accord at the White House on April 30, 1996. Though more symbolic than substantive, the accord reflected the determination of the two parties to press ahead with the peace process, despite the obstacles, and to commit their governments to close cooperation in the ongoing struggle against terrorism. Only two days earlier, Clinton had delivered just such a message to the American Israel Public Affairs Committee (Speech 7-4).

On May 31, 1996, the election of Benjamin Netanyahu, the leader of the Likud Party, put a damper on Washington's hope for rapid progress in the Israeli-Palestinian negotiations. Nearly a year passed before Clinton met with Israel's new Prime Minister. Concerned over the stalled peace process, Secretary of State Madeleine Albright (who had assumed the post in January 1997) made her first trip to the Middle East in that capacity on

September 1997, to try to accelerate the peace process. She called on Israel to refrain from taking steps that could forestall meaningful final-status negotiations (in particular, over the status of Jerusalem) and urged the PLO leadership to curb terrorist attacks on Israelis, but returned with little to show from either side.

The Clinton administration's relationship with Netanyahu's government was testy. In a joint press conference with Netanyahu held in London on November 14, 1997, Albright complained that the absence of peace between Israel and its neighbors made it more difficult to deal with Saddam Hussein's challenge to the UN's inspections of Iraq's suspected caches of weapons of mass destruction. In early December, Clinton echoed Albright's criticism. None of this made for easy going in the numerous meetings that the US officials held with Israeli and PLO leaders in the spring and summer of 1998.

After more than a year and a half, on October 15 – 23, 1998, President Clinton succeeded in bringing Netanyahu and Arafat together at the Wye River Conference Center in Maryland. The negotiations resulted in the Wye Memorandum, which committed the two sides to exchange land for security in "steps [that were] to be carried out in a parallel phased approach." Among its provisions, the agreement required the following: Israel was to allow the Palestinians to open the Gaza International Airport, return an additional 13 percent of West Bank territory to Palestinian control, and release some 750 Palestinians from detention; the Palestinian Authority was to outlaw and combat terrorist organizations, prohibit illegal weapons, prohibit all forms of incitement to violence and terror, and convene the Palestine National Congress to nullify all anti-Israeli provisions of the Palestinian National Charter. At its signing, Clinton expressed his hope that both sides would abide by the agreements (Speech 7-5).

Critics of the Wye Memorandum questioned whether it would be implemented as crafted. Their concerns were twofold. First, Arafat might not be able to prevent terrorist attacks by militants with interests and agendas different from his. In such an eventuality, the best intentions would not be enough to guarantee a further normalization of Israeli-Palestinian relations. Second, the intractable issues remain untouched, with no solution in sight: the status of Jerusalem, the refugees, the division of water resources, and, of course, security and the final boundaries. In addition, Clinton undertook to arrange financial packages to help Israel defray the expense of troop redeployments, as land was turned over to the Palestinian Authority, and to help the PA promote economic developments. He also committed the CIA to help monitor the accords, thereby thrusting it into a policy implementation role that might cause trouble in the future.

Still, the importance of timing and just plain luck in the successes of policy and the political fortunes of leaders should never be underestimated. In early 1999, Netanyahu's unstable coalition collapsed, leaving him without a working majority in the Knesset and forcing a new election. In mid-May 1999, Ehud Barak, a highly decorated General, led the Labor Party to victory on a platform that pledged to pursue peace more vigorously than had his predecessors. After visiting Egypt and Jordan, extending an olive branch to Syria, and meeting with Yasir Arafat in mid-July, Prime Minister Barak flew to Washington, where his extensive discussions with President Clinton and American officials were apparently cordial and candid. He promised to withdraw Israeli forces from Southern Lebanon within a year, and suggested a framework that he said should show within fifteen months "whether we have a breakthrough, and are really going to put an end to the conflict, or, alternatively, ... we are stuck again."

Pleased with the Prime Minister's initiative, Clinton expressed new hope for the Israeli-Palestinian peace process and committed himself to providing Israel with all the support he could and to playing the role of an active facilitator.

* * *

Another major source of unfinished business in the Middle East with which the Clinton administration had to contend was Saddam Hussein's Iraq and, to some extent, post-Khomeini Iran. On May 19, 1993, amidst considerable fanfare, the administration elaborated a policy toward Iraq and Iran that it called "dual containment." Implicitly critical of the Reagan-Bush policy of tilting toward Iraq, it asserted the intention to use US power and influence to contain both Iraq and Iran. In the case of Iraq, this meant a commitment to upholding UN-mandated sanctions and to continuing "flexible" interpretations of some UN resolutions under which Washington stipulated "no-fly zones" for Iraqi aircraft over Iraq's Kurdish-populated area in the North and Shiite-populated area in the South. With respect to Iran, dual containment meant preventing that country from obtaining foreign investment capital or advanced dual-use equipment, especially nuclear-related technology from Russia.

As with so many post-Cold War issues, knowing the historical context within which Clinton's policy unfolded is essential for a clear perspective. Whereas Iran had been a "pillar" of US policy in the Persian Gulf region during much of the US-Soviet Cold War era, Iraq, from 1959 on, increasingly relied on the Soviet Union for weapons and advisers, and posed a threat to those Arab states, such as Saudi Arabia, Jordan, and Kuwait, that looked to the United States for varying degrees of security. However, in January 1979, Ayatollah Ruhollah Khomeini's populist-theocratic revolution toppled the pro-US Shah of Iran and established a regime that was intensely anti-American.

War broke out between Iran and Iraq in September 1980 and lasted until August 1988, with more than 1 million killed. During the war, the Reagan administration surreptitiously aided Iraq, even though Saddam Hussein used poison gas against Iran as well as against Kurdish rebels in his own country. After the war, the Bush administration courted Saddam, hoping through loans and political interactions to moderate his hostility toward Israel and the peace process and in this way also to deepen Iran's isolation. But this policy greatly misread Saddam's ambitions. In August 1990, Iraq invaded and occupied its southern neighbor, tiny but oil-rich Kuwait. To safeguard Saudi Arabia and the free flow of oil to the West and Japan, President Bush organized a multinational coalition, including Egypt, Syria, and key NATO allies, and enlisted the cooperation of the Soviet Union to reverse Saddam's aggression. With UN Security Council approval for the use of military force, the US-led force began operations in mid-January 1991 and by early March forced Saddam to sue for peace.

To survive, Saddam Hussein accepted terms for a permanent cease-fire set forth by the UN Security Council Resolution 687 on April 3, 1991. This resolution required Iraq to renounce terrorism, free all prisoners, restore all seized assets, establish a fund based on oil revenues to provide reparations to Kuwait, and permit inspection designed to ensure that all weapons of mass destruction were destroyed. The last provision was of particular significance: Iraq was required to accept the destruction, removal, and dismantling of all nuclear, chemical, and biological weapons, to terminate all research and development of such weapons, to destroy all stocks of chemical and biological agents, and to divest itself of ballistic missiles with ranges beyond 100 miles. To supervise and monitor Iraq's compliance, the UN established a UN Special Commission (UNSCOM).

Sensitive to congressional concerns about the possibility of heavy loss of American lives, the Bush administration skillfully managed the military phase of Saddam's defeat, but was overly optimistic about what would be required to depose the dictator. Saddam mobilized his remaining forces effectively to suppress uprisings by the Kurds and the Shiites. When Clinton took office, Saddam was isolated abroad and hamstrung by UN Security Council resolutions and economic sanctions, but firmly in control at home and still a dangerous threat.

In April 1993, Clinton was confronted with what was perceived as an undeniable challenge—evidence that Iraq was planning to assassinate President Bush during his visit to Kuwait City in June. Convinced that the threat was credible, Clinton ordered the headquarters of Iraq's Intelligence service bombed and spoke to the nation about the Iraqi threat and the measures taken to counter it (Speech 7-6). His reaction to the first serious challenge to his administration reflected a determination to hold Iraq accountable for its criminal actions.

Undeterred by Clinton's air-strikes, in early October 1993, Saddam moved a large number of troops to the border with Kuwait. Within days, several thousand US troops were flown to Kuwait. When even Saddam's former supporters, PLO leader Yasir Arafat and King Hussein of Jordan, declined to back him, Iraq pulled back its units, and recognized Kuwait's sovereignty and the existing Iraq-Kuwait border. Notwithstanding this retreat, the UN Security Council kept all sanctions in place.

In March 1995, over 35,000 Turkish soldiers launched attacks across the Iraqi border (possibly, with Baghdad's tacit approval) against the Kurdish Workers Party (PKK), a Turkish terrorist group using bases in Northern Iraq to strike at targets in Turkey. At the same time, fighting continued between Iraqi Kurdish factions in Northern Iraq, the "no-fly" zone under US, UK, and French air protection. The two main Kurdish parties, the Kurdish Democratic Party (KDP) and the Patriotic Union of Kurdistan (PUK), feuded over leadership. The United States tried, unsuccessfully, to mediate their bitter, long-standing inter-clan and ideological quarrel.

Iraq's refusal to cooperate with UN weapons inspections resurfaced in the summer of 1996. In June, Iraq barred UN weapons inspectors from examining three of eight sites outside of Baghdad, citing national security considerations. Although Iraq yielded to UN pressure and readmitted the inspectors by the end of the month, the UN chief weapons inspector warned that Iraq continued to conceal important weapons components and incriminating documents. His caution proved justified when, in July, Iraq again delayed UN teams from inspecting suspicious areas.

At the end of August 1996, Iraqi forces swept into the Kurdish area that the United States had declared a "no-fly" zone in order to protect the Kurds from Saddam's air force. Using troops and armored divisions, Saddam ousted the pro-Iranian PUK from control of the provisional capital of Irbil and left the more amenable KDP as the leading faction of the region. A few days later, the United States launched a series of cruise missiles at military targets, began a major military buildup in the area, and warned Saddam to abide by the UN ceasefire resolutions. In this setting, the President used his regular Saturday radio broadcast, generally a low-key event, to explain the latest attack on the Iraqi military (Speech 7-7).

As UNSCOM reports accumulated, they conveyed a disturbing picture. Iraq, it appeared, was engaged in a systematic effort to conceal proscribed activities and mislead UN inspectors from UNSCOM and the International Atomic Energy Agency, for example, regarding secretly produced SCUD-type missile engines and the regime's ongoing work on chemical and biological agents. Inspectors alleged that Iraq retained a considerable capability to produce a variety of chemical agents, including the advanced nerve agent VX.

By 1997, the cat-and-mouse game between Iraqi authorities and UN-SCOM became routine. UNSCOM reported new caches of suspected sites of chemical and biological agents; Iraq insisted that all such weapons had been destroyed. Inspections were often postponed, cancelled, then as abruptly resumed. The aim was, evidently, to limit the effectiveness of the inspectors, and to cause friction in the UN Security Council between the United States and Britain on the one hand, and Russia and France, who generally favored a more lenient approach to Saddam, on the other. The net effect of Iraq's behavior was to impede and subvert UNSCOM's activities. It was obvious that Saddam's tactics were not without some limited successes. His hope was that "sanctions fatigue" would prompt more conciliatory UN Security Council compromises, lead to the relative isolation of the United States with its pinprick military attacks, and enhance Saddam's prestige in the Arab world among those who had little interest in seeing a US condominium in the region.

A major crisis developed in October 1997, when UNSCOM submitted a devastating report on Iraqi evasiveness and duplicity. The report noted the following:

- that Iraq had not given an adequate account of its proscribed missile assets
- that Iraq continued to lie about its chemical and biological weapons arsenal
- that Iraq may well be hiding special missile warheads capable of being filled with chemical and biological warfare agents
- that Iraq must be presumed, in the absence of solid evidence, to still have ample supplies of VX nerve gas, notwithstanding the considerable stockpile supposedly destroyed during the Gulf War.

After a lengthy debate, the UN Security Council condemned Iraq but did little else. Iraqi arrogance brought criticism even from Russia and France, but Saddam was gradually undermining the effectiveness of the UN inspection system in Iraq.

The UN Security Council permitted Iraq to export a limited amount of oil biannually in order to purchase food, medicine, and other necessities, as well as to provide reparations to victims of the war against Kuwait, and as payment for the costs of UN operations in Iraq. But sanctions were not lifted because of Saddam's continued obstructionism.

On June 21, after several incidents of interference with UNSCOM activities, the Security Council threatened Iraq with stiffer sanctions, but Saddam paid little heed. In October, the crisis worsened when Iraq announced that it would expel the American members of the UNSCOM team. The Security Council condemned Iraq and insisted that inspectors of all nationalities remain. In November, Iraq agreed to postpone the date when the Americans would be expelled, but proceeded to expel six American weapons inspectors several days later. Only after the United States threatened military action were the American inspectors allowed to return. A conflict then arose over sites, particularly the many palaces of Saddam Hussein, which remained closed to the inspectors. At the year's end the issue had not been resolved.

The struggle between Saddam Hussein and the UN Security Council over Iraq's evasiveness regarding UNSCOM inspection continued until December 1998, when Saddam ended all cooperation. Refusing to allow any type of weapon inspection on Iraqi territory any longer, he forced UNSCOM to pull out of the country. On December 16, 1998, President Clinton told the American people of his decision to bomb Iraq once again (Speech 7-8). Critics noted that although the UN Security Council had voted unanimously in September and October, as Clinton noted in his address, to condemn Saddam's actions and lack of cooperation, it had not authorized any recourse to military action. In Resolution 1154 of March 2, 1998, the Security Council had warned of severe consequences in the event of Iraqi interference with UNSCOM inspections, but whether this meant that unilateral military measures could be used remained a much-argued point. It was not clear what a bombing limited to four days (out of regard for the Muslim holy season of Ramadan) was expected to accomplish. On some occasions, Clinton talked of deposing Saddam; on others, he spoke of wanting him to live up to the terms of UN resolutions.

US military options for dealing with Saddam were limited: bombing for brief periods to weaken Saddam's infrastructure and military support capability; launching an all-out invasion to depose Saddam; or undertaking an all-out bombing campaign of indeterminate duration (as was done against Yugoslavia/Serbia in the March/June 1999 period), until Saddam was either overthrown or acceded to all demands for full and unfettered inspections. Increasingly, Clinton resorted to military action, relying on the first option. However, there was no evidence that these air attacks were having the desired political effect of weakening Saddam's grip on power. Moreover, a major dilemma continued to worry US planners: as was discovered during the Gulf War, strikes against arms depots might unintentionally hit stockpiles of chemical and biological agents, unleashing highly toxic substances into the atmosphere with catastrophic fall-out.

The Clinton strategy of "dual containment" was a failure. The policy toward Iraq seemed primarily to have divided the Western allies, angered large segments of the Arab world, which condemned the victimization of the Iraqi people, and alienated Russia. Despite the most comprehensive system of sanctions ever imposed by the United Nations against a country,

Iraq was exporting oil illicitly through brokers in Syria, Iran, Turkey, Lebanon, and the Persian Gulf emirates, and importing all kinds of good and armaments.

After UNSCOM pulled out in August 1998 in response to Iraq's restriction on inspections and inspectors, Secretary of State Albright insisted that, for any of the sanctions against Iraq to be lifted, UNSCOM must have full and complete access, and that the process of inspections must be maintained. But after the US bombing in December 1998, Iraq's Vice-President told reporters in Baghdad that "the issue of UNSCOM is in the past. Its mission is over."

The situation was stalemated.

In Iran, Clinton's policy of dual containment also came to a dead end. Far from being isolated, Iran showed signs of steadily improving relations with former important trading partners, such as Britain, Germany, and Russia, and it nurtured closer ties with Turkey, Turkmenistan, and Kazakhstan. It desperately needed foreign investment and expanded trade in order to overcome the devastation wrought by the war with Iraq (1980 – 1988) and to provide employment and a better life for its rapidly growing population of almost seventy million people. In the early 1990s, under President Hashemi Rafsanjani, and after 1997, under President Mohamed Khatami, the Iranian government moved cautiously to encourage foreign investment in the oil and natural gas sectors of the economy and to ease repressive controls over social and political life by the still all-powerful inner circle of clerics who sought to perpetuate the theocratic state established by Ayatollah Ruhollah Khomeni in 1979. Khatami's efforts at internal liberalization suffered setbacks, whether permanent or temporary it is too early to tell.

The Clinton administration was aware of the ferment in Iran, but was reluctant to launch any initiatives to test Khatami's intentions—or, indeed, his power. Some tentative reactions to the developments in Iran came from State Department officials, but President Clinton did not deliver an official speech on US policy toward Iran. Officially, the US government position was that before US-Iran relations could improve, Tehran must renounce terrorism, cease its opposition to the Arab-Israeli peace process, and demonstrate its opposition to the production and use of weapons of mass destruction.

Washington was also deeply concerned over Russia's building of Iran's nuclear and missile capabilities. Eager to earn hard currency, individual Russian ministries and firms entered into their own arrangements with Iranian authorities. The Ministry of Atomic Energy helped Iran build two light-water nuclear reactors in Bushehr, on the Persian Gulf. The government arms exporting agency acknowledged selling Iran advanced aircraft, air defense systems, and T-72 tanks. In addition, US sources alleged that Russia supplied Iran with components for the development of inter-mediate-range missiles, with a range of 800 miles to 1,300 miles, notwith-standing Russian legislation that forbade such transactions. The net effect of all of this was to reinforce suspicions in US political and military circles that Iran's aims in the region were not congenial to US interests.

Clinton's policy of political inertia toward Iran enjoyed tacit support in the Congress, in large measure because the President's critics were unable to provide a better solution. Short of the unlikely triumph of re-formers over the entrenched, anti-American, ultra-conservative clerics, Washington was prepared to adopt a watch-and-wait attitude.

7-1 Moving Beyond Oslo: The Israeli-Palestinian Declaration of Principles

Remarks at the Signing Ceremony
The White House
September 13, 1993

... Today we bear witness to an extraordinary act in one of history's defining dramas, a drama that began in the time of our ancestors when the word went forth from a sliver of land between the river Jordan and the Mediterranean Sea. That hallowed piece of earth, that land of light and revelation is the home to the memories and dreams of Jews, Muslims, and Christians throughout the world.

As we all know, devotion to that land has also been the source of conflict and bloodshed for too long. Throughout this century, bitterness between the Palestinian and Jewish people has robbed the entire region of its resources, its potential, and too many of its sons and daughters. The land has been so drenched in warfare and hatred, the conflicting claims of history etched so deeply in the souls of the combatants there, that many believed the past would always have the upper hand.

Then, fourteen years ago, the past began to give way when, at this place and upon this desk, three men of great vision signed their names to the Camp David accords. Today we honor the memories of Menachem Begin and Anwar Sadat, and we salute the wise leadership of President Jimmy Carter. Then, as now, we heard from those who said that conflict would come again soon. But the peace between Egypt and Israel has endured. Just so, this bold new venture today, this brave gamble that the future can be better than the past, must endure.

Two years ago in Madrid, another President took a major step on the road to peace by bringing Israel and all her neighbors together to launch direct negotiations. And today we also express our deep thanks for the skillful leadership of President George Bush.

Ever since Harry Truman first recognized Israel, every American President, Democrat and Republican, has worked for peace between Israel and her neighbors. Now the efforts of all who have labored before us bring us to this moment, a moment when we dare to pledge what for so long seemed difficult even to imagine: that the security of the Israeli people will be reconciled with the hopes of the Palestinian people and there will be more security and more hope for all.

Today the leadership of Israel and the Palestine Liberation Organization will sign a declaration of principles on interim Palestinian self-government. It charts a course toward reconciliation between two peoples who have both known the bitterness of exile. Now both pledge to put old sorrows and antagonisms behind them and to work for a shared future shaped by the values of the Torah, the Koran, and the Bible....

We know a difficult road lies ahead. Every peace has its enemies, those who still prefer the easy habits of hatred to the hard labors of reconciliation. But Prime Minister Rabin has reminded us that you do not have to make peace with your friends. And the Koran teaches that if the enemy inclines toward peace, do thou also incline toward peace.

Therefore, let us resolve that this new mutual recognition will be a continuing process in which the parties transform the very way they see and understand each other. Let the skeptics of this peace recall what once existed among these people. There was a time when the traffic of ideas and commerce and pilgrims flowed uninterrupted among the cities of the Fertile Crescent. In Spain and the Middle East, Muslims and Jews once worked together to write brilliant chapters in the history of literature and science. All this can come to pass again.

Mr. Prime Minister, Mr. Chairman, I pledge the active support of the United States of America to the difficult work that lies ahead. The United States is committed to ensuring that the people who are affected by this agreement will be made more secure by it and to leading the world in marshaling the resources necessary to implement the difficult details that will make real the principles to which you commit yourselves today.

Together let us imagine what can be accomplished if all the energy and ability the Israelis and the Palestinians have invested into your struggle can now be channeled into cultivating the land and freshening the waters, into ending the boycotts and creating new industry, into building a land as bountiful and peaceful as it is holy. Above all, let us dedicate ourselves today to your region's next generation. In this entire assembly, no one is more important than the group of Israeli and Arab children who are seated here with us today.

Mr. Prime Minister, Mr. Chairman, this day belongs to you. And because of what you have done, tomorrow belongs to them. We must not leave them prey to the politics of extremism and despair, to those who would derail this process because they cannot overcome the fears and hatreds of the past. We must not betray their future. For too long, the young of the Middle East have been caught in a web of hatred not of their own making. For too long, they have been taught from the chronicles of war. Now we can give them the chance to know the season of peace. For them we must realize the prophecy of Isaiah that the cry of violence shall no more be heard in your land, nor wrack nor ruin within your borders. The children of Abraham, the descendants of Isaac and Ishmael, have embarked together on a bold journey. Together today, with all our hearts and all our souls, we bid them shalom, salaam, peace....

7-2 Toward Peace Between Israel and Jordan

Remarks on Departure for the Middle East
The White House
October 25, 1994

... Tomorrow, in the desert between Israel and Jordan, two neighbors will agree to lay to rest age-old animosities and give a new future to their countries.... King Hussein and Prime Minister Rabin will enter into an historic peace treaty. By their courage, they help their peoples, their region, and the entire world. They help to begin a final journey to peace in one of the most perilous conflicts of our age. By taking part in that ceremony, I will help to fulfill a mission pursued vigorously by the United States, by Presidents of both parties, since the end of World War II.

Peace in the Middle East is in our fundamental interests, and our continued participation in the peace process is crucial to its success. The signing ceremony I will witness grows out of the peace process we have helped to build.

The treaty between Israel and Jordan will be only the second full peace treaty between Israel and one of its Arab neighbors and the first ever signed in the Middle East itself. The roots of this process reach back to the Camp David accords between the late Anwar Sadat of Egypt and Menachem Begin of Israel, in which President Carter played such a pivotal role, and to the historic peace treaty they signed here fifteen years ago.

But this trip is more than a celebration of another important step toward peace, it's an opportunity to pursue new steps. Israel and Jordan have shown that contact can overcome conflict and that direct talks can produce peace. My goal is to make clear that the time has arrived for all parties to follow the brave and hopeful inspiration of Israel and Jordan. With so much at stake, it is more important than ever for the United States to stand shoulder-to-shoulder with those who are taking risks for peace.

For all the progress toward peace, indeed, because of that progress, we have witnessed a new wave of terrorism and violence. No step on this long journey requires more patience, more discipline, more courage than the steps still to come. At this crucial moment, the people of the Middle East stand at a crossroads. In one direction lies the dark past of violence, terrorism, and insecurity that desperate enemies of peace seek to prolong. In the other lies a brighter future, a brighter future that Israel and all her Arab neighbors can achieve if they have the courage to stand up to violence, to terrorism, to mistrust, to build that future.

Above all else, I go to the Middle East to deliver one clear message: The United States stands by those who, in the words of the Psalms, "seek peace and pursue it." And we stand up to those who threaten to destroy the dream that has brought us to this historic moment.

Standing up for peace in this region includes countering the aggressive acts of Iraq's toward its neighbors. Like our troops around the world, the men and women of our Armed Forces stationed in Kuwait are the strength behind our pledge to support peace and security. They are doing a magnificent job, and I want them to know how proud all Americans are of their efforts. When I visit them on Friday, I know I'll carry the good wishes of all their fellow Americans, just as I know all Americans will pray this week for the progress toward peace as we witness this historic treaty and carry the peace process forward.

7-3 The Quest for a Wider Middle Eastern Security

Remarks to the American Israel Public Affairs
Committee Policy Conference
Washington DC
May 7, 1995

The United States, and I believe all the Western nations, have an overriding interest in containing the threat posed by Iran. Today Iran is the principal sponsor of global terrorism, as the Prime Minister has said. It seeks to undermine the West and its values by supporting the murderous attacks of the Islamic Jihad, Hezbollah, and other terrorist groups. It aims to destroy the Middle East peace process.

You know the need for firm action here as well as I do. And I thank you for your long history of calling attention to Iran's campaign of terror. I thank you for urging a decisive response, and I thank you for supporting the action we have taken. We have worked to counter Iran's sponsorship of terrorism, its efforts to acquire nuclear weapons. We led our G-7 allies to ban weapons sales, tightening restrictions on dual-use technology and in preventing Iran from obtaining credit from international financial institutions. But more has to be done. That's why I ordered an end to all US trade and investment with Iran.

I understand this will mean some sacrifice for American companies and our workers. But the United States has to lead the way. Only by leading can we convince other nations to join us. I hope you will help us convince other nations to join us.

Let me mention two other nations. We have also taken a strong stand against Libya. We remain determined to bring those responsible for the bombing of Pan Am 103 to trial. And make no mistake about it, though UN sanctions have weakened Saddam Hussein, he remains an aggressive, dangerous force. He showed that last October, menacing Kuwait until our Armed Forces' swift and skillful deployment forced him to back down. As long as he refuses to account for Iraqi weapons programs, past and present, as long as he refuses to comply with all relevant Security Council resolutions, we cannot agree, and we will not agree, to lift the sanctions against Iraq. We will not compromise on this issue, and we value the support we have received from the Prime Minister and the State of Israel....

Now I want to go over some of the things that the Prime Minister has said because it is important that we be seen as one voice on these issues. ... [B]efore I was elected to office I vowed to be an unshakable supporter of Israel. I have kept that commitment. We have maintained current levels of security and economic assistance. We've made clear to all that our commitment to the security and well-being of the Jewish state is absolutely unwavering, and will continue to be.

In any agreement, in any agreement Israel concludes with Syria it will have the means to defend itself by itself. And no child in Kiryat Shemona or Metulla will go to bed afraid for his or her safety.

Today, Israel's military edge is greater than ever because the United States has kept its word. We approved the purchase of F-15-E's for the Israeli Air Force because Israel should have the world's best long-range, multiple-role fighter. We have continued the transfer of 200 fighter aircraft and attack helicopters that began after the Gulf war. We are committing over $350 million, the major share of development costs, for the Arrow missile system to assure that Israel never again is left defenseless in the face of a missile attack.

We delivered the most advanced multiple-launch rocket system in the world to give Israel defense forces the fire power they need. And to help enhance Israel's high-tech capabilities, we approved the sale of supercomputers, and we allowed access for the first time to the American space launch vehicle markets.

... [T]his is a two-way relationship that has real benefits for both our nations. Our strategic and intelligence cooperation is now deeper than ever. This year we conducted the largest ever joint military exercise[s] ... We are pre-positioning more military hardware in Israel. And the Pentagon has signed contracts worth more than $3 billion to purchase high-quality military products from Israeli companies.

The landmark events of the last two years were, in part, possible because the United States worked to ensure Israel's strength, because we helped to give Israel the confidence to make peace by minimizing those risks, because we built a relationship of trust, and because we made it clear that no one could drive a wedge between us. And, Mr. Prime Minister, as long as I'm here, no one will ever drive a wedge between us.

But we have a new problem here at home to which others have alluded. Here in the United States and in positions of authority, there are those who claim to be friends of Israel and supporters of peace and people who believe they are friends of Israel and supporters of peace, whose efforts would make Israel less safe and peace less likely. Under the cover of budget cutting, back-door isolationists on the left and the right want to cut the legs off of our leadership in the Middle East and around the world. They want to deny the United States the resources we need to support allies who take risks for peace.

Legislation being prepared in Congress could reduce by as much as 25 percent our foreign policy spending, which is now just a little over one percent of the Federal budget and is clearly, as a percentage of our income, by far the smallest of any advanced nation in the world. We did not win the Cold War to walk away and blow the peace on foolish, penny-wise, pound-foolish budgeting.

... If we have to abandon that role simply because we are denied the tools of foreign aid and security assistance, one of the first to be affected is Israel, because Israel is on the frontline of the battle of freedom and peace, and Israel's strength is backed by America's strength and our global leadership.

... Let me say just a few words about where we are now in the Middle East. The conflict of decades will not end with the stroke of a pen, or even two pens, but consider how far we have come. No one who was there will ever forget that brilliant day on the White House lawn when Prime Minister Rabin and Chairman Arafat resolved to end their conflict. No one who was there will ever forget the magnificent ceremony in the Araba on the ground at the Patriarch's Walk when Israel and Jordan made peace after forty-six years. Those were two of my proudest moments as President. They should be two of every American's proudest moments for our country in the last two years.

There is a constituency for peace in the Middle East growing stronger and stronger. Thanks in large measure to the tireless efforts of Secretary Christopher, Israel and Syria are engaged in serious, substantive negotiations on the terms of a treaty which can both secure another of Israel's borders and put an end to the entire conflict. A number of Arab countries, Morocco, Tunisia, Oman, Qatar, have begun to normalize relations with Israel. We have begun to dismantle the Arab boycott, and I think we'll see its end before too long. I will not rest until we do see the end of the boycott. It is high time, and it should be ended....

We are encouraging Chairman Arafat to continue and to intensify his efforts to crack down on extremists. He is now taking concrete steps to prosecute those who plan and carry out acts of violence. These measures and others to confront terror and establish the rule of law must be continued. The peace will never succeed without them.

... [T]he enemies of peace will not succeed because they are the past, not the future. We will continue to do everything in our power to make that statement true....

In the Middle East, as nowhere else, these two forces of integration and disintegration are locked in a deadly struggle, a strong Israel backed by a strong America, building peace with its neighbors, a new openness in the region but, on the other side, these continuing desperate attempts of fanatics, eager to keep old and bloody conflicts alive....

7-4 Overcoming the Obstacle of Terrorism

Remarks to the American Israel Public
Affairs Committee Policy Conference
Washington DC
April 28, 1996

… As the Prime Minister said, we had an agreement back in 1993, but it wasn't in writing, and it was shattered. For the first time now, there is an agreement in writing that will be more effective in preventing further outbreaks. The violence has stopped. There is now a monitoring mechanism to which Israel and Lebanon can refer complaints. And now it is our fond hope that civilians on both sides of the border can resume their lives with greater confidence and security. And we will not tolerate further efforts to disrupt the calm.

When I came into office, I was determined that our country would go into the twenty-first century still the world's greatest force for peace and freedom, for democracy and security and prosperity. We have to promote these values just as vigorously as we did in the Cold War. Indeed, in some ways, our responsibilities as Americans are now greater....

We have made a lot of progress with the Declaration of Principles of the Palestinians, the peace of the Arabs with Jordan, the interim accord that was signed in Washington. I have watched in these very difficult months since Prime Minister Rabin's assassination Prime Minister Peres rise to this moment. He has been a true and reliable friend of our country, and a true and reliable leader of his own....

I know that in Israel and Lebanon, throughout the Middle East and throughout the world, it would be so easy after yet another round of violence and death to give up, to think that the very best we could expect is a future of separate armed camps. It is that sort of bunker mentality that we fight, indeed, all across the world in different ways today. It would be easy to give into it in the Middle East, but it would be wrong....

We can still achieve a peace if we conquer fear and restore security and deal honestly with those with whom we have differences. We know it will not be easy. Peace requires in some ways more strength than war. And

219

we must have the patience to endure a few more setbacks along the way. We know that it takes great courage to press forward into an unknown future. It's harder than retreating into a familiar past. It takes great bravery to reach out to a former enemy. It's easier to stay in the false security of isolation....

If the Jewish people have endured centuries of exile, persecution, the ultimate evil of the Holocaust, flourishing against all the odds, surely— surely—together they can throw back their shoulders and raise their heads and say, after all this, Hezbollah and Hamas will not succeed where others have failed.

Even as the Katyushas were falling, we saw proof of peace taking hold. We saw it in the meeting between Prime Minister Peres and Chairman Arafat ten days ago, when they vowed to move ahead on the goals set by the accords. We saw it in the Prime Minister's path-breaking trips to Qatar and Oman this month. And I salute again the Prime Minister for the strength and commitment he has shown in pursuing the peace in this difficult period.

And of course, last Wednesday, on the forty-eighth anniversary of Israeli independence, the Palestinian National Council finally did change the PLO charter and deleted the hateful clause calling for the destruction of Israel. Now, think about that. That symbol of hatred had endured since 1964, before some people in this room were even born. It's a moment we have long waited and worked for. The Palestinian leadership followed through on its commitments and made a better move to a better day. All friends of peace should be heartened by this, and especially by the large margin of the vote in support of Chairman Arafat's policy....

I say again, I want to hammer this home, not only to you who know, but to people beyond this room; this progress for peace is the reason the enemies of peace are lashing out. We must restore peace. We must restore security. But we must not be diverted from our ultimate goal, else we will hand them the victory that they have sought all along.

We know the circle of peace cannot be closed only by an end to the fighting in Lebanon. It can be closed only when the Arab-Israeli conflict is truly over; when normalization takes hold in the entire Arab world; when Israel's security is completely assured; when Israel is fully accepted in every way in the region. The circle of peace will be closed only—and I say only—when the people of Israel are confident that what they are getting is worth the risks they must take. Peace and security are indivisible. And Israel must feel comfortable and confident about both in order to achieve either over the long run.

... [T]he breakthroughs of the past were possible because we built together a bond of trust. And I pledge to you today that this relationship will remain strong and vital, so strong and so vital that no one will ever drive a wedge between us.

Our commitment to Israel's security is unshakable. It will stay that way because Israel must have the means to defend itself by itself. In a time of shrinking resources, we have maintained our economic assistance. We have sought to enhance Israel's security to lessen the risks it has taken and still takes every day for peace.

Israel's qualitative military edge is greater than ever because we have kept our word. Earlier today, Prime Minister Peres and Secretary Perry signed an agreement to expand our theater missile defense program so that we can detect and destroy incoming missiles. That way Israel will have not only the advantage it needs today, but will be able to defeat the threats of tomorrow.

As part of this effort, we are proceeding with the third phase of the deployment of the Arrow missile program. The United States is committing $200 million to this effort so that the children who lived through the Scud attacks of the Gulf War will never again face that fear. We also pledge to expand work on the Nautilus high-energy laser system, which is designed to destroy Katyushas in flight. Our air forces are working together so that the first of the F-15-I's are delivered as planned next year. And we have offered Israel the AMRAAM, our most advanced air-to-air missile system, so that Israel's air power remains unmatched in the region.

Our strategic cooperation is greater than ever. We are continuing to help build Israel's high-tech capacity through the sale of supercomputers. We are even expanding cooperation in space and preparing to train Israeli astronauts....

We are also working, as the Prime Minister has said, more closely than ever to defeat terrorism. This week we will complete the agreement to combat extremist violence that we began work on during my visit to Israel last month. Almost as soon as we received word of the bombings we began sending new equipment to detect explosives. Now we are committing more than $100 million to this program for equipment and training, for development of new technologies and improved communications and co-ordination. And I am very pleased that in the budget I signed just two days ago, the first $50 million was included in our common antiterrorist efforts.

... Israel should have every tool at its disposal in the fight against terror. And we all know that the organized forces of hatred and terror threaten people not only in the Middle East, but here at home and around the world.... Fighting terrorism will remain one of our top law enforcement priorities for many years to come. And in order to be successful, we have to have the tools we need here, and we have to work together....

7-5 On the Road to Peace: The Arrival at Wye

Remarks at the Wye River Memorandum
Signing Ceremony
Wye River, Maryland
October 23, 1998

... After some very difficult negotiations, very long, dare I say, quite sleepless, the Israelis and Palestinians here have reached an agreement on issues over which they have been divided for more than seventeen months. This agreement is designed to rebuild trust and renew hope for peace between the parties. Now both sides must build on that hope, carry out their commitments, begin the difficult, but urgent journey toward a permanent settlement....

This agreement is good for Israel's security. The commitments made by the Palestinians were very strong, as strong as any we have ever seen. They include continuous security cooperation with Israel and a comprehensive plan against terrorism and its support infrastructure.

This agreement is good for the political and economic well-being of Palestinians. It significantly expands areas under Palestinian authority to some 40 percent of the West Bank. It also offers the Palestinian people new economic opportunities, with an airport, an industrial zone, soon safe passage between Gaza and the West Bank, and in time, a seaport. The Palestinian people will be able to breathe a little easier and benefit from the fruits of peace.

Most importantly, perhaps, this agreement is actually good for the peace process itself. For eighteen months it has been paralyzed, a victim of mistrust, misunderstanding, and fear. Now, ordinary Israelis and Palestinians once again can become partners for peace.

To bolster this effort, Chairman Arafat will invite members of the Palestinian National Council and other important political entities to reaffirm his prior commitments and their support for the peace process. I have agreed to address that meeting, several weeks hence, and to underscore the values of reconciliation, tolerance, and respect, and my support for those commitments and this process.

People around the world should be heartened by this achievement today. These leaders and those with whom they work have come a very long way. The Israeli and Palestinian peoples, whose bitter rivalry in this century has brought so much suffering to both sides, have moved yet another step closer toward fulfilling the promise of the Oslo accords, closer to the day when they can live peacefully as true neighbors, with security, prosperity, self-governance, cooperation, and eventually, ... genuine friendship.

No doubt, as peace gains momentum, forces of hate, no matter how isolated and disparate, will once again lash out. They know this, the leaders, and they are prepared to face it. Staying on the path of peace under these circumstances will demand even greater leadership and courage.

The work at Wye River shows what can happen when the will for peace is strong. But let me say once again to all the rest of you, everyone who is tempted to handicap every little twist and turn over the last nine days, you need to know one overwhelming thing: The Prime Minister and the Chairman and the members of their delegation who supported this process, even when there were things about it they did not agree with, are quite well aware that the enemies of peace will seek to extract a price from both sides. They are quite well aware that in the short run, they themselves may have put themselves at greater risk. But by pledging themselves to the peaceful course for the future, to the same values and, ultimately, to the same enemies, they have given both Israelis and Palestinians a chance to have the future we all want for our children and our children's children.

Every effort will have to be exerted to ensure the faithful implementation of this agreement—not because the parties do not want to do so, but because the agreement covers many things, was developed over many days, involved many discussions and sleepless nights. It will test whether the Palestinian people are prepared to live in peace, recognizing Israel's permanence, legitimacy, and a common interest in security. It will tell us whether Israelis want to help build a strong Palestinian entity that can fulfill the aspirations of its people and provide both real security and real partnership for Palestinians and Israelis.

The United States is determined to be of whatever help we can to both sides in their endeavors. I will consult with Congress to design a package of aid to help Israel meet the security costs of redeployment and help the Palestinian Authority meet the economic costs of development. I hope we will have support from Republicans and Democrats in that endeavor....

7-6 Containing Iraq

Address to the Nation
The White House
June 26, 1993

My fellow Americans, this evening I want to speak with you about an attack by the Government of Iraq against the United States and the actions we have just taken to respond.

This past April, the Kuwaiti Government uncovered what they suspected was a car bombing plot to assassinate former President George Bush while he was visiting Kuwait City. The Kuwaiti authorities arrested sixteen suspects, including two Iraqi nationals. Following those arrests, I ordered our own intelligence and law enforcement agencies to conduct a thorough and independent investigation. Over the past several weeks, officials from those agencies reviewed a range of intelligence information, traveled to Kuwait and elsewhere, extensively interviewed the suspects, and thoroughly examined the forensic evidence.

... [T]here is compelling evidence that there was, in fact, a plot to assassinate former President Bush and that this plot, which included the use of a powerful bomb made in Iraq, was directed and pursued by the Iraqi intelligence service.

We should not be surprised by such deeds, coming as they do from a regime like Saddam Hussein's, which is ruled by atrocity, slaughtered its own people, invaded two neighbors, attacked others, and engaged in chemical and environmental warfare. Saddam has repeatedly violated the will and conscience of the international community. But this attempt at revenge by a tyrant against the leader of the world coalition that defeated him in war is particularly loathsome and cowardly. We thank God it was unsuccessful. The authorities who foiled it have the appreciation of all Americans.

It is clear that this was no impulsive or random act. It was an elaborate plan devised by the Iraqi Government and directed against a former President of the United States because of actions he took as President. As such, the Iraqi attack against President Bush was an attack against our country and against all Americans. We could not and have not let such action against our Nation go unanswered....

Therefore, ... I ordered our forces to launch a cruise missile attack on the Iraqi intelligence service's principal command-and-control facility in Baghdad.... And I have called for an emergency meeting of the United Nations Security Council to expose Iraq's crime.

These actions were directed against the Iraqi Government, which was responsible for the assassination plot. Saddam Hussein has demonstrated repeatedly that he will resort to terrorism or aggression if left unchecked. Our intent was to target Iraq's capacity to support violence against the United States and other nations and to deter Saddam Hussein from supporting such outlaw behavior in the future. Therefore, we directed our action against the facility associated with Iraq's support of terrorism, while making every effort to minimize the loss of innocent life.

There should be no mistake about the message we intend these actions to convey to Saddam Hussein, to the rest of the Iraqi leadership, and to any nation, group, or person who would harm our leaders or our citizens. We will combat terrorism. We will deter aggression. We will protect our people.

The world has repeatedly made clear what Iraq must do to return to the community of nations. And Iraq has repeatedly refused. If Saddam and his regime contemplate further illegal provocative actions, they can be certain of our response....

7-7 The Struggle Continues: The Kurdish Problem

The President's Radio Address
The White House
September 14, 1996

... I want to speak with you about why ten days ago I ordered our Armed Forces to strike Iraq, what we have accomplished, and where we go from here.

America's vital interests in the Persian Gulf are constant and clear: to help protect our friends in the region against aggression, to work with others in the fight against terrorism, to preserve the free flow of oil, and to build support for a comprehensive Middle East peace. Any group or nation that threatens the stability of the region threatens those interests.

For the past five years, Saddam Hussein has repeatedly threatened the stability of the Persian Gulf and our allies Saudi Arabia and Kuwait. Time and again, he has lashed out recklessly against his neighbors and against his own people. America's policy has been to contain Saddam, to reduce the threat he poses to the region and to do it in a way that makes him pay a price when he acts recklessly. That is why when Saddam sent his troops into the Kurdish city of Urbil in Northern Iraq two weeks ago, we responded strongly, immediately, and strategically.

If we had failed to answer Saddam's provocation, he would have been emboldened to act even more recklessly and in a manner more dangerous to our interests. That is why we did respond and why we did so in a way that made our interests more secure. We acted in southern Iraq, where our interests are the most vital and where we had the capacity to increase the international community's ability to deter aggression by Saddam against his neighbors.

I ordered the attacks in order to extend the no-fly zone in Iraq, the air space through which Iraq's military is not allowed to fly. Now, we control the skies over Iraq from the border of Kuwait to the southern suburbs of Baghdad. This action tightened the strategic straightjacket on Saddam, making it harder for him to threaten Saudi Arabia and Kuwait and easier for us to stop him if he does. In so doing, we advanced America's fundamental interests in the region.

Of course, our interests also must include protecting the safety of our own pilots who are patrolling the expanded no-fly zone. That is why our cruise missiles struck the bulk of Saddam's air defense system in southern Iraq. The United States will take whatever steps are necessary to protect our pilots as they enforce the expanded no-fly zone and to defend our strategic interests. I have ordered sufficient forces to the region to give us that capability.

On another note, let me say that I deeply regret the very week our Armed Forces advanced America's interests halfway around the world. Here at home, the Senate missed an historic opportunity to make our soldiers and citizens safer by failing to vote on the Chemical Weapons Convention. The fact that our troops are facing off against Saddam Hussein, who once amassed stockpiles of chemical weapons and still seeks to develop them, should have underscored the importance of this treaty. But the treaty seems to have gotten caught up in election year politicking.

It's been nearly four years since the Bush administration signed the Chemical Weapons Convention and three years since I submitted it to the Congress. We've been at this a long time, and I have no intention of letting this treaty die....

7-8 Battling the Rogue State: The Weapons Inspection Crisis

Address to the Nation
The White House
December 16, 1998

... Earlier today I ordered America's Armed Forces to strike military and security targets in Iraq. They are joined by British forces. Their mission is to attack Iraq's nuclear, chemical, and biological programs and its military capacity to threaten its neighbors. Their purpose is to protect the national interest of the United States and, indeed, the interest of people throughout the Middle East and around the world. Saddam Hussein must not be allowed to threaten his neighbors or the world with nuclear arms, poison gas, or biological weapons.

I want to explain why I have decided, with the unanimous recommendation of my national security team, to use force in Iraq, why we have acted now, and what we aim to accomplish.

Six weeks ago Saddam Hussein announced that he would no longer cooperate with the United Nations weapons inspectors, called UNSCOM. They are highly professional experts from dozens of countries. Their job is to oversee the elimination of Iraq's capability to retain, create, and use weapons of mass destruction and to verify that Iraq does not attempt to rebuild that capability. The inspectors undertook this mission, first, seven and a half years ago, at the end of the Gulf War, when Iraq agreed to declare and destroy its arsenal as a condition of the cease-fire.

The international community had good reason to set this requirement. Other countries possess weapons of mass destruction and ballistic missiles. With Saddam, there's one big difference: He has used them, not once but repeatedly, unleashing chemical weapons against Iranian troops during a decade-long war, not only against soldiers but against civilians; firing Scud missiles at the citizens of Israel, Saudi Arabia, Bahrain, and Iran, not only against a foreign enemy but even against his own people, gassing Kurdish civilians in northern Iraq.

The international community had little doubt then, and I have no doubt today, that left unchecked, Saddam Hussein will use these terrible weapons again.

The United States has patiently worked to preserve UNSCOM, as Iraq has sought to avoid its obligation to cooperate with the inspectors. On occasion, we've had to threaten military force, and Saddam has backed down. Faced with Saddam's latest act of defiance in late October, we built intensive diplomatic pressure on Iraq, backed by overwhelming military force in the region. The UN Security Council voted fifteen to zero to condemn Saddam's actions and to demand that he immediately come into compliance. Eight Arab nations—Egypt, Syria, Saudi Arabia, Kuwait, Bahrain, Qatar, United Arab Emirates, and Oman—warned that Iraq alone would bear responsibility for the consequences of defying the UN.

When Saddam still failed to comply, we prepared to act militarily. It was only then, at the last possible moment, that Iraq backed down. It pledged to the UN that it had made, and I quote, "a clear and unconditional decision to resume cooperation with the weapons inspectors." I decided then to call off the attack, with our airplanes already in the air, because Saddam had given in to our demands. I concluded then that the right thing to do was to use restraint and give Saddam one last chance to prove his willingness to cooperate.

I made it very clear at that time what "unconditional cooperation" meant, based on existing UN resolutions and Iraq's own commitments. And along with Prime Minister Blair of Great Britain, I made it equally clear that if Saddam failed to cooperate fully, we would be prepared to act without delay, diplomacy, or warning.

Now, over the past three weeks, the UN weapons inspectors have carried out their plan for testing Iraq's cooperation. The testing period ended this weekend, and last night, UNSCOM's Chairman, Richard Butler, reported the results to UN Secretary-General Annan. The conclusions are stark, sobering, and profoundly disturbing.

In four out of the five categories set forth, Iraq has failed to cooperate. Indeed, it actually has placed new restrictions on the inspectors. Here are some of the particulars:

Iraq repeatedly blocked UNSCOM from inspecting suspect sites. For example, it shut off access to the headquarters of its ruling party and said it will deny access to the party's other offices, even though UN resolutions make no exception for them and UNSCOM has inspected them in the past.

Iraq repeatedly restricted UNSCOM's ability to obtain necessary evidence. For example, Iraq obstructed UNSCOM's effort to photograph bombs related to its chemical weapons program. It tried to stop an

UNSCOM biological weapons team from videotaping a site and photo-copying documents and prevented Iraqi personnel from answering UN-SCOM's questions.

Prior to the inspection of another site, Iraq actually emptied out the building, removing not just documents, but even the furniture and the equipment. Iraq has failed to turn over virtually all the documents requested by the inspectors; indeed, we know that Iraq ordered the de-struction of weapons-related documents in anticipation of an UNSCOM inspection.

So Iraq has abused its final chance. As the UNSCOM report con-cludes, and again I quote, "Iraq's conduct ensured that no progress was able to be made in the fields of disarmament. In light of this experience and in the absence of full cooperation by Iraq, it must, regrettably, be recorded again that the Commission is not able to conduct the work man-dated to it by the Security Council with respect to Iraq's prohibited weap-ons program."

In short, the inspectors are saying that, even if they could stay in Iraq, their work would be a sham. Saddam's deception has defeated their effec-tiveness. Instead of the inspectors disarming Saddam, Saddam has dis-armed the inspectors.

This situation presents a clear and present danger to the stability of the Persian Gulf and the safety of people everywhere. The international community gave Saddam one last chance to resume cooperation with the weapons inspectors. Saddam has failed to seize the chance.

And so we had to act, and act now. Let me explain why.

First, without a strong inspections system, Iraq would be free to re-tain and begin to rebuild its chemical, biological, and nuclear weapons programs in months, not years.

Second, if Saddam can cripple the weapons inspections system and get away with it, he would conclude that the international community, led by the United States, has simply lost its will. He will surmise that he has free rein to rebuild his arsenal of destruction. And some day, make no mistake, he will use it again, as he has in the past.

Third, in halting our airstrikes in November, I gave Saddam a chance, not a license. If we turn our backs on his defiance, the credibility of US power as a check against Saddam will be destroyed. We will not only have allowed Saddam to shatter the inspections system that controls his weapons of mass destruction program; we also will have fatally under-cut the fear of force that stops Saddam from acting to gain domination in the region.

That is why, on the unanimous recommendation of my national security team, including the Vice President, Secretary of Defense, the

Chairman of the Joint Chiefs of Staff, the Secretary of State, and the NationalSecurity Adviser, I have ordered a strong, sustained series of airstrikes against Iraq. They are designed to degrade Saddam's capacity to develop and deliver weapons of mass destruction, and to degrade his ability to threaten his neighbors. At the same time, we are delivering a powerful message to Saddam: If you act recklessly, you will pay a heavy price.

We acted today because, in the judgment of my military advisers, a swift response would provide the most surprise and the least opportunity for Saddam to prepare. If we had delayed for even a matter of days from Chairman Butler's report, we would have given Saddam more time to disperse his forces and protect his weapons.

Also, the Muslim holy month of Ramadan begins this weekend. For us to initiate military action during Ramadan would be profoundly offensive to the Muslim world and, therefore, would damage our relations with Arab countries and the progress we have made in the Middle East. That is something we wanted very much to avoid without giving Iraq a month's headstart to prepare for potential action against it....

... [S]o long as Iraq remains out of compliance, we will work with the international community to maintain and enforce economic sanctions. Sanctions have cost Saddam more than $120 billion, resources that would have been used to rebuild his military. The sanctions system allows Iraq to sell oil for food, for medicine, for other humanitarian supplies for the Iraqi people. We have no quarrel with them. But without the sanctions, we would see the oil-for-food program become oil-for-tanks, resulting in a greater threat to Iraq's neighbors and less food for its people.

The hard fact is that so long as Saddam remains in power, he threatens the well-being of his people, the peace of his region, the security of the world. The best way to end that threat once and for all is with a new Iraqi Government, a Government ready to live in peace with its neighbors, a Government that respects the rights of its people.

Bringing change in Baghdad will take time and effort. We will strengthen our engagement with the full range of Iraqi opposition forces and work with them effectively and prudently.

8. Weapons of Mass Destruction: Coping with Twenty-first Century Threats

An enduring analogy for the relationship between the United States and the Soviet Union during the Cold War period is that of two scorpions in a bottle, each being the focus of the other's attention, aware that one wrong move would be fatal for both. The collapse of the Soviet Union broke the bottle, and the "scorpions" have scuttled apart, but their deadly power remains a threat to the world. The arsenal of weapons of mass destruction (WMD) links the United States and Russia (the successor of the USSR) for the indefinite future in a shared search for a suitable long-term security architecture. For analytical purposes, it may be useful to discuss the Clinton administration's policy regarding WMD along three parallel tracks: nuclear weapons and efforts to control their proliferation; chemical weapons; and biological weapons and threats.

The first aspect of the overall nuclear issue involves curtailing and reversing "vertical proliferation," that is, preventing nuclear states from further enhancing their nuclear capability and encouraging reduction of existing nuclear arsenals. On May 26, 1972, the first Strategic Arms Limitation Treaty (SALT) was signed in Moscow by President Richard M. Nixon and the Soviet Union's political leader, CPSU Secretary Leonid Brezhnev. There were two basic agreements. The first one was a five-year interim accord, setting quantitative limits on each side's strategic delivery systems, that is, intercontinental ballistic missiles (ICBMs) and submarine-launched ballistic missiles (SLBMs) capable of striking the other's homeland. Long-range bombers were not included. The second was a treaty of unlimited duration on the limitation of anti-ballistic missile (ABM) systems. It prohibited the development of such systems, though originally permitting each side to protect its national capital and one ICMB silo launcher area. A protocol, added in 1974, formally restricted each side to only one ABM deployment.

Under the Reagan administration, the United States and the Soviet Union took the first strides toward eliminating an entire category of nuclear weapons. On June 1, 1988, they signed the Treaty on the Elimination of Intermediate Range and Shorter Range Missiles (INF treaty), which rid superpower arsenals of nuclear-capable missiles having a range of 300 to 3,000 miles.

On July 31, 1991, President George Bush and Soviet President Mikhail Gorbachev signed the Strategic Arms Limitation Agreement (START I)—the preferred name for SALT adopted during the Reagan administration (1981 – 1989). Under START I, long-range nuclear warheads were to be reduced to levels of approximately 6,000 and delivery systems to 2,000. By the end of the year, the issue was complicated when the Soviet Union broke up into fifteen independent republics. Of these, Russia, Belarus, Ukraine, and Kazakhstan were now nuclear states with sizable stockpiles of nuclear weapons. Because of the need to obtain their accession to a denuclearized status, START I was not formally ratified until December 5, 1994, by which time Washington and Moscow had persuaded the three smaller countries to move all of their nuclear weapons to Russia.

At the end of 1991, shortly before the Soviet Union collapsed, Congress passed farsighted and unprecedented legislation for underwriting the dismantlement of Moscow's nuclear weapons—the Soviet Nuclear Threat Reduction Act, also known as the Cooperative Threat Reduction (CTR) program, but generally referred to as the Nunn-Lugar bill in recognition of its two co-sponsors, Senator Sam Nunn (D-GA) and Senator Richard Lugar (R-IN). It allotted funds to help Russia, Ukraine, Belarus, and Kazakhstan improve accountability systems and storage facilities for dismantled nuclear warhead components and to establish effective verification systems. CTR has remained a key program that has had continuing support in Washington and Moscow, notwithstanding serious political disagreements in other areas.

On January 3, 1993, shortly before leaving office, President Bush signed a follow-up START II agreement with Russian President Boris Yeltsin, which called for both sides to reduce their nuclear arsenals still further, to no more than 3,500 warheads by early in the twenty-first century. These cuts would eliminate approximately 70 percent of the two countries' Cold War levels of nuclear warheads, by far outreaching START I, which had cut the US and Soviet warheads by no more than 30 percent.

Continuing the reduction of nuclear warheads has been a major concern of President Clinton, who made nonproliferation a top priority. Thus, the discussions started between Bush and Yeltsin continued between Clinton and Yeltsin. In his remarks at the Nixon Center for Peace and Freedom Policy Conference on March 1, 1995, Clinton spoke of the accomplishments of the American foreign policy and the challenges faced with regard to the former Soviet Union (Speech 8-1). He lauded the success of START I, the wisdom of the Nunn-Lugar program, and the decision of the United States and Russia no longer to point their missiles at each other—admittedly, a symbolic gesture, since retargetting missiles is a matter of minutes. Clinton also expressed hope that START II would be ratified promptly. The obstacle proved to be Yeltsin's troubled relationship with the Duma, which was dominated by Communists and ultra-conservatives, who were mistrustful of the president who had ordered the military assault on the parliament building in October 1993.

In June 1995, Yeltsin submitted START II to the Duma, but a number of other concerns caused postponement of its ratification. START II was ratified by the US Senate in January 1996. Many Russian legislators felt that Russia had signed a disadvantageous agreement. Soon after Washington's decision to push NATO enlargement, the ultra-nationalist Vladimir Zhirinovsky denounced the policy as evidence of "American expansionism in the Slav world." Aleksandr Lebed, retired Lieutenant-General and elected Governor of a province in Siberia, argued that NATO's action would require Russia to rely more heavily on its nuclear deterrent, in order to compensate for the weakness of its conventional forces. Mikhail Gorbachev, writing in the *New York Times* on February 10, 1996, warned of the consequences for nuclear disarmament of the widespread beliefs among Russians that NATO was "a war machine that is trying to take advantage of our troubled political and economic situation" and that its expansion was "a fundamental violation of Western guarantees after Russia dissolved the Warsaw Pact and agreed to German unification." More criticism came from the Duma, which claimed the START II treaty placed an excessive financial burden on the budget: Russia would have to commit scarce resources to destroy the land-based multiple-warhead intercontinental ballistic missiles (ICBMs), replace or downsize some of them to carry single warheads, and make them silo-based rather than mobile.

Repeated appeals by President Clinton found an unresponsive Duma. At their summit meeting in Helsinki, Finland, in March 1997, on the eve of NATO's move to formally propose the admission of new members, Clinton and Yeltsin agreed to extend the period of the reductions called for under START II by five years. However, given the legislative impasse in Moscow, their public statements about pushing negotiations for a START III treaty seemed little more than window dressing. Deteriorating US-Russian relations left the future of START II uncertain.

START II was not a model agreement. For one thing, it called for the destruction only of delivery systems (missiles and bombers), not the warheads they carry; cuts in warheads were to be carried out by removing them from missiles. For another, the permissible limits at the end of the downsizing would leave each side with 3,000 to 3,500 long-range (strategic) nuclear weapons—far more than the minimum requirement for deterrence. Still, the treaty's advantages may, in time, come to be accepted even by the ultranationalists, because its terms are such as to leave Russia with nuclear equivalence with the United States, a deterrent potent enough to safeguard Russia against any prospective enemy for decades to come, a central role in the global management of nuclear issues, and a military expenditure on nuclear forces that would be affordable under Russia's straitened economic circumstances.

The second aspect of the overall nuclear issue in which the United States has invested much effort relates to halting "horizontal proliferation," or the birth of new nuclear weapons states. A convergence of US and USSR interests led to their support for a Nuclear Non-Proliferation Treaty (NPT), which came into effect in March 1970 for a period of twenty-five years. (France and China did not become signatories until 1992.) Article One of the treaty states that "each nuclear state undertakes not to transfer nuclear weapons or other nuclear explosive devices, or in any way help non-nuclear weapons states to develop a nuclear weapons capability." Non-nuclear weapons states accepted periodic inspections by the UN International Atomic Energy Agency (IAEA) of their peaceful nuclear activities.

Successive American presidents urged indefinite extension of the treaty's provisions and called on non-member threshold states (Israel, Brazil, North Korea) and nuclear non-member states (India and Pakistan) to join the NPT. President Clinton, too, placed utmost importance on extending the treaty indefinitely, as illustrated by the following excerpt from his remarks to the Nixon Center for Peace and Freedom Policy Conference on March 1, 1995:

> Nothing is more important to prevent the spread of nuclear weapons than extending the treaty indefinitely and unconditionally. ... The NPT is the principal reason why scores of nations do not now possess nuclear weapons, why the doomsayers were wrong. One hundred and seventy-two nations have made NPT the most widely subscribed arms limitation treaty in history for one overriding reason: it's in their self-interest to do so. ... Failure to extend NPT infinitely could open the door to a world of nuclear trouble. Pariah nations with rigid ideologies and expansionist ambitions would have an easier time acquiring terrible weapons, and countries that have chosen to forgo the nuclear option would then rethink their position. They would certainly be tempted to reconsider that decision.

In late 1995, a permanent extension of the NPT was voted by member states, including Russia. However, over the years, US intelligence has indicated that both Russia and China have sold relevant technologies and equipment to Pakistan and Iran.

A particularly vexing problem for the United States on the NPT issue has been North Korea. In 1985, North Korea, then closely allied with the Soviet Union, signed the NPT. During the Gorbachev period (1985 – 1991), expectations of declining tensions on the Korean Peninsula were reinforced by the admission of the two Koreas to membership in the United Nations, their nonaggression accord in December 1991, and the US decision to withdraw all of its nuclear weapons from South Korea, which followed North Korea's pledge to work toward a nuclear-free Peninsula. In January 1992, North Korea signed a safeguards agreement with the IAEA for international inspection of its nuclear facilities.

But the end of the Cold War resulted in new uncertainty and tension on the Korean Peninsula. North Korea refused to permit full and unfettered inspection. IAEA had reason to believe that North Korea possessed weapons-grade nuclear material and took seriously its announcements of pulling out of the Nuclear Non-Proliferation Treaty. Adding to rising tensions, in May 1993, North Korea successfully tested a nuclear-capable missile, the Ro Dong 1, with a range of approximately 600 miles.

At first, Clinton adopted a tough line with North Korea, mounting a military buildup in East Asia and raising the possibility of UN sanctions, coupled with only a marginal attempt at negotiations. In his remarks in Seoul on July 10, 1993, he reassured South Korea of American support for a nonnuclear Korean Peninsula and made it clear that the United States expected North Korea to comply with existing nonproliferation arrangements (Speech 8-2). Nevertheless, North Korea continued a policy of defiance and in June 1994 withdrew from the IAEA and threatened war against South Korea.

A visit to Pyongyang on June 15, 1994, by former President Jimmy Carter helped ease tensions. North Korea agreed to resume compliance with inspections in return for a number of concessions from the United States. Not overly pleased, Clinton expressed his annoyance, at one point stating that Carter was not an official spokesman for American policy.

On July 8, 1994, Kim Il Sung, the leader of North Korea since the end of World War II, died. His son, Kim Jong Il, continued his father's policy. On October 21, 1994, the United States and North Korea signed the Agreed Framework, under which Kim Jong Il agreed to adhere to the NPT and dismantle the graphite-moderated nuclear reactors that produce large amounts of weapons grade plutonium. In return, the United States committed itself to building two light-water nuclear reactors, financed mostly by Japan and South Korea. (Light-water reactors would generate relatively small quantities of plutonium, which North Korea would export periodically.) The United States also agreed to supply North Korea with 500,000 metric tons of heavy fuel oil annually, starting in 1995, as a compensation for forfeited energy production during the transition period. The Korean Peninsula Energy Development Organization (KEDO), founded in 1995 by the United States, South Korea, and Japan, was tasked with carrying out both parts of the agreement. Though seemingly solving the problem peacefully, the agreement was criticized in Congress, where opponents alleged that it rewarded nuclear blackmail and failed to obtain full access for inspections to prevent North Korean cheating.

Iraq also posed a threat of "horizontal proliferation." In defiance of UN Security Council resolutions passed at the end of the 1991 Gulf War, Saddam Hussein in February 1998 denied UNSCOM inspectors access to "presidential sites" and "sensitive areas." A few days later, President Clinton outlined the history of Hussein's noncompliance with the United Nations and warned of a possible strike against Iraq (Speech 8-3). UN Secretary-General Kofi Annan managed to work out a peaceful solution with Hussein on February 22, and Iraq promised to allow unhindered inspections. However, on December 14, Richard Butler, the UN chief weapons inspector, reported to the United Nations that Iraq failed to cooperate. On December 17, the United States and Great Britain launched Operation Desert Fox, whose goal, according to Clinton, was to "attack Iraq's nuclear, chemical, and biological weapons programs, and its military capacity to threaten its neighbors" and "to protect the national interest of the United States, and indeed the interests of people throughout the Middle East and around the world."

NPT seemed in trouble when the newly elected French President Jacques Chirac announced on June 13, 1995, that France would conduct a series of nuclear tests before deciding whether to renew it. To allay the concerns of member states, both France and China promised to work toward an unconditional Comprehensive Test Ban Treaty. Only after the rest of the major nuclear powers made similar promises was the NPT extended indefinitely by a unanimous vote of the 174 signatories of the treaty.

Another concern of the Clinton administration in the nuclear field has been to gain international acceptance for a Comprehensive Test Ban Treaty (CTBT). Formal negotiation on a comprehensive ban on all nuclear weapons tests took place at the UN Conference on Disarmament in January 1994. China, however, dismayed the global community by conducting two nuclear tests on June 10 and October 7, 1994, despite declaring its support for such a ban. Countries hesitant to stop nuclear testing forever—among them Russia and China—attached a provision (Article XIV) to CTBT that all forty-four states in possession of nuclear power, research reactors, nuclear weapons programs, or other equipment that would render them "nuclear-capable" deposit their instruments of ratification before the treaty would become effective. If this did not happen by September 1999, treaty signatories could convene a conference charged with finding a way to accelerate the treaty's coming into force. Twenty-three of the required forty-four states had not ratified the treaty by the middle of 1999; another three—North Korea, India, and Pakistan—had yet to sign it.

In May 1998, India and Pakistan tested nuclear weapons, intensifying pressures from signatories for their accession to the treaty. The United States briefly imposed sanctions on both nations, but its leverage was weakened by its own failure, thus far, to ratify the CTBT treaty. President Clinton had transmitted the treaty to the Senate in 1996, but the Chairman of the Foreign Relations Committee, Senator Jesse Helms (R-NC), refused to hold hearings, convinced that the treaty undermined US sovereignty. In his State of the Union Address on January 19, 1999, Clinton asked the Senate to "approve the Treaty now to make it harder for other nations to develop nuclear arms, and to make sure we can end nuclear testing forever," but the Senate was still not inclined to consider ratifying CTBT.

Chemical and biological weapons have grown in importance relative to their nuclear counterparts and become a priority matter for the US government in the post-Cold War world. The first major utilization of chemical weapons dates back to April 22, 1915, when the Germans used chlorine gas in an attack at Ypres during World War I. In all, 100,000 tons of chemical agents were used as weapons by both sides during the four years of the war (1914 – 1918).

After the war, the use of "asphyxiating, poisonous, or other gases and of bacteriological methods of warfare" was prohibited by the 1925 Geneva Gas Protocol, signed by over 140 nations, including all the major powers. Though stockpiled, chemical weapons were not used in World War II, in part because of their ineffectiveness, the availability of countermeasures such as gas masks, and the fear of retaliation against civilian populations.

During the Cold War, the United States and the Soviet Union stockpiled significant quantities of liquid nerve gas, including sarin—which rapidly evaporates and thus is extremely dangerous to the respiratory system. These liquids could be spread among the enemy lines in the form of a cloud or spray released by explosion of a bomb or missile warhead; aircraft and tanks could also be used for purposes of chemical warfare.

Negotiated by the Reagan and Bush administrations, the 1993 Chemical Weapons Convention prohibited developing, producing, stockpiling, and using chemical weapons and required the destruction of existing stocks over ten years. The treaty, prepared by the United Nations Disarmament Conference, was signed by 167 nations, ratified by 81 nations, and put into force on April 29, 1997. The two acknowledged chemical weapons states—the United States and Russia—ratified it on April 24 and October 31, respectively, both having done so after the required sixty-five nations had already adopted the treaty.

The US Senate ratified the Chemical Weapons Convention in April 1997, following heavy lobbying by President Clinton (Speech 8-4) and a number of concessions to the Republican conservatives led by Senate Foreign Relations Committee Chairman Jesse Helms. Helms and his supporters attached thirty-three "understandings" to the resolution of the treaty, five of which were rejected by the Senate. The most important of the five called for a renegotiation of Article X, which gave the member countries "the right to request and ... to receive" assistance against chemical attack from other members and called upon them to "facilitate ... the fullest possible exchange" of chemical technologies. The major criticism was that the United States would have to share its chemical weapons defenses with potential enemies, who might be able to figure out ways to penetrate them. President Clinton responded to this and other criticisms in a news conference on April 18, 1997 (Speech 8-5).

Like chemical weapons, biological weapons were prohibited by the 1925 Geneva Protocol from use in war, but no international arrangement stood in the way of their manufacture. Great Britain authored a Biological Weapons Convention in 1968, and in March 1971 a twelve-member Committee of the Conference on Disarmament agreed on a compromise draft and forwarded it to the UN General Assembly. On December 18, 1971, the draft was approved. The development, production, and stockpiling of biological weapons were prohibited in 1972 by the Biological Weapons Convention, signed by over 100 nations, including the five permanent members of the United Nations Security Council. However, the reported 1980 outbreak of anthrax in the Soviet city of Sverdlovsk signified one weakness of the Convention—the lack of verification mechanisms. Nevertheless, to date, biological weapons have never been used.

Still, the question remains how the United States will be able to deal with this problem in the future. Biological weapons such as anthrax are easy to produce and obtain, while defenses are time-consuming and difficult to develop. Currently, vaccines and rapid diagnoses are the primary defenses against biological weapons. In remarks to the National Academy of Science on January 22, 1999, Clinton expressed his confidence in the projects being developed to enhance America's protection against biological and chemical attacks (Speech 8-6). Though not mentioned by him, one such project initiated by the US military in 1997 was a plan to vaccinate all military personnel against anthrax within eight years. Not all reactions to this plan were positive: several hundred military personnel refused inoculation despite the expected consequence of being dishonorably discharged for disobeying orders; and critics in the scientific community cautioned against the unanticipated consequences of the mass use of such a potent vaccine.

With vaccines remaining the key protection against biological weapons, it was not surprising that both the United States and Russia—officially the sole remaining possessors of smallpox virus—resisted eliminating their stocks despite pressure from the World Health Organization in its decades-old campaign to rid the planet of smallpox. The fear in Washington and Moscow was that smallpox might be hidden away in other places in the world, and could be released accidentally or intentionally; the development of vaccines would require live smallpox viruses. Since most people today have no immunity to the disease and since producing vaccines in sufficient quantities to vaccinate the entire population would take months, a smallpox epidemic could prove disastrous.

In the post-Cold War world, weapons of mass destruction pose new threats. No longer does the possession of these technologies indicate a first-class high-tech military; instead weapons of mass destruction are increasingly turning into "weapons of the weak"—the resort of terrorist organizations and inferior armies. Trained scientists and engineers from economically depressed areas of the former Soviet Union are looking for work, and a variety of rogue terrorist organizations as well as regimes with a history of endorsing terror are all potential employers.

Because of its enormous wealth and influence in the world, the United States is an exposed and vulnerable target for those hostile to its aims, values, and institutions. The times call for vigilance and a farsighted diplomacy. At the fifty-first session of the UN General Assembly on September 24, 1996, President Clinton spoke of the goals he hoped would make the world more secure (Speech 8-7). They are the challenges of the twenty-first century.

8-1 Nonproliferation Efforts in the Former Soviet Union

Remarks to the Nixon Center for Peace
and Freedom Policy Conference
Washington DC
March 1, 1995

... Over the past two years, the United States has made real progress in lifting the threat of nuclear weapons. Now, in 1995, we face a year of particular decision in this era, a year in which the United States will pursue the most ambitious agenda to dismantle and fight the spread of weapons of mass destruction since the atom was split.

We know that ours is an enormously complex and difficult challenge. There is no single policy, no silver bullet, that will prevent or reverse the spread of weapons of mass destruction. But we have no more important task. Arms control makes us not only safer, it makes us stronger. It is a source of strength. It is one of the most effective insurance policies we can write for the future of our children.

Our administration has focused on two distinct but closely connected areas, decreasing and dismantling existing weapons and preventing nations or groups from acquiring weapons of mass destruction and the means to deliver them. We've made progress on both fronts.

As the result of an agreement President Yeltsin and I reached, for the first time in a generation Russian missiles are not pointed at our cities or our citizens. We've greatly reduced the lingering fear of an accidental nuclear launch. We put into force the START I treaty with Russia that will eliminate from both our countries delivery systems that carry more than 9,000 nuclear warheads, each with the capacity to incinerate a city the size of Atlanta.

START I, negotiated by two Republican administrations and put into force by this Democratic administration, is the first treaty that requires the nuclear powers actually to reduce their strategic arsenal. Both our countries are dismantling the weapons as fast as we can. And thanks to a far-reaching verification system, including on-site inspections which began in Russia and the United States today, each of us knows exactly what the other is doing.

And again, through the far-sighted program devised by Senators Nunn and Lugar, we are helping Russia and the other newly independent states to eliminate nuclear forces in transport, safeguard and destroy nuclear weapons and material.

Ironically, some of the changes that have allowed us to reduce the world's stockpile of nuclear weapons have made our nonproliferation efforts harder. The breakup of the Soviet Union left nuclear materials dispersed throughout the newly independent states. The potential for theft of nuclear materials, therefore, increased. We face the prospect of organized criminals entering the nuclear smuggling business. Add to this the volatile mix, the fact that a lump of plutonium the size of a soda can is enough to build a bomb and the urgency of the effort to stop the spread of nuclear materials should be clear to all of us.

That's why from our first day in office we have launched an aggressive, coordinated campaign against international terrorism and nuclear smuggling. We are cooperating closely with our allies, working with Russia and the other newly independent states, improving security at nuclear facilities, and strengthening multilateral export controls.

One striking example of our success is Operation Sapphire, the airlift of nearly 600 kilograms of highly enriched uranium, enough to make dozens of bombs from Kazakhstan to the United States for disposal. We've also secured agreements with Russia to reduce the uranium and plutonium available for nuclear weapons, and we're seeking a global treaty banning the production of fissile material for nuclear weapons.

Our patient, determined diplomacy also succeeded in convincing Belarus, Kazakhstan, and Ukraine to sign the Non-Proliferation Treaty and give up the nuclear weapons left on their territory when the Soviet Union dissolved. One of our administration's top priorities was to assure that these new countries would become non-nuclear nations, and now we are also achieving that goal.

Because of these efforts, four potential suppliers of ballistic missiles, Russia, Ukraine, China, and South Africa, have all agreed to control the transfer of these missiles and related technology, pulling back from the nuclear precipice has allowed us to cut United States defense expenditures for strategic weapons by almost two-thirds, a savings of about $20 billion a year, savings which can be shifted to vital needs such as boosting the readiness of our Armed Forces, reducing the deficit, putting more police on our own streets. By spending millions to keep or take weapons out of the hands of our potential adversaries, we are saving billions in arms costs and putting it to better use.

Now, in this year of decision, our ambition for the future must be even more ambitious. If our people are to know real lasting security, we have to redouble our arms control, nonproliferation, and antiterrorism efforts. We have to do everything we can to avoid living with the twenty-first century version of fallout shelters and duck-and-cover exercises to prevent another World Trade Center tragedy.

A ... key goal of ours is ratifying START II. Once in effect, that treaty will eliminate delivery systems from Russian and American arsenals that carry more than 5,000 weapons. The major reductions under START I, together with START II, will enable us to reduce by two-thirds the number of strategic warheads deployed at the height of the Cold War. At my urging, the Senate has already begun hearings on START II, and I am encouraged by the interest of the Senators from both parties in seeking quick action. I commend the Senate for the action taken so far, and I urge again the approval of the treaty as soon as possible.

President Yeltsin and I have already instructed our experts to begin considering the possibility after START II is ratified of additional reductions and limitations on remaining nuclear forces. We have a chance to further lift the nuclear cloud, and we dare not miss it....

8-2 Toward a Non-Nuclear Korean Peninsula

Remarks to the Korean National Assembly
Seoul, South Korea
July 10, 1993

... [One] security priority for our new Pacific Community is to combat the spread of weapons of mass destruction and their means of delivery. We cannot let the expanding threat of these deadly weapons replace the Cold War nightmare of nuclear annihilation. And today, that possibility is too real. North Korea appears committed to indiscriminate sales of the SCUD missiles that were such a source of terror and destruction in the Persian Gulf. Now it is developing, testing, and looking to export a more powerful missile with a range of 600 miles or more, enough for North Korea to threaten Osaka or for Iran to threaten Tel Aviv....

The Pacific nations simply must develop new ways to combat the spread of biological, chemical, and missile technologies. And in the coming weeks, the US will propose new efforts aimed at that goal. But no specter hangs over this peninsula or this region more darkly than the danger of nuclear proliferation. Nearly 160 nations have now joined to resist that threat through the Nuclear Non-Proliferation Treaty, the most universally supported treaty in all history.

Now, for the first time since that treaty was open for signatures, one of its members has threatened to withdraw. Our goals remain firm. We seek a nonnuclear Korean Peninsula and robust global rules against proliferation. That is why we urge North Korea to reaffirm its commitment to the Non-Proliferation Treaty, to fulfill its full-scope safeguards obligations to the International Atomic Energy Agency, including IAEA inspections of undeclared nuclear sites, and to implement bilateral inspections under the South-North nuclear accord.

Our goal is not endless discussions but certifiable compliance. North Korea must understand our intentions. We are seeking to prevent aggression, not to initiate it. And so long as North Korea abides by the UN Charter and international nonproliferation commitments, it has nothing to fear from America.

The US has worked to bring North Korea back within the fold of nuclear responsibility. But your nation, too, has a critical role to play. The future of this peninsula is for you and North Korea to shape. The South-North nuclear accord you negotiated goes even further than existing international accords. It not only banishes nuclear weapons from the peninsula, it also bans the production of nuclear materials that could be used to make those weapons. We urge full implementation of this path-breaking accord which can serve as a model for other regions of nuclear tension....

8-3 The "Crime and Punishment" of Iraq

Remarks at the Pentagon
Arlington, Virginia
February 17, 1998

... We have to defend our future from ... predators of the twenty-first century. They feed on the free flow of information and technology. They actually take advantage of the freer movement of people, information, and ideas. And they will be all the more lethal if we allow them to build arsenals of nuclear, chemical, and biological weapons and the missiles to deliver them. We simply cannot allow that to happen.

There is no more clear example of this threat than Saddam Hussein's Iraq. His regime threatens the safety of his people, the stability of his region, and the security of all the rest of us....

Remember, as a condition of the cease-fire after the Gulf War, the United Nations demanded—not the United States, the United Nations demanded—and Saddam Hussein agreed to declare within fifteen days ... his nuclear, chemical, and biological weapons and the missiles to deliver them....

The United Nations set up a special commission of highly trained international experts, called UNSCOM, to make sure that Iraq made good on that commitment. We had every good reason to insist that Iraq disarm. Saddam had built up a terrible arsenal, and he had used it, not once but many times. In a decade-long war with Iran, he used chemical weapons against combatants, against civilians, against a foreign adversary, and even against his own people. And during the Gulf War, Saddam launched Scuds against Saudi Arabia, Israel, and Bahrain.

Now, instead of playing by the very rules he agreed to at the end of the Gulf war, Saddam has spent the better part of the past decade trying to cheat on this solemn commitment. Consider just some of the facts. Iraq repeatedly made false declarations about the weapons that it had left in its possession after the Gulf War. When UNSCOM would then uncover evidence that gave lie to those declarations, Iraq would simply amend the reports. For example, Iraq revised its nuclear declarations four times within just fourteen months, and it has submitted six different biological warfare declarations, each of which has been rejected by UNSCOM.

In 1995, Hussein Kamel, Saddam's son-in-law and the chief organizer of Iraq's weapons of mass destruction program, defected to Jordan. He revealed that Iraq was continuing to conceal weapons and missiles and the capacity to build many more. Then and only then did Iraq admit to developing numbers of weapons in significant quantities and weapons stocks. Previously it had vehemently denied the very thing it just simply admitted once Saddam Hussein's son-in-law defected to Jordan and told the truth.

Now, listen to this. What did it admit? It admitted, among other things, an offensive biological warfare capability, notably 5,000 gallons of botulinum, which causes botulism; 2,000 gallons of anthrax; 25 biological-filled Scud warheads; and 157 aerial bombs. And I might say, UNSCOM inspectors believe that Iraq has actually greatly understated its production. As if we needed further confirmation, you all know what happened to his son-in-law when he made the untimely decision to go back to Iraq.

Next, throughout this entire process, Iraqi agents have undermined and undercut UNSCOM. They've harassed the inspectors, lied to them, disabled monitoring cameras, literally spirited evidence out of the back doors of suspect facilities as inspectors walked through the front door, and our people were there observing it and have the pictures to prove it.

Despite Iraq's deceptions UNSCOM has, nevertheless, done a remarkable job. Its inspectors, the eyes and ears of the civilized world, have uncovered and destroyed more weapons of mass destruction capacity than was destroyed during the Gulf War. This includes nearly 40,000 chemical weapons, more than 100,000 gallons of chemical weapons agents, 48 operational missiles, 30 warheads specifically fitted for chemical and biological weapons, and a massive biological weapons facility at Al Hakam equipped to produce anthrax and other deadly agents.

Over the past few months, as they have come closer and closer to rooting out Iraq's remaining nuclear capacity, Saddam has undertaken yet another gambit to thwart their ambition by imposing debilitating conditions on the inspectors and declaring key sites which have still not been inspected off limits, including, I might add, one palace in Baghdad more than 2,600 acres large....

It is obvious that there is an attempt here, based on the whole history of this operation since 1991, to protect whatever remains of his capacity to produce weapons of mass destruction, the missiles to deliver them, and the feedstocks necessary to produce them. The UNSCOM inspectors believe that Iraq still has stockpiles of chemical and biological munitions, a small force of Scud-type missiles, and the capacity to restart quickly its production program and build many, many more weapons.

Now, against that background, let us remember the past, here. It is against that background that we have repeatedly and unambiguously made clear our preference for a diplomatic solution. The inspection system works. The inspection system has worked in the face of lies, stonewalling, obstacle after obstacle after obstacle....

We have no business agreeing to any resolution ... that does not include free, unfettered access to the remaining sites by people who have integrity and proven competence in the inspection business. That should be our standard. That's what UNSCOM has done, and that's why I have been fighting for it so hard. That's why the United States should insist upon it....

If Saddam rejects peace and we have to use force, our purpose is clear: We want to seriously diminish the threat posed by Iraq's weapons of mass destruction program. We want to seriously reduce his capacity to threaten his neighbors. I am quite confident from the briefing I have just received from our military leaders that we can achieve the objectives and secure our vital strategic interests.

Let me be clear: A military operation cannot destroy all the weapons of mass destruction capacity. But it can and will leave him significantly worse off than he is now in terms of the ability to threaten the world with these weapons or to attack his neighbors. And he will know that the international community continues to have the will to act if and when he threatens again.

Following any strike, we will carefully monitor Iraq's activities with all the means at our disposal. If he seeks to rebuild his weapons of mass destruction we will be prepared to strike him again. The economic sanctions will remain in place until Saddam complies fully with all UN resolutions....

8-4 Lobbying for the Ratification of the CWC

Remarks to the American Society of Newspaper Editors
Washington DC
April 11, 1997

... For the last fifty years, Americans have lived under the hair-trigger threat of mass destruction. Our leadership has been essential to lifting that global peril, thanks in large measure to the efforts of my predecessors, and during the last four years also when we have made remarkable progress....

We helped to win the indefinite extension of the Nuclear Non-Proliferation Treaty, a powerful global barrier to the spread of nuclear weapons and their technology. We led in concluding the Comprehensive Test Ban Treaty, which will bring to life a decades-old dream of ending nuclear weapons testing. President Yeltsin and I agreed in Helsinki to a roadmap through the START treaties to cut our nuclear arsenals over the next decade by 80 percent from their Cold War peaks and actually to destroy the warheads so they can never be used for destructive ends.

Now America must rise to the challenge of ratifying the Chemical Weapons Convention and doing it before it takes effect on April 29, less than three weeks from today.

This century opened with the horror of chemical warfare in the trenches of World War I. Today, at the dawn of a new century, we have the opportunity to forge a widening international commitment to begin banishing poison gas from the Earth, even as we know it remains a grave, grave threat in the hands of rogue states or terrorist groups.

The Chemical Weapons Convention requires other nations to do what we decided to do more than a decade ago—get rid of all chemical weapons. In other words, the treaty is about other nations destroying their chemical weapons. As they do so and renounce the development, production, acquisition, or use of chemical arms, and pledge not to help others acquire them or produce them, our troops will be less likely to face one of the battlefield's most lethal threats. As stockpiles are eliminated and the transfer of dangerous chemicals is controlled, rogue states and terrorists will have a harder time getting the ingredients for weapons. And that will protect not only military forces but also innocent civilians.

By giving us new tools for verification, enabling us to tap a global network for intelligence and information, and strengthening our own law enforcement, the treaty will make it easier for us to prevent and to punish those who seek to violate its rules....

America has led the effort to establish an international ban against chemical weapons. Now we have to ratify it and remain on the right side of history. If we do, there will be new momentum and moral authority to our leadership in reducing even more the dangers of weapons of mass destruction.

Within my lifetime we've made enormous strides. Stepping back from the nuclear precipice, from the bleak time of fallout shelters and air-raid drills. But we have so much more to do. We have to strengthen the world's ability to stop the use of deadly diseases as biological weapons of war. We have to freeze the production of raw materials used for nuclear bombs. We must give greater bite to the global watchdogs responsible for detecting hidden weapons systems and programs. Continuing this progress demands constant work, nonstop vigilance, and American leadership....

8-5 Responding to Criticisms: The Lobbying Continues

The President's News Conference
The White House
April 18, 1997

... Less than two weeks from today, the Chemical Weapons Convention goes into effect, with or without the United States. The bottom line is this: Will the United States join a treaty we helped to shape, or will we go from leading the fight against poison gas to joining the company of pariah nations this treaty seeks to isolate?

With this treaty, other nations will follow the lead we set years ago by giving up chemical weapons. Our troops will be less likely to face poison gas on the battle field. Rogue states and terrorists will have a harder time acquiring or making chemical weapons, and we'll have new tools to prevent and punish them if they try. But if we fail to ratify, other countries could back out as well. We won't be able to enforce the treaty's rules or use its tools, and our companies will face trade sanctions aimed at countries that refuse to join....

By going the extra mile, we've reached agreement on twenty-eight conditions that will be included in the treaty's resolution of ratification, for example, maintaining strong defenses against chemical attacks, toughening enforcement, allowing the use of riot control agents like tear gas in a wide range of military and law enforcement situations, and requiring search warrants for any involuntary inspections of an American business.

These agreed-upon conditions resolve virtually all of the issues that have been raised about this treaty. But there are still a handful of issues on which we fundamentally disagree. They will be voted on by the full Senate as it takes up the treaty next week. We should all understand what's at stake. A vote for any of these killer amendments will prevent our participation in the treaty. Let me quickly address four of them.

The first would prohibit the United States from joining the treaty until Russia does. That is precisely backwards. The best way to secure Russian ratification is to ratify the treaty ourselves. Failure to do so will only give hardliners in Russia an excuse to hold out and hold on to their chemical weapons.

A second killer condition would prohibit us from becoming a party until rogue states like Iraq and Libya join. The result is we'd be weaker, not stronger, in our fight to prevent these rogue states from developing chemical weapons because we would lose the ability to use and enforce the treaty's tough trade restrictions and inspection tools. No country, especially an outlaw state, should have a veto over our national security.

A third killer condition would impose an unrealistically high standard of verification. There is no such thing as perfect verifiability in a treaty, but this treaty's tough monitoring, reporting, and on-site inspection requirements will enable us to detect militarily significant cheating. Our soldiers on the battlefield will be safer. That, clearly, is an advance over no treaty at all.

Finally, the opponents would force us to reopen negotiations on the Chemical Weapons Convention to try to fix two concerns that have already been resolved. First, they claim that a treaty expressly devoted to eliminating chemical weapons somehow would force its parties to facilitate the spread of chemical weapons.

This interpretation is totally at odds with the plain language of the treaty. I have committed to the Senate that neither the United States nor our allies share this interpretation and that we will reaffirm that fact annually.

The opponents also misread the treaty to require that we share our most advanced chemical defensive technology with countries like Iran and Cuba, should they join the Chemical Weapons Convention. I have committed to the Senate that in the event such countries are threatened by chemical attack, we would limit our assistance to providing nothing more than emergency medical supplies.

America took the lead in negotiating the Chemical Weapons Convention, first the Reagan administration, then the Bush administration. Every Chairman of the Joint Chiefs of Staff for the past twenty years supports it, as do the overwhelming majority of our veterans, the chemical industry, and arms control experts. Now we must lead in bringing this bipartisan treaty to life and enforcing its rules. America should stand with those who want to destroy chemical weapons, not with those who would defy the international community. I urge every Member of the Senate to support the convention when it comes to a vote next week....

8-6 If Biological and Chemical Weapons Do Spread ...

Remarks at the National Academy of Science
Washington DC
January 22, 1999

... Four years ago, the world received a wake-up call when a group unleashed a deadly chemical weapon, nerve gas, in the Tokyo subway. We have to be ready for the possibility that such a group will obtain biological weapons. We have to be ready to detect and address a biological attack promptly, before the disease spreads. If we prepare to defend against these emerging threats we will show terrorists that assaults on America will accomplish nothing but their own downfall.

Let me say first what we have done so far to meet this challenge. We've been working to create and strengthen the agreement to keep nations from acquiring weapons of mass destruction, because this can help keep these weapons away from terrorists, as well. We're working to ensure the effective implementation of the Chemical Weapons Convention, to obtain an accord that will strengthen compliance with the Biological Weapons Convention, to end production of nuclear weapons material. We must ratify the Comprehensive Test Ban Treaty to end nuclear tests once and for all.

As I proposed Tuesday in the State of the Union Address, we should substantially increase our efforts to help Russia and other former Soviet nations prevent weapons material and knowledge from failing into the hands of terrorists and outlaw states. In no small measure we should do this by continuing to expand our cooperative work with the thousands of Russian scientists who can be used to advance the causes of world peace and health and well-being but who, if they are not paid, remain a fertile field for the designs of terrorists.

But we cannot rely solely on our efforts to keep weapons from spreading. We have to be ready to act if they do spread. Last year, I obtained from Congress a 39 percent budget increase for chemical and biological weapons preparedness. This is helping to accelerate our ongoing effort to train and equip fire, police, and public health personnel all across our country to deal with chemical and biological emergencies. It is helping us to ready Armed Forces and National Guard units in every region to meet this challenge and to improve our capacity to detect an outbreak of disease and save lives, to create the first ever civilian stockpile of medicines to treat people exposed to biological and chemical hazards, to increase research and development on new medicines and vaccines to deal with new threats.

Our commitment to give local communities the necessary tools already goes beyond paper and plans. For example, parked just outside this building is a newly designed truck we have provided to the Arlington, Virginia, Fire Department. It can rapidly assist and prevent harm to people exposed to chemical and biological dangers....

Today, I want to announce the new initiatives we will take, to take us to the next level in preparing for these emerging threats. In my budget, I will ask Congress for $10 billion to address terrorism and terrorist emerging tools. This will include nearly $1.4 billion to protect citizens against chemical and biological terror—more than double what we spent on such programs only two years ago.

We will speed and broaden our efforts, creating new local emergency medical teams, employing in the field portable detection units the size of a shoe box to rapidly identify hazards; tying regional laboratories together for prompt analysis of biological threats. We will greatly accelerate research and development, centered in the Department of Health and Human Services, for new vaccines, medicines and diagnostic tools.

I should say here that I know everybody in this crowd understands this, but everyone in America must understand this: the government has got to fund this. There is no market for the kinds of things we need to develop; and if we are successful, there never will be a market for them. But we have got to do our best to develop them. These cutting-edge efforts will address not only the threat of weapons of mass destruction, but also the equally serious danger of emerging infectious diseases. So we will benefit even if we are successful in avoiding these attacks....

We are doing everything we can, in ways that I can and in ways that I cannot discuss, to try to stop people who would misuse chemical and biological capacity from getting that capacity. This is not a cause for panic. It is a cause for serious, deliberate, disciplined, long-term concern....

8-7 The Bottom Line of the WMD Nonproliferation

Remarks to the Fifty-first Session of
the United Nations General Assembly
New York, New York
September 24, 1996

... The CTBT is the shared work of hard negotiation. Some have complained that it does not mandate total nuclear disarmament by a date certain. I would say to them, do not forsake the benefits of this achievement by ignoring the tremendous progress we have already made toward that goal. ...

The United States and other nuclear weapons states have embraced the South Pacific and African nuclear free zones. Now half the world's land area is nuclear free by international agreement. And the world community extended indefinitely the Nuclear Non-Proliferation Treaty.

Yet some of the very changes that have made this progress possible have also created new risks. The breakup of the Soviet Union left nuclear materials dispersed throughout the New Independent States. As barriers have come down around the world, the danger of nuclear smuggling has gone up. So even as we reduce the global stockpiles of weapons of mass destruction, we must also reduce the danger that lethal materials could wind up in the wrong hands, while developing effective defenses for our people if that should happen.

The United States has six priority goals to further lift the threat of nuclear weapons destruction and the threat of weapons of mass destruction and to limit their dangerous spread:

First, we must protect our people from chemical attack and make it harder for rogue states and terrorists to brandish poison gas by bringing the Chemical Weapons Convention into force as soon as possible. I thank the nations here that have ratified the Chemical Weapons Convention. I deeply regret that the United States Senate has not yet voted on the convention, but I want to assure you and people throughout the world that I will not let this treaty die and we will join the ranks of nations determined to prevent the spread of chemical weapons.

Second, we must reduce the risk that an outlaw state or organization could build a nuclear device by negotiating a treaty to freeze the production of fissile materials for use in nuclear weapons. The Conference on Disarmament should take up this challenge immediately. The United States, Russia, France, and the United Kingdom already have halted production of fissile materials for weapons. I urge other nations to end the unsafeguarded production of these materials pending completion of the treaty.

Third, we must continue to reduce our nuclear arsenals....

Fourth, we must reinforce our efforts against the spread of nuclear weapons by strengthening the Nuclear Non-Proliferation Treaty. We should give the International Atomic Energy Agency a stronger role and sharper tools for conducting worldwide inspections. Our law enforcement and customs officials should cooperate more in the fight against nuclear smuggling. And I urge all nations that have not signed the NPT to do so without delay.

Fifth, we must better protect our people from those who would use disease as a weapon of war, by giving the Biological Weapons Convention the means to strengthen compliance, including on-site investigations when we believe such weapons may have been used or when suspicious outbreaks of disease occur. We should aim to complete this task by 1998.

Finally, we must end the carnage caused by antipersonnel landmines, the hidden killers that murder and maim more than 25,000 people a year. In May I announced a series of actions the United States would take toward this goal. Today I renew my appeal for the swift negotiation of a worldwide ban on the use, stockpiling, production, and transfer of antipersonnel landmines. Our children deserve to walk the Earth in safety....

Selected Bibliography

Allison, Graham T., Cote, Owen R., et al., *Avoiding Nuclear Anarchy: Containing the Threat of Loose Russian Nuclear Weapons and Fissile Material* (Cambridge: MIT Press, 1996).

Bebler, Anton A., ed., *The Challenge of NATO Enlargement* (Westport, CT: Praeger, 1999).

Bilinsky, Yaroslav, *Endgame in NATO's Enlargement: The Baltic States and Ukraine* (Westport, CT: Praeger, 1999).

Blackman, Ann, *Seasons of Her Life: A Biography of Madeleine Korbel Albright* (New York: Scribner's, 1999).

Boutros-Ghali, Boutros, *Unvanquished: A US-UN Saga* (New York: Random House, 1999).

Carpenter, Ted Galen and Conry, Barbara, eds., *NATO Enlargement: Illusions and Reality* (Washington DC: CATO Institute, 1998).

Christopher, Warren, *In the Stream of History: Shaping Foreign Policy for a New Era* (Stanford: Stanford University Press, 1998).

Clemens, Clay, *NATO and the Quest for Post-Cold War Security* (New York: St. Martin's 1997).

Clinton, Bill, *Between Hope and History* (New York: Random House, 1996).

Cockburn, Andrew and Cockburn, Patrick, *Out of the Ashes: the Resurrection of Saddam Hussein* (New York: Harper-Collins, 1999).

Cockburn, Andrew and Cockburn, Leslie, *One Point Safe: A True Story* (New York: Anchor, 1998). (Deals with nuclear weapons)

Cordesman, Anthony H., *Iraq and the War of Sanctions: Conventional Threats and Weapons of Mass Destruction* (Westport, CT: Praeger, 1999).

Dobbs, Michael, *Madeleine Albright: A Twentieth Century Odyssey* (New York: Henry Holt, 1999).

Drew, Elizabeth, *Showdown: The Struggle Between the Gingrich Congress and the Clinton White House* (New York: Simon and Schuster, 1996).

Feldman, Shai, *Nuclear Weapons and Arms Control in the Middle East* (Cambridge: MIT Press, 1997).

Gertz, Bill, *Betrayal: How the Clinton Administration Undermined American Security* (Washington DC: Regnery, 1999).

Gow, James, *Triumph of the Lack of Will: International Diplomacy and the Yugoslav War* (New York: Columbia University Press, 1997).

Grayson, George W., *Strange Bedfellows: NATO Marches East* (Lanham, MD: University Press of America, 1999).

Owen, David, *Balkan Odyssey* (Harcourt Brace & Company, 1995).

Physicians for Human Rights, *Winds of Death: Iraq's Use of Poison Gas Against Its Kurdish Population* (New York: Human Rights Watch, 1989).

Ritter, Scott, *Endgame: Solving the Iraq Problem—Once and for All* (New York: Simon and Schuster, 1999).

Roberts, Brad, *Terrorism with Chemical and Biological Weapons* (Alexandria, VA: Chemical and Biological Weapons Control Institute, 1997).

Tanter, Raymond, *Rogue Regimes: Terrorism and Proliferation* (New York: St. Martin's Press, 1998).

Ullman, Richard H., ed., *The World and Yugoslavia's Wars* (New York: Council on Foreign Relations, 1996).

Wurmser, David, *Tyranny's Ally: America's Failure to Defeat Saddam Hussein* (Washington DC: American Enterprise Institute, 1999).

Yost, David S., *NATO Transformed: The Alliance's New Roles in International Security* (Washington DC: United States Institute of Peace, 1998).

Zimmermann, Warren, *Origins of a Catastrophe: Yugoslavia and Its Destroyers* (New York: Random House, 1996).

Guide to Further Research

The paucity of books devoted to Clinton's foreign policy is a function of time and preoccupation with his personal problems. The periodical literature, however, offers an ample amount of information on specialized aspects of his policy. Among the key journals, the following are especially useful:

- *Asian Survey*
- *Bulletin of Atomic Scientists*
- *Foreign Affairs*
- *Foreign Policy*
- *International Affairs*
- *International Security*
- *Middle Eastern Forum*
- *Middle Eastern Quarterly*
- *Middle Eastern International*
- *Orbis*
- *Problems of Post-Communism*
- *Strategic Review*
- *Survival*
- *The National Interest*
- *The New Republic*
- *The New York Review of Books*
- *Washington Quarterly*
- *World Policy Journal*

Online Research Guide

Below is a list of online US government databases that are major sources of data on foreign policy of the Clinton administration.

The White House:

Press Briefings and Speeches by the Principals
http://www.pub.whitehouse.gov

US Government Printing Office:

Weekly Compilations of Presidential Releases
http://www.access.gpo.gov/nara/nara003.html

Department of State:

Daily Press Briefings
http://dosfan.lib.uic.edu/ERC/briefing.html

Central Intelligence Agency (CIA):

Press Releases and Statements
http://www.odci.gov/cia/public_affairs/press_release/news.html

Speeches and Testimony
http://www.odci.gov/cia/public_affairs/speeches/speeches.html

Department of Defense (DOD):

Public Statements of the Secretary of Defense
http://web2.whs.osd.mil/SPEECHES/SECSTATE.HTM

Reports on International Affairs
http://www.defenselink.mil/pubs/#REPORTS

Pentagon Library Online Databases
http://www.hqda.army.mil/library/databases.html

General Accounting Office (GAO):

Reports and Testimony
http://www.gao.gov/reports.htm

US Congress:

Congressional Documents Database
http://clerkweb.house.gov/docs/docs.htm

Index